TREELINE AND BEYOND

Published by
WHITEWATER PUBLISHING CO.
17910 87th Street
Becker, Minnesota USA 55308

Printed in Canada by
Friesens
Altona, Manitoba, Canada

Pre-press by
North Star Press of St. Cloud, Inc.
St. Cloud, Minnesota

TREELINE AND BEYOND

by

Dan D. Gapen, Sr.

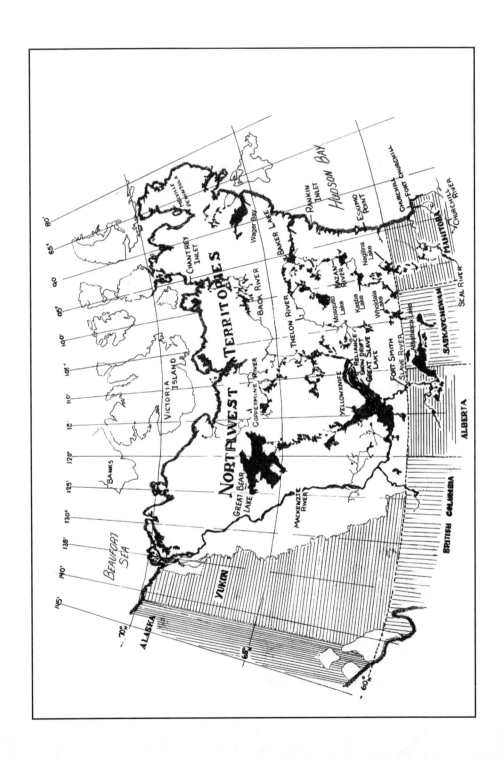

to
ROSS GEORGE

~ a friend ~

~ a mentor ~

~ a man of spirit ~

~ a man of fairness ~

~ the gooseman ~

and

~ Waldo's buddy ~

FOCUS ON THE VOICES OF . . .

river waters
Arctic winds
still summer days
aspen in a breeze
drifting snow
booming ice
crunching snowshoes
panting wood stove
gas lantern buzz
yelping geese
howling wolves

THEY ARE WILDERNESS!

Table of Contents

Foreword

I begin this book because I must . . . because I must attempt to tell my readers the tales of the world I love so dearly . . . because this may well be the last book I write . . . because life takes from the human body, not its spirit, but the physical texture to do that one more project.

Within these hardback covers, I would like to tell the tales of those spiritual gifts passed on by the land I love so much, to tell tales of how my readers might attain what, for me, has been a true gift from the land of my youth, tales of how one might survive and live within the land I hold so close to my heart, tales of how the reader might take, as well as give back to this land of the north, tales of what I wish might remain after this author has left the world of Mother Nature and Great Spirit.

It was the land at *Treeline and Beyond* that gifted this man with an appreciation and love for the real meaning of why the creature, man, was placed upon our earth. An appreciation that spells out why we came, how we should conduct ourselves, and why someday we must depart.

Today our world moves too fast, consumes too much, and destroys that which has come before. No longer are humans content to be stewards of the world about them. Instead, humans must change and reshape the world in which they live. Nature has no place. Humans have become smarter than the earth that gave them life. Humans have become intolerant of the wind, the flow of water, the growth of fauna, and the warmth of Mother Sun. What earth has sewn together, the human is bent on ripping apart to be resewn to his needs. Computers rule. Materialism, a sign of wealth; caring, a sign of weakness; truthfulness, a forgotten trait; and lessons of years past, a myth to cast aside. Only today and tomorrow seem to matter. To cast one's friend aside to accomplish tomorrow has become the law of the human creature.

I hope, within these covers, that I, Dan Gapen, Sr., a man of senior status, will inject within the heart and soul of you, my reader, that days of old and lessons of the past matter . . . that past knowledge is important, mellowed knowledge can be cherished, wrinkled knowledge can be strengthening, and all which came before has a place in this modern world of hurry-scurry.

Having read these words, reader, you have my permission to read on . . . to become part of and enter into the northern natural world where the human intruders are tolerated only if they come with humility.

Dan Gapen, Sr.

About the Author

Many who know the author will call him *fisherman*. Some may make claim to his fight for running water and call him *environmentalist*. But, to those who really know the man, he's a *caring naturalist*. To us, the publishers, Dan Gapen, Sr., is a man whose roots reach far back into another time and another world. Dan could be called the conscience of Mother Nature.

Born April 9, 1934, on the shores of North America's giant Lake Superior, Dan D. Gapen, Sr., is considered one of the land's top anglers. To most he is the continent's number one river fisherman.

During the late 1930s and 1940s and most of the 1950s, young Gapen learned about the wilderness, its treasures, its waterways, and its demands. Don Gapen, Dan's father and the originator of the world famous Muddler Fly, saw to it that his son was exposed to this wilderness at a point on the map called the Nipigon River in northern Ontario, Canada. Here young Gapen was worm boy, fishing guide, charter boat operator, river runner, and lure creator. At the age of six, young Dan learned the art of fly tying. At eight, his spending money came from lures and flies he created in his father's tackle shop. At fourteen, he became a fishing guide and worked closely with several old Indians who were eager to teach. During Ontario's cold and bitter winter months when his father's fishing resort was closed, young Gapen learned to trap and understand the need to conserve wildlife and its habitat. At a point in history when America's wilderness had not yet expanded beyond young Gapen's home, there was time to transform his lessons into lasting moods and lifestyle. Today, these moods, these lessons learned, are still an intricate part of his life. Attempting to pass this love of nature on to his readers is part of the man.

Over the years, Gapen has fought desperately to save running water. Every facet of governmental bureaucracy has felt his sting . . . from those who would rip off the upper Mississippi, a waterway he loves desperately, to those farmers who would drain wetland and the small life-giving creeks they birth. Gapen has been a staunch supporter of the National Wild and Scenic River system since its inception, a legislative bill he helped mold and support along waterways such as the upper Mississippi.

Many who read this book will recognize Dan's name in conjunction with fishing tackle (lures), which are so synonymous with it. For twenty-five years, Gapen directed the manufacturing and supply of his American-made products. But, as was the case with so many good American companies, the early 1980s saw a need to limit production of American goods and allow foreign imports to supply most of the market. Gapen lures are still made and can be found, but their numbers are limited to those on which a proud American firm can compete.

By using the skills and heritage handed down through generations, Dan Gapen has been able to make a living. These same outdoor skills now include photography and writing, two which Gapen openly admits he prefers. When asked, this man places fishing first, waterfowl gunning second, and his photography next.

Regarding his writing, Dan makes no bones about his ability. He readily admits to being a romantic and that his writing style may not please the educated writers of the world. But, it's not these people to whom he wishes to give pleasure. It's you, the average outdoor person and fisherman to whom he speaks. It's you and your enjoyment he seeks with his stories, tales, and fishing know-how. He hopes he has succeeded with *Treeline and Beyond*.

The Publisher

Dan D. Gapen, Sr.

Illustrations
by

Sue Beutz
Margaret Caldwell
Heidi Knoop
Michele Steffen

Chapter 1

Wholdaia

"Gagon." The raven squawked his irritation at the two humans who scurried about gathering dry wood to feed the cabin aerotight. Lead-gray skies hung low, ominous with icy rain. Winds had shifted three times this day. They now blew from the northeast. It would rain this night—cold, sleet-laden rain. Dry wood would bring the necessary comfort to get the two outsiders through the night. Nothing beats the warmth created by a buffeting aerotight stove when late fall winds blow in the first onslaught of winter.

At dock's end, a mother seagull and a gray chick, as large as the mother, watched in patient silence. The youngster squatted low, periodically stretching its neck and flaring its mouth open, hoping mother might magically regurgitate food of some kind. The begging was for naught. The mother only blinked yellow eyes at the youngster's gestures. If food was to be had, it would have to come in the form of fish carcasses left by these two humans, who had come so late in the season. All other gulls had long since departed south, migrating to warmer water and a more bountiful food supply.

Overhead, a hundred late-leaving Canadian geese yelped their way south, following the path taken by thousands of their kind during the past six days.

The northeast winds increased in velocity. The wind, moaning low, objected to the breaking of its path by the Wholdaia cabin walls. Rain began to patter upon the cabin's eastern windows. Flecks of sleet pelted hard upon the soft, fine sand before the cabin's steps, held a moment, then melted away.

Shortly, within the cabin's kitchen, a woman's voice sang softly some mostly forgotten tune. Cabin windows began to steam, and the fresh warm scent of frying lake trout danced away downwind to disappear over the frothing lake. The dim glow of a propane light illuminated the cabin windows fogged completely by the warmth.

Squawking came from downwind. The mother and fledgling lifted into the turbulent wind, drawn by the tantalizing smell of frying fish. They would soon settle back, their quest lost as winds blew harder.

Fishing had been good, too good. Lake trout now seeking gravel washes in which to spawn, had left the ninety- and one-hundred-foot, rocky holding areas of August. They now cruised within the four- to ten-foot deep, rocky shoreline reefs. Wherever a combination of gravel, round rock, and access to waterwash existed, the huge females crowded. With them came the long-nosed males, large and small. Once these fish were located, the fishermen were hard pressed to draw a lure through such an area without having it viciously attacked by one or more of the highly stressed males.

In many instances, the hooked trout would be accompanied by three or more fish aggressively attempting to rip the intruder's lure from its mouth. Bigger trout—the females—often followed but lost the race to the more active males. Every so often, when a lure was placed just right, a trophy female would be hooked, landed and released.

Yes, fishing had been good, but now the wind increased, and the temperature dropped. Shelter created by the small plywood cabin and its wood-burning stove was warm and rewarding. The late guests at Wholdaia settled into a hot meal of red-fleshed lake trout, mashed potatoes, boiled carrots, and steaming hot coffee. Fishing would have to wait till the weather cleared.

Across the bay, a ghostly gray form appeared, then disappeared beneath the yellowing shoreline willow and golden-needled tamarack. Lonely yellow eyes paused, gazed intently at the flickering window light, and then turned away. Slowly an Arctic wolf nosed his way past the fish-cleaning board wedged between a pair of stunted black spruce. For weeks the young male had rousted ravens and seagulls from pike and trout entrails left by the guests of Wholdaia. Today he found no food. The good times of summer had come to an end. He would turn his attention to the coming of caribou.

Chatter from the cooking cabin soon ended. The golden light faded to black. Only a flickering of candlelight from the sleeping cabin glittered faintly in the darkened Arctic night. Beneath it the male guest jotted notes in a daily diary.

The storm would pass, and the last two guests of the season at the Wholdaia Lake Camp would fish two more days. Northern pike by the dozens would be caught above the big grayling rapids. The cabbage weed bed, which once held so many trophy summer pike, had begun to fade but continued to hold a goodly number of late fall fish. Several over forty-two inches were caught and released. The two fishermen presumed that these monster fish remained to feed on the late migration of grayling heading into deeper lake water. Only below and above the Dubawnt River rapids did these concentrations of pike still hold. In the main lake, pike had moved to deep off points, a more normal late fall/winter staging.

Another storm was beginning its descent on Wholdaia the day the last visitors of the season left. Snowflakes, driven by a strong northwestern wind, raced horizontally between the camp cabins.

With much happiness and great sadness, the two visitors greeted the sight and sound of the Otter aircraft as it topped Wholdaia's southeastern shoreline. They would leave behind a challenge unfulfilled, a wonder never soothed. "Just how long might two such last as they endure and happily survive at a place called Wholdaia in a land North of Sixty?"

For information on the Wholdaia Lake camp turn to the information page at book's end.

Chapter 2

Rafting the Kamilukuak

The unknown—sometimes frightening, forever exciting, always bewitching—best describes Northwest Territory's Kamilukuak River system. It is a world fossilized by time and harsh environment. Past and present lie exposed along the land's 4,000-year-old caribou trails, on graying glacial stone, and in quilt-like brown bogs. It is a world, once traveled, that will haunt the outside visitor forever. It is the world into which Laurie Dickhart and I traveled in August of 1995. We did so via float plane, rubber raft, sleeping bag, and nylon tent. It was to be a trip never forgotten, forever rewarding.

Longitude: 102.32°W

Latitude: 61.30°N

The flexible skin of the zodiac rolled smoothly upwards, then down, reacting to strong winds and cresting waves. Skies overhead glistened cobalt blue, disturbed only by the flight of passing Arctic terns. There was a sharp, fresh smell to the air as gust after gust of wind drove icy cold spray upwards past the raft's handrails.

5

Laurie Dickhart sat rigidly erect upon a wooden seat, gasping to catch her breath whenever a cresting wave sprayed too high. Her eyes always lit up when she would tell me about the antics of her young son, so I recognized that same sparkle in her eyes and the wide-eyed wonder as she drank in the beauty of the great northern country.

Both Laurie and I had anxiously awaited this trip into the world of giant fish, moaning wolves, restless caribou, and yelping geese —a land far from the bothersome honk of horns, clattering phones, aggravating traffic, and the stench of pollution. For the two of us, it would be eight days away from all this, days void of contact with the outside world, days that would thrust us back into a sphere of primitive yesterday.

Slowly the bobbing raft made its way across the wind-swept bay, heading for a small, open-water island. The massive landscape seemed to gradually swallow up the red dot of the raft and its passengers. Time held still as it so often does in the Arctic.

The portable locator screen showed fifty-three feet of water. It was late August, and even here, above the treeline, lake trout continued to seek shelter in the lake's deeper holes. Only small fish remained in the shallows, fish in the three-to-eight-pound class. We proved this the night before while fishing for our supper. Oh, we hooked a goodly number of fish and selected a near five pounder to fillet and fry—but nary a trophy lake trout did we find. Today we sought bigger fish in water depths exceeding eighty feet.

Slowly, deeper water began to chart. Down past sixty, then seventy, and finally eighty feet flashed on our locator. At eighty-four feet, four feet off the bottom, a pair of large, red blips showed. At eighty-seven feet, the screen showed fish in pairs and multiple numbers, all suspended four to seven feet off bottom.

"Lake trout! Large ones!"

Moments later, 100 yards south of the gray-stone island, we graphed a maximum depth of 116 feet. Kamilukuak's ancient riverbed patterned directly below. Along the 10,000-year-old stream bed's northern edge, where island rock etched clear beneath crystal water, water depth plunged straight down. This plunge into darkness was interrupted only twice. Once at the sixty-eight-foot level and again at eighty-seven feet. Both these interruptions showed masses of fish staging. The lower edge, a structure some fifty feet wide, held the largest specimens. On the graph, huge trout showed up as red bars, surrounded in black. We would begin fishing here.

Laurie readied equipment. I snapped a large, two-ounce, fluorescent red jig with a gold mylar tail, tipped with a long strip of belly meat, onto my line. My casting reel was loaded with fourteen-pound, "no stretch" line, mounted to a six-and-a-half-foot sturdy rod. Such equipment is needed to set a hook into deep-water lakers. If possible, and it sometimes is, an ultra-light rod and reel, loaded with six-pound line, might work, but plan on missing eight out of ten strikes.

However, when you are after large, twenty-pound-plus fish, you need large bait and sturdy equipment to do the best job. Next, we marked an eighty-seven-foot deep ledge with a yellow float marker and backed the raft upwind and allowed it to drift. Approach would begin slowly from upwind.

Quickly I reached for a second rod and reel. As our raft rolled past the marker, both strip-loaded jigs plummeted toward bottom. Once there, we reeled up six feet of line and commenced jigging action. Elevating and lowering the rod tip in twenty-four-inch thrusts seems to best entice lake trout under such conditions.

It took but ten feet of drift for the first fish to strike. There was a hard pull on the rod tip, a fast rush sideways and then a downward run. The fish was small, a fact indicated by the jerking, twisting action at the rod tip.

Ten seconds into my fight with this lake trout, Laurie set hook in a much larger fish. We knew it was large because there wasn't the normal, sporadic jerking at the rod tip. Instead, a heavy, steady run along the bottom into deeper water was followed by a series of stubborn, upward lifts and back-to-bottom rushes.

My fish came to the boat and was released as Laurie continued to struggle. It took ten minutes more of heavy lifting before the first erupting bubbles surfaced, an indicator that Laurie's fish may have been ready to give ground.

Red-faced and gasping for air, Laurie desperately held on, her rod arched within inches of the surface. Whatever fought below was no lightweight. The raft drifted into deeper water. Once again, line inched off Laurie's reel, the fish edging ever deeper.

"Okay, Hon. Lift and reel, lift and reel. If you can ever get him started up, the battle is half won."

"Half won? What do you mean . . . half won?" she gasped.

Grunting, Laurie heaved hard, lifting the rod tip some twenty-four-inches above the water's surface . . . but not for long. Feeling the pressure, the huge fish darted forward and deeper. Laurie's shoulders shuddered. It was going to be a long fight.

"He's got to be a big 'un, partner. You haven't gained an inch since hooking him . . . maybe over thirty? Maybe the biggest lake trout you've ever caught . . . if you land him!"

"I . . . I . . . don't think . . . I can land him. My arms are burning," complained Laurie, forcing her rod tip high once again.

This time the monster broke from his routine and began a slow circle. It was a sign of weakening. Slowly now, along with brief, stubborn runs, the huge trout began to circle toward the surface.

Minutes passed. Fight between woman and trophy dragged on. Who would give up first?

Finally, in a burst of rolling, thrashing water, the monster trout floundered to the surface. Laurie had won, but none too soon. Her arms were all but ready to drop off . . . or so she said.

Without an accurate scale, we could only measure the prize. Length: 49.5 inches. Girth: 24.25 inches. Estimated weight: about thirty-nine pounds. Never before had she caught such a lake trout. But, it would not be her biggest. Another would attack her offering two days later and surpass this monster in girth size.

That morning, Laurie and I caught and released fifty-three trout, the largest her near-thirty-nine pounder. My largest was estimated at twenty-eight, an excellent specimen but not my largest of the trip.

Arms tired, we headed back to camp. Other things, equally as important as catching fish, awaited investigation.

We were camped above the treeline where tundra environment prevailed. Caribou might be on the lake's largest islands. It was likely we could photograph them in their natural habitat, but we would consume a shore lunch of golden fried trout fillets first.

Shortly after lunch, we selected the lake's largest island and began an upward walk into its Eden-like central region. Once past the dwarfed spruce along the shoreline, the island's environment took on a more barrenland appearance, and once we crossed the first stony esker, a small Walt Disney-style oasis appeared directly below us. Four miniature lakes glimmered in a valley of lush greenery.

Between two of the lakes, three caribou grazed on tundra foliage. On one of the lakes, seven Canadian honkers swam.

Above, several Arctic terns buzzed back and forth over the lake surface. To the west, high upon a gray sand esker, two orange-breasted Arctic marmots stood up high above their mounds, startled by our intrusion. A world of Shangri-La lay below, one to be photographed. We drifted farther back in time, the modern world all but vanquished from our minds.

Minutes later the three caribou trotted off to join seven more grazing just out of sight over the next esker. Eventually, a mere 200 feet would separate man and beast. The balance of our day was spent walking the land, absorbing its beauty and peacefulness.

Too many anglers heading into the northern world fail to stop long enough to enjoy all the other things that mold this wilderness into the wondrous place it is. Catching fish seems to take up all their time. Thus, when slow fishing days occur, and they do, no matter where you are or how "hot" the lake you fish, many fishermen become disgruntled. Trophy pike, lake trout, and grayling aren't caught on every cast . . . or even every day. You may cut down the odds by traveling into these far northern lands, but here luck also plays a big part in taking a trophy fish.

On day three, a heavy, northern storm descended on our paradise. Cold rain, heavy winds, and a falling barometer made travel impossible. Twice Laurie and I attempted to leave the sheltering tent, and twice we were forced to return.

Nevertheless, there is something comforting about a warm sleeping bag, the shelter provided by a flapping tent, and the sound of rain on canvas.

As evening descended, a pair of caribou left an island point across from our camp. Laurie and I managed to catch up with them just as their hooves touched the shoreline shallows. Once again, I snapped my camera, and the day became a success.

On the fourth day, we boated and released a number of big lake trout, the largest a 49-inch-long (26.5-inch girth) fish, which we estimated at 46 to 49 pounds. The trophy was enticed by vertical jigging in water nearly 100 feet deep. It was this same day I boated my biggest fish of the trip, a near 36 pounder. The 49 pounder, Laurie's fish, was landed after a hard, twenty-minute battle that left her arms exhausted for several hours.

In all cases, lake trout and pike were boated without the help of a net. Many feel landing nets tend to destroy outer protective slime on a lake trout, which may eventually cause fungus and the fish's death. Landing these larger fish isn't nearly as difficult as one might suspect when a net isn't used. It takes a bit more time to wear the prize fish down, but it can be done with patience. Even when barbless hooks were used, a practice now recommended in most of these primitive waters, nary a fish was lost. Preventing such a loss is simply a matter of keeping a constantly tight line between your rod tip and the fish. Laurie lifted her forty-nine pounder, caught on a barbless white Ugly Bug jig, into the boat, by placing one hand under the fish's gill plate and the other beneath its belly.

Certainly any lake trout taken after that monster would have been anti-climactic. Neither Laurie nor I tried very hard to beat her record during our remaining four days. Much time was spent photographing, hiking, being lazy, sleeping in, studying wildlife and searching out ancient artifacts.

Photography took up most of our last two days. Canada's central sub-arctic region, the area in which Laurie and I traveled, hosts an historical legacy some 10,000 years old. Since the days of receding glaciers, man has shown his presence via a trail of artifacts scattered across this land. Ancient Inuit tribes, ravaging Native American bands, and primitive land-bridge natives have all come and gone, leaving behind signs of their passing. Chipping stations, spear heads, quartz ax heads, tent stones, inuksuks, stone food caverns, hide tent poles, log cabins, and rotting watercraft carcasses can be found if you know the signs.

I remember best this part of our trip north of the sixtieth parallel during the summer of 1995. On the sixth day we were high atop a sandy, rock esker that overlooked the entire lake and its inner island structures. After researching a map provided by our outfitter, Clark Jenney, we came to the conclusion that if a caribou migration were to occur within this area, it would have to pass just beneath this very esker where the lake structure narrowed. Primitive man searching for caribou would have sought the highest land points available for viewing game and avoiding summer insects. Below was an ideal spot to have constructed summer and fall hunting camps.

11

Within minutes of reaching the esker's highest point, I discovered the first chipping station. It contained many quartz chips and a pair of small, broken game bird spear heads. Within another thirty minutes, we'd discovered eight more chipping stations. I'd never found anything like this in all my days of Arctic travel. Later, it was determined these artifacts dated back to 2,000 B.C.

Laurie found the first set of tent stones. They formed a nearly perfect circle on which she gaily skipped from stone to stone. Several of the stones were nearly buried by sand and grit, but they definitely were skin tent stones. Later we found four more sets of tent rings within several feet of the first. We walked the stones several times, happily dreaming of those who once slept within such structures. If only we could regress in time to see those hardy, five-foot-tall humans who once lived and hunted this ancient place.

In the end, we discovered a quartz ax head, a fleshing stone, and a spearhead. We left them as we found them. Years of travel in these Arctic and sub-Arctic lands have left me with a great many superstitions. Ghosts, evil spirits, unexplained happenings, and mythological events may be my excuses. Whatever they are, I have strong feelings about disturbing what comes from so far in the past. I prefer to leave such things as I find them. Why tempt fate and all those spirits who walk the land North of Sixty?

Toward trip's end, we caught and released a number of trophy-sized northern pike. The biggest tipped the scales near twenty pounds. They were found far back in the hidden bays on the Kamilukuak River system. All were released to fight another day.

Sub-Arctic and Arctic waters support fewer weeds than water systems farther to the south. When they are found in an Arctic watershed, it's a good bet northern pike will be close at hand. The use of flashy spoons, brightly colored spinner baits, or bucktail spinners seem to produce the best action.

Those traveling into this world of trophy fish may wonder which rod and reel combos to take along. It's simple! Anything you'd use on large-mouth bass, for walleye trolling, or northern pike fishing here in the United States will work in the far north. Jigs (three-eighths- to two-ounce sizes), flashy spoons (four-to-seven-inch), spinner baits (three-eighths- to one-ounce) in chartreuse, white, and yellow, and large blacktails will do for lures. Line weights from eight to fourteen pounds on spinner gear, twelve to twenty on casting gear, are best. Along with these, make sure to take a good electronic depth sounder along. It can be an LCR or a digital unit.

Early on the eighth day, we engaged in a bit of deep-water trolling, trying once more for that once-in-a-lifetime trophy. For five hours we roamed the deepest water Kamilukuak had to offer. We boated several fish over fifteen pounds, the largest a twenty-two pounder. As before, all were carefully released. In eight days, only seven lake trout were kept, these for eating. Yes, Laurie's forty-nine pounder continues to swim beneath the waters of Kamilukuak, hopefully to thrill another fisherman some day in the distant future. Trolling gear consisted of a six-ounce Bait-Walker sinker and a heavy, fluorescent red/chartreuse Dardevle spoon.

There are no words to stress how important it is to vary activities on your next trip into the far northern world. Certainly there are a great number of trophy fish to be had, many more than you might find elsewhere. Pike and lake trout in the twenty-pound class are not unusual. However, this wilderness world has much more to enrich a vacation long after the stories about trophy fish have faded. Too many who venture north fail to recognize this fact and return home disheartened when fishing results decline below expectations.

Laurie Dickhart and I left our time-held paradise at noon on the eighth day. The float-mounted Otter aircraft arrived on schedule. Our camp was dismantled with help from the pilot, and within minutes of his arrival, we headed south toward the base camp at Obre Lake.

It had been a wonderful vacation, one neither of us would forget
. . . one made not only by Laurie's forty-nine pounder, but also the
soft-eyed caribou, ancient chipping stations, wind-swept and rainy
nights spent in the warm sanctuary of a darkened tent, fond
visions of a hard and entrepreneurial people who loved, lived and
then perished doing what they did to get through life under the
toughest of conditions. This land, with its extreme beauty and
extreme hardships, made us more aware of our own immortality.
We came away with a renewed zest for life, rested and at peace,
feeling very fortunate indeed.

*Note: For information on how the reader might involve
himself in a trip to the Kamilukuak basin turn to the
information page at book's end. The lake fished on the
Kamilukuak River system in this chapter is named
Casimir, a body of water hosting hundreds of rocky
islands covered in tundra fauna.*

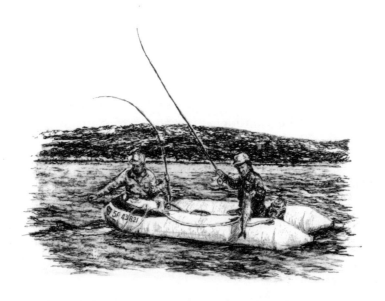

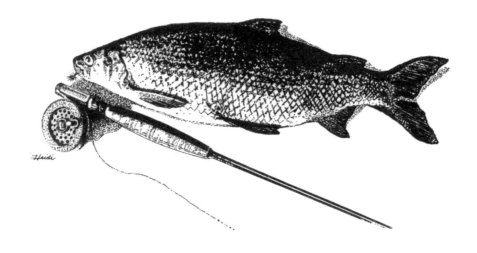

Chapter 3

Fly Rodding Challenge
"The Northern Whitefish"

It took an entire summer vacation for the ten-year-old lad to land his first silver-sided, moon-eyed fish. Many had been hooked, then lost. Each day, as the evening sun disappeared and Lake Helen calmed, huge schools of Lake Superior whitefish invaded the shallow lake bays near his family's resort.

Each evening the anxious young man would head down to dockside, shove off in a flat-bottom, plywood punt toward the calm, surface water-feeding fish and begin working a wooden fly rod.

At age ten, the young man had already accomplished the fine art of fly fishing. The area's many native brook trout, up to slightly over six pounds—a trophy in anyone's book—fell victim to his skill. But, so far, the one fish that had failed to come to boatside, often lost due to the absence of a net, was the soft-rising fish of midsummer.

Two fish had been viciously torn off by prowling northern pike. His four-pound leader and #12 dry flies were no match for a toothy northern pike bent on dinner.

One night in late August 1944, the lad would succeed, not once, but twice. Rowing some 100 yards west of the boat dock, oars were set to rest, and the boat slowly glided to a halt. A small, brown, bivisible dry fly was cast directly ahead of an oncoming school of fish. The lad had learned that placement of his fly was important. His first cast saw twenty-five feet between fly and oncoming fish. With thousands of mayflies hatching, there was much competition. The best chance of hooking one of these fish would be to set the fly by itself in an open pocket where no natural flies floated. When placed directly next to or in a group of natural flies, percentages of attaining a strike diminish greatly.

Moments dragged by as silver tails and dorsal fins appeared and disappeared. Slowly the school's position advanced toward the lad's solitary fly. The school was large, twenty fish at least. Then, as only whitefish can do, a three-pound silver fish gently rolled where the fly held. Mystically, the small, brown fly disappeared. Only the upper half of a silver-gray, forked tail was seen cutting the water. The hook was set, not hard as would be the case with trout, but with a slightly soft, foot-long lift of rod tip. The tiny hook dug in. A stubborn fight began. It was a battle that lasted nearly ten minutes.

Previously lessons had been learned: You cannot horse or force this soft-mouthed fish. Too much pressure would see the hook barb rip loose and a trophy lost.

The lad grimaced under each hard, surging, twisting run. The hook held. Twice the silver fish leaped long and far, a jump like none other the lad had seen, a leap that carried the silver fish horizontally across water some five to six feet.

Finally, with thick, muscular body quivering from exhaustion, the silver prize came to net. The lad was ecstatic. He wanted desperately to race to the hilltop and show off his prize, but somehow composure was regained, and the limber bamboo fly rod was placed again in action.

Six more fish were hooked that night, and only one of these, a four pounder, would be brought to boat. It was a moment in time that began a quest that would last a lifetime.

As years slipped by, the lad pursued the mighty whitefish wherever he went. From Lake Michigan to the turbulent waters of tundra rivers, whenever whitefish rose to the fly, all other species were instantly forgotten, and the pursuit of the whitefish was taken up. This writer knows . . . for it was he who so proudly displayed that first pair of glittering white fish for all to see some fifty years ago.

Yes, even today the quest and challenge of landing just one more whitefish remains. Let lake surface calm, a bug hatch begin, and the dimpling rings made by soft mouths commence, and there's no holding me back! No matter what fish I then pursue, it is immediately forgotten in favor of the challenging fish of my youth.

Whitefish abound throughout the northern half of North America. They are found as far west as Oregon and as far east as Maine. Their range begins in Illinois and extends far into the Arctic. Being a larva and insect feeder, they are not readily taken on standard fishing gear. Being a deep-water fish, found to suspend in forty to eighty feet, whitefish are seldom seen by the angler except on a flashing depth-finding machine. Often whitefish are mistaken for other species that refuse to strike. Such encounters can be most frustrating to the angler. Only when this silvery fish heads to the surface is he easily caught and then only by a tiny fly identically matching the current hatching insects.

In the far north, whitefish find the taste of pesky blackflies most rewarding. Can you imagine how many of these bothersome critters a five-pound fish must eat to fill his stomach? But, for the most part, whitefish prefer shad flies, dun, or mayflies, insects with a bit more bulk than the tiny-bodied, bothersome blackfly. It is at these times, usually in late June, July, and early August that an angler is able to cash in on Mr. Whitefish.

Ardent fly-fishing anglers are advised to select dry fly patterns such as (in order of effectiveness) Black Gnat, Adams, Black Ant "Dry," Coachman, March Brown, Gray Hackle, Hendrickson Light, Water Walkers, Beaverkill, or a Mosquito. There are others such as a Royal Wolf or an Irresistible that work well and ride high due to their heavy dressing, but if these are selected, do so in very small sizes . . . #14s preferred.

Nymph and wet fly patterns that will work on whitefish are March Brown nymphs, Ed Burke nymphs, Mosquito Larvae nymphs, Black Gnat wet, Hare's Ear wet, and a Quill Gordon wet. Select these flies in #12 and #14 sizes.

During a 1985 outing, my fishing partner, Bob Vos, and I found a huge school of whites working a large slick of white foam below a rapids on the Dubawnt River in the Northwest Territories. As normal in this case, the colorful grayling for which we were angling were immediately forgotten. The fact that we'd taken a dozen or so trophy-size fish made little difference. What was a four-pound grayling in comparison to a six-pound whitefish?

Not having worked whitefish before, Bob found leaving the colorful, leaping grayling a bit hard. That only lasted until he set hook in his first white.

"You're right, Gapen! They fight like the devil!" Vos acknowledged as his first fish twisted and rolled its way into deeper water.

"Did you see that? That fish jumped across water nearly ten feet! He must have come down so hard it tore the hook loose," exclaimed the startled angler.

It was true; the fish had torn loose, but in doing so, it had instantly converted another fly fisherman to the art of angling whitefish.

That day on the Dubawnt, Bob and I caught but five whites. The largest tipped the scales at near six pounds. We lost a dozen and a half and failed to hook another dozen. One of the lost was estimated near nine pounds. They didn't come easy. The school had come to feed on blackflies beneath and within misty surface foam in circulating eddies. Imitating such an insect is not easily done.

Finally, after a dozen or so flies and nymphs were tried, Bob came up with the idea that only the red floss and peacock hurl of a Royal Coachman dry fly body be used. It worked! Why it worked, I'm not sure. Possibly the bunched peacock hurl reminded the feeding fish of a pair of tiny, gray-black blackfly insects. No matter . . . it didn't take long to trim the brown hackle, white wings, and golden pheasant tail off one of the #12 Royal Coachman dries.

At one point, a rising fish, later weighed in at five-and-one-half pounds, missed my fly and accidentally foul hooked himself in the dorsal fin. You would have thought Jonah and the Whale had been set upon. Round and round our boat, far out of range, the fish circled. Each time he was brought within seeing distance, there came another tremendous burst of power, and thirty more feet of flyline was lost. It took nearly fifteen minutes to bring that fish to net. At the beginning, before he was seen, I was convinced a fifteen pounder had been hooked. Such was not the case. However, it did establish how much power and stamina these thick, bulky fish have.

Fishermen, those familiar with the art of fly fishing, wanting to give whitefish a try, can easily do so without ever adding to the equipment they now possess. A seven-to-eight-foot fly rod, line to match, a standard assortment of dry flies and nymphs, plus some good dry fly floatant are all that's needed.

The tough part about whitefish angling is locating the fish, getting him to hit, and controlling his fight. As previously stated, whitefish have an extremely tender mouth, paper-thin along its outer sides. Only in the upper portion of the jaw and nose is there enough gristle to adequately hold a hook. Setting hook becomes a most critical feat in taking whitefish. It must be done . . . not too hard . . . and not too softly. A gentle lift of rod tip as the fish rolls over and ingests the fly is all that's needed. Often this is a hard act to accomplish, since whitefish have a slow, rolling strike that lasts two seconds. Anglers unaccustomed to the sight of such action react hard and fast, too hard and fast to properly place a hook in this fish.

Once hooked, the use of force must be curtailed during the first portion of the fight. At this point whitefish do most of their rolling and twisting. As with lake trout, whose battle is made up of a great many rolling twists, the whitefish begins his fight for life in a similar manner.

Not being successful at freeing himself, the tactics will change in midstream, and there now begins a steady, driving, forceful battle. Often during this latter portion of the fight, a whitefish will elect to leap high above surface a time or two. In the end, a hooked whitefish exhausts himself completely, coming to net belly up or on his side.

To locate whitefish, look for lakes that are deep, rocky, contain sand and gravel, are relatively clear, and prone to fly hatches in silted bays. Lakes that contain lake trout generally harbor whitefish. River systems throughout northern Canada normally hold this species. Here whitefish are found feeding directly below rapid water in circulating eddies, especially those where pockets of frothy white foam gather.

Whitefish are easily identified by their slow, rolling feeding patterns as they ingest insect life from the surface. The telltale dorsal and tail fin slicing surface water targets these feeding fish as a whitefish. In some instances, soft sucking pops will accompany the visual sighting of feeding whitefish.

In lakes, their feeding pattern takes on a pattern similar to that of a school of porpoises gliding along a sandy ocean beach at high tide. Look for whitefish to form a similar pattern along lake bays. Once a block of shoreline has been traversed, the school of whitefish reverses course and returns along its previous route, feeding as it goes. Each fish will suck a fly from the surface, roll a swooping pattern deep and come to the surface once again to ingest another fly. Generally the space between surface breaks extends a length of fifteen to twenty feet. Knowing this, the angler is able to place himself and his boat ahead of the advancing school and places his fly the correct distance ahead of the targeted fish. The hardest part is the wait as a school passes. Never fear—if you fail to obtain a strike this time, the moon-eyed fish will soon return.

Feeding time seems to last as long as the hatch continues. Attempting to draw this fish to the surface, as you would do with trout, when there aren't any hatching insects, is a quest in futility. Pursue whitefish only when there is natural competition.

There are times when whitefish take nymphs even better than dry flies. Such times occur prior to a hatch or during premature hatching of insects that have failed to make it to surface and adulthood. During such times, whitefish can be seen carrying on in a similar feeding pattern but without breaking the water surface in such a visible manner as when feeding on adult dry flies.

Flies representing duns, shad, and mayfly nymphs generally do the best job of enticing whitefish at this time. Work your offering closer to the water surface than you would do in the case of nymphing trout. A similar erratic action is given to the nymph worked for whitefish as that given to a fly fished for trout. There is no need for sinking wet tip lines.

When it comes to eating, there is no better fish than Mr. Whitefish. Baked, broiled, fried, smoked, or boiled, he is a table delicacy beyond compare. Bob "Banjo" Ecker, our host and guide on the Dubawnt River trip, smoked several whitefish using a family recipe. Using only brown sugar, salt, and birchwood smoke, Banjo turned those silver whitefish into meals of golden brown tablefare, the likes of which you can't imagine! There aren't words to describe just how delicious those smoked white-fish were.

Bob and I enjoyed ten days on the Dubawnt River. Much of our time was taken up fly fishing huge northern pike and trophy-sized grayling . . . but, whenever whitefish were spotted, all others were forsaken, and the two of us would take off immediately after the fish of my youth. In all we caught about three dozen, far fewer than grayling or northern pike. However, the challenge of catching whitefish was greater; the rewards were unbelievably better! Our largest whitefish tipped the scales at eight-and-one-quarter pounds—not a monster, but still a trophy—a trophy even better than several pike in the fifteen to twenty-seven-pound class, caught on the same fly rod with giant poppers.

Angling for whitefish with a fly rod and fly spans a period of time between mid-June and late August throughout most of its range. In the north, this time is narrowed to a period between July and August. In its southern range, sightings of whitefish feeding on the surface may begin as early as May and last well into late September. Sightings depend entirely on the availability of hatch-ing insects—insects this fish find palatable.

If there are doubts about the fish you have spotted breaking the surface on your local lake or stream, and if all lures of enticement are rejected, most likely they are whitefish. If the surface break is slow and rolling, the feeding pattern dolphin-like in manner, and the fishes' fins sparkle silver reflections, they must be whitefish. If you're fooled, you're not alone. Whitefish can baffle even the best of anglers. From Maine to Minnesota to Oregon, this fish is often mistaken for other species.

Thus a rule of thumb: When in doubt, assume the rising fish to be whitefish and break out your fly fishing gear. Check out the hatching fly pattern. Match it, and go to work. The rewards are beyond belief. Whitefish angling is a sport every fly rodder can do . . . a sport, once tried, that will stay with you as long as you're able to lift a rod.

> *NOTE: For information on a rafting trip on the Dubawnt River for grayling and giant whitefish turn to the Information Page at the end of the book.*

The Mayfly or Shad Fly (*Hexagenia limbata*)

The far northern reaches of North America host nearly a hundred different species of mayflies. From two inches in length to less than a quarter of an inch, these whitefish-enticing bugs hatch periodically in northern waters. Unlike some of the other insects, the mayfly species can draw deepwater whitefish from the coldest depths of northern lakes. No one can say why this is. Hatching caddis, dunns, or mosquitoes never have the pulling power to draw the cold-water whitefish into the uncomfortable warmer surface waters like the *Hexagenia* species does. No one has ever been able to explain this. It may be the taste, the over-abundance of their hatch, or the protein enhancement whitefish gain from this particular insect that causes this fish species to go against all rules of nature. Whatever it is, whitefish respond to the hatching of mayflies like no other food on which they feed.

Dry flies in the colors of brown, gray, tan, yellowish-brown or any combination of those will work. Fishermen must match the size of the fly more than the color to the size of the hatch. It is also a good idea to adapt the outlining details of the natural fly to the fly used, as well. Remember, what the whitefish sees from below is silhouetted against that sky. Thus, what they see is more form than color.

23

Tips and Bits
OF THE NORTHERN NATURAL WORLD

During the hot months of summer, Arctic polar bears hunt seals by swimming underwater and emerging directly in front of the targeted seal as it sits at the edge of an iceberg. So adept at swimming underwater are these white bears that they can literally end up face to face with their prey. What makes this tactic so advantageous is that a seal cannot back up; they can only propel themselves forward, and seals always face open water when resting on an ice flow. This gives the polar bear a heavy advantage. The seal is always forced to jump forward, and that action propels it directly into the bear's grasp.

Chapter 4

The Horn

The terrain along the western shoreline of Wager Bay is, for the most part, blackened and evil. Few trees grow from the ominous volcanic layers of hardened fire rock. Near the oddity known as "reversing falls," cliff structures have been rounded by time and weather, their surfaces salted by millions of crystal-black fragments. Between the deviled jewels, occasional cuttings of tundra berry and mosses grow. It is a world of troubled beauty.

West of the reversing falls, the hills of Ford Lake have a similar vertical, tilted look. They are gray and aged with patches of burnt orange lichen, attached as if sprayed upon the rock face by some air brush artist gone amuck.

Near water's edge, the base stone is smooth and slick, still vertical in construction, rising bold and square to meet the base of structures towering above. Vertical lines meet, divide, and reach ever upwards dramatically toward the heavens. Wall construction along much of Ford Lake appears to have been created by some giant contractor using the largest building block the world has ever seen. Wherever the upper portions of these palisades allow, Arctic vegetation covers the narrow, flat spaces with blankets of green moss.

Tens of thousands of years of wind, rain, and ice have chipped away at the once-towering altars of molten firestone. The coming and going of expanding ice has taken the greatest toll.

Halfway up the southern shoreline of Ford Lake, a small, rock-tormented, clear water stream enters. It is a system that sees a torrent of raging, boulder-smashing water cascade down its length as spring melt reaches peak runoff.

On such a day, as runoff peaked, a small band of bearded muskox attempted to cross the raging torrent two miles upstream from Ford Lake.

The date was long ago, long before the coming of the white man. The time . . . midday. The weather . . . blustery with scattered snow showers.

The herd, diminished by the loss of an ancient bull four months earlier, numbered only nine. The bitter cold of February had been the undoing of the aging herd bull. Leadership of the herd had yet to be designated between the two remaining mature bulls. Mating season would see this matter settled. The remainder of the herd consisted of a pair of yearlings, two newly born calves, and three cows.

As often is the case, the oldest cow led the herd to water. She chose a gradual, sloping, gravel riff between a pair of bouldered bars on which to enter the swollen stream.

Years of experience and timeless instinct had instructed the cow well. This place was the only option the herd of nine had to cross the raging river. All others, for a mile upstream and a mile downstream would surely bring certain death to one or all of the herd's members.

Downstream from the gravel riff, a raging torrent dropped off into a chasm of roaring white death.

The old cow's entry point selection would allow even the youngest herd members enough time to reach the far shoreline with no fear of being swept away. The adults would need to swim a mere ten yards, while the yearlings and current year's youngsters would have nearly three times the distance before their feet touched bottom once again.

As often happens with any animal species, there are those who refuse to follow. So it was with one of the teenage muskox. With the lead cow entering water, the impatient youngster darted back past a trailing bull and raced off down along the shoreline to a point halfway between the riff and the raging torrent. It was here he'd enter.

Caution thrown to the wind, the young muskox raced into the swiftly flowing waterway. His goal: beat the herd across.

Upstream, the herd with its leader's front legs touching the far shoreline bottom, appeared to be crossing without incident. They had drifted downstream to a point across from where the wayward youngster entered. The youngest of the herd began to emerge safely from the river, though they were extremely tired and panting, tongues lolling from their mouths.

Safe, the eight animals now glanced toward the struggling yearling. He'd have all but made it . . . were it not for a pair of submerged rocks. These were rocks normally placed high and dry on shoreline riverbed. This day they held eighteen inches below the surface and were an obstruction the young bull could not surmount. Try as he would, his legs were not able to find solid footing atop the submerged boulders. Each time he made an effort, the current racing across, around, and over the boulders ripped his front hooves away. Fear filled the dark, round eyes; the youngster's mouth gaped open.

Had the young muskox allowed his body to shift a few feet downstream, he might have had a chance. But, fifty feet away, water crested into a roaring torrent and broke away down the gorge. Instinct dictated that the youngster advance no closer to the death-dealing menace. The struggle continued, each attempt becoming less effective, more futile.

The herd watched, nervous tension rippling through their ranks. Then, with the yearling continuing to struggle, the herd of eight walked slowly uphill and over the horizon. The fate of the young one was already sealed in their minds. The youngster would soon perish and no longer be one of them. Instinct had taken over.

With a final effort, the young muskox lunged up upon the flooded boulders. He had seen his herd's departure. His effort failed, he slipped away one final time, then slipped on downstream.

Frightened, black eyes glazed over as the roaring waters rolled the young animal under. In a moment his life would be lost.

Pounded and battered, the young body tumbled and bounced about, striking stone after stone. Bones crunched, and skin ripped. Within moments, the once-proud youngster became a mass of broken, battered flesh.

The right horn finally made solid contact within a gap created by a vertical rock crevice at the chasm's lower end. With a tearing wrench, the animal's right horn was ripped from its head, the skull broken and exposed. Here it would stay, lodged firmly between two large vertical walls. The carcass would now plunge on downstream, eventually ending up in Ford Lake to sink into the unforgiving depths. Thus, the yearling would disappear from the land yet still remain part of it. So it is with nature.

The torn horn would remain behind, deposited within its craggy rock grave, solid as the bitter cold of an early fall descended on the land.

Ten years later, the eight inches of sharpened horn would be uncovered as shifting riverbed allowed exposure. The broken horn would remain in this state for countless years, its outer mass turning green under a growth of Arctic fungus.

Not until a wandering adventurer, Laurie Dickhart, discovered the horn tip during the summer of 1990 did the story become complete. Today the young muskox's horn rests in a place of prominence far to the south. He's not forgotten. The spirit lives on.

Tips and Bits
OF THE NORTHERN NATURAL WORLD

Eskimo means "man who eats raw meat." This is a term few Arctic natives like. They prefer to be called *Inuit*, a term derived from the name of the native tribes who roamed the interior tundra plains. The "true" Inuit followed the caribou herds, living completely off the herds. The last of the true Inuits disappeared in 1952 when they were extracted from the land by the Canadian government. They were deposited at the coastal town of Eskimo Point. The term, Inuit, means "The People" in the native tongue.

Chapter 5

The Hunt . . .

2,000 Years Ago

The Kamilukuak River departs open water north of an island known to hold a large herd of summer caribou. It does so through a pair of narrow channels, the western one nearly unnavigable, the eastern exit a bit deeper. Each has a slight current as northeast-bound waters glide over volcanic stones of gray and black. The water runs crystal clear.

Nearby swims a brutish, hook-nosed fish, its search for food an endless task. It matters little that its food often is a similar species. The immense brownish-gray lake trout eats anything that cannot escape its curved jaws and canine-like teeth. This is a savage land. Only the most vicious creatures survive. Such is the law in this wilderness place. So it has been for thousands of years.

Today, little has changed. Caribou continue to migrate north and south with the changing seasons, a happening that has changed little in thousands of years. Their passage follows the trails laid before them by generations of ancestors. Dwarfed spruce continue to grow and die along bogs and water-laced draws, as well as in those areas protected by the land's rock and sand eskers. Marmots scurry down well-worn tunnels beneath enormous boulders deposited by the melting of the icecap 10,000 years before as it receded northward. Wolves, white fox, and snowy owls remain the unchanging balance factor in this sub-Arctic region. Arctic hare, lemming, and ptarmigan hold keenly aware of such predators.

No, not much has changed! Not much, that is, except loss of the "people" creatures who once migrated through the land. They are gone, vanished, nearly without a trace.

So, this chapter is born 2,000 years after it began.

61.32° Latitude

102.30° Longitude

As It Was Then

Otok and his brother, Atertak, along with their wives, five small children, and an aging grandmother, selected Heronhead escarpment for their camp with good reason. It held higher than any other land mass along the Kamilukuak River and reached eastward into the river farther than any others. Constant tundra breezes, from all directions, swept across its face, a feature that kept pesky gnats and mosquitoes to a minimum. During the time of late snow melt and early summer sun, bugs could be the people's worst enemy. Skin tents, no matter how well constructed, provided little protection from these insect hordes.

Heronhead esker had been the summer hunt camp for as far back as the people could remember. Otok's aging grandmother, Attago, a leather-skinned, wrinkled old woman, had met her man there countless summers before. Even then, the people remembered back to a time when their ancestors told tales of summers spent along the waters of Kamilukuak.

Heronhead esker was a place of great advantage during the spring and fall hunt. *Tuktu*, the-deer-who-swims, was seen to cross directly beneath its easternmost point. Here the esker structure jutted farthest into the waterways. Observing *tuktu*'s single-file approach was easily done from the highest point on Heronhead. There was always sufficient time to ready for the hunt, soon to follow.

Heronhead provided an excellent area from which to gather the pink-fleshed fish that swam beneath the surface in the two large bodies of water north and south of the campsite. The northern water was open, wide, and carried as far as an eye could see. It had few islands and often erupted in great waves when northern storms descended. It was not a place on which to be caught in a skin canoe.

The southern water was more peaceful. It ran for several days south and was choked with mind-distorting islands. Several times, men of the people lost their way among these islands, only to return weeks later with whispered tales of evil places and fiendish monsters. Otok's wife's great uncle once became lost upon the southern water and never returned. Some claimed he was eaten by a devil monster. Others claim to have seen him a year after his disappearance, paddling the skin canoe within a great cloud of fog, which often persists above these waters. However, as he was approached, the old man paddled off to rise rapidly into the sky and disappear within the sun.

The bird-shaped esker, at its highest point, provided a large, gravel flat fifty feet in diameter capable of housing several skin tents. Numerous head-size stones, gathered years before, lay patterned to provide anchoring points when tents were erected. The flat open area was ideal for setting up housekeeping.

At a point where the high escarpment began to fall away eastward into the river bottom, several large volcanic boulders had been deposited thousands of years before. They made an ideal outlook station and provided excellent platforms to cool one's self on hot windy days. These same rocks, smaller ones, provided work tables on which the peoples' spear makers engaged in their art. Hundreds of white quartz stone chips, deposited beneath these work benches over the centuries, provided proof of this.

The Story of the People Who Came

Name	Story Character	Name Meaning
Otok	main man	Seal Basking on Ice
Atertak	Otok's brother	Bear Cub
Attago	grandmother	Let Us Endeavor
Unark	fourteen-year-old son of Otok	Lance
Anana	Unark's younger sister	Beautiful
Kayok	thirteen-year-old son of Atertak	Yellow Hawk

Heavy ice remained in north lake as Otok and Atertak arrived. Snow in ravines, drifted full during winter storms, remained deep in many hollows. Warm spring sun glazed their outer covers into nearly half-inch-thick ice, the edges consisting of icy razor-sharp crystals. Cold spring nights reversed any softening by the warm daylight melting. Snow on open areas had receded. With the snow's disappearance had come biting insects, millions of them.

The trip that led the people to Heronhead esker began sixteen days before, far to the south. Twice, young children nearly perished while forging icy cold rivers. Current-driven ice chunks rammed into the children as they waded waist deep in water, causing them to stumble and be swept away. Atertak was nearly lost when breaking through thin ice on a lake called Napartok. Had it not been for Otok and his quick response with a muskox hair rope, the people's finest hunter may have perished beneath rotted spring ice.

Two days before arriving at Heronhead, Otok's oldest son, a boy of fourteen springs, was nearly trampled to death by an angry bull muskox that mistook the youngster for a predator bent on attacking one of its herd's newly born calves. Tragedy was averted because of the animal's poor eyesight and the child's fast reflexes. It was a lesson never to be forgotten by the small forty-three-inch human. Unark, the boy child, had been warned by Otok several times about the anger of the hairy, brute-like animals. Angered and red of eye, this beast could be dangerous. Next to the barrens brown bear, who had no equal when it came to being mean and ferocious, *Omingmak*, the muskox, was feared most.

Unark had first spotted the small herd of muskox while exploring a tundra valley for edible roots and bulbs with his younger sister, Anana. Knowing his father would be interested in how many animals the herd contained and if there was a way one might be ambushed, Unark had elected to scout them. Being armed with such information would certainly make the young man worthy of praise by father, Otok. But, as eager children often do, Unark had tried a bit too hard and creep a bit too close.

Unark's stalk took him to within fifty feet of the closest animal, an enormous flat-nosed, shaggy-chested cow. Close beneath the female's hairy flank trotted a newborn, light-brown calf. The boy achieved his position next to the herd by scurrying up a rubble rock ravine, which ran 200 feet into the rocky boulder-strewn hillside where the muskox fed.

Before beginning the stalk, Unark had stationed Anana behind a huge, square, flat-faced boulder near the ravine's bottom end.

Slowly, the boy's beady, black eyes, shielded by long shaggy hair, lifted up and above the last rock. The eyes blinked. There, not more than four spear lengths away, stood a monstrous bull. The beast had been sheltered from sight by a slight dip in the land just above the ravine's uppermost point.

Unark froze in terror! Otok's words rang loud in the youth's mind. This hairy, musty-smelling beast was surely a killer of the people.

Time stood still!

The beast's eyes glowed red and appeared to stare directly at Unark. Body stench from the herd washed over the youth. He remained frozen, unable to move or blink an eye.

Without warning, the wind direction switched, and the omnipotent beast expelled a thundering grunt. Twice he pawed the ground, lowered the enormous shaggy head, then raced towards the boy. Rocks, gravel, and dust engulfed the coming charge. Unark could see only a heavy wall of hair supported by a huge set of black curving horns bearing down upon him.

Nerves stretched, then released, causing Unark to leap sideways just as the beast catapulted forward, instantly closing the distance between them. Nerves, armed by fear, had snapped and none too soon. Where Unark held a second before, there now stomped a very angry bull muskox. Head and horns pivoted from side to side; cloven hoofs trampled up clouds of dust. The beast had covered the short distance between them faster than a white bird of the tundra flushed from a mound of drifted snow.

Luckily, poor eyesight and another shift in wind direction allowed Unark to race off the escarpment undetected. Retreat was accomplished, but not without a series of hard falls and stumbling steps. Escape was not without damage. The panicked boy had torn skin and ripped clothing in his escape.

Back with the walking band, Unark sadly reported the find, his sister adding things Unark somehow failed to tell. There was no need to pursue the herd. By now they would have circled, positioning themselves against any intrusion by predators. Vulnerable calves and young cows would have been herded to the center of a circle with bulls and older cows forming the protective outer ring. Heads would be lowered and facing out, a position nearly impossible to penetrate. The herd would remain this way for hours, or even days if need be, to protect itself.

Unark was reprimanded, assigned to help Anana and their mother with women's chores. Otok would decide when the punishment ended.

Once the small band of people reached Heronhead, skin tents were quickly wrapped around aging wood poles, left behind the fall before. Skin thongs held each set of four pole tops tightly together while the outer skin shell was rolled around the structure. Next, pole bottoms were wedged tightly apart in four separate directions to form a perfect teepee-like shelter.

Around the structure's base, holding stones, used for countless generations, were rolled into place up and onto the hide's lower edges. The distance between each stone was one stride, twenty-eight inches. The distance across structure's middle, at its base, was eight feet. In some peoples' bands' encampments, this distance could reach twelve feet across, and winter homes might be even smaller.

With tents erected, fires—sparked by flint and dry moss—soon were lit. Each fire, constructed upon small flat stones, was manufactured low in profile and small in structure. It was the women's duty to keep these insect-rebuffing fires burning throughout all hours of the day. Special mosses and tundra vegetation were the ingredients that warded off marauding insects.

Inside the tents, a line of head-sized stones were placed directly across the structure's middle. These would be a barrier against slippage of bedding mosses stored at the structure's rear. Bedding material consisted of foot-deep tundra moss. During the use of this structure, mosses would be periodically replaced as needed.

In the structure's forward semicircle, fresh gravel was laid down. This eliminated, or partially eliminated, the intermingling of esker sand and food. Sand and cooked meat make for a poor meal.

The forward portion of the skin structure wasn't always used for cooking. Much of the time cooking was accomplished on outside fires. Only during inclement weather was it necessary to cook inside. Often, fresh meat was eaten without cooking, a habit inherited by the people from their ancestors. There was no better treat than the hot, steaming heart or liver of a freshly killed caribou.

With summer camp set, the people of Otok's band began a residency that would last until departure in the fall when the last of the caribou migrated south past this place. The only happening which would alter this habitation would be the failure of the caribou herds to come.

Unark, the boy who failed to properly scout the muskox herd, was given first day watch for caribou. He would sit atop a huge boulder near the esker's eastern edge and watch for the coming of *tuktu*.

Spring migrating caribou herds came from the southeast to cross the water only ten spear throws beneath the lookout stone. The first sighting of the herd's lead animals always came three hills to the southeast, some half day's travel away. Such advance sighting gave band hunters plenty of time to plan an ambush.

Unark would fail this time. Gleaming black eyes held riveted towards the southeast where the first horns would rise above the skyline. In nearly all cases, an aging cow would lead the herd.

Six days came and went. Each morning the boy took his place atop the giant rock. Each morning Unark was allowed this honor only after promising his father he would not blink an eye. Otok, being a wise father, knew his son would work harder than all others to right the mistake made previously.

The sun was near its highest point on day six when *tuktu* came. Unark, dazed by the sun's warmth, gazed in disbelief. Twice eyelids blinked closed, then reopened, while his head shook to eliminate the daze. Faint etchings along the southeastern skyline moved.

It was true, movement came again. Moments later seven shapes appeared above the far hilltop.

"*Tuktu . . . tuktu . . .* he comes!" yelped the fully awake lad.

Leaping from his perch, Unark raced down towards the lake below. Here his father and uncle were patiently waiting on the migration of giant trout through the narrow passage of water between the large lakes. In six days these men had speared fourteen large fish and eight small "fish-with-high-fin" species.

"*Tuktu*, Father. He comes," panted the youth as he stumbled to a halt.

"How many, Son? From where do they approach?" questioned Otok quietly while stepping down from a large, flat rock that had provided an excellent station from which to eye fish passing below.

"There are as many as there are days in winter," the child exclaimed excitedly.

"Are you sure, Son?" Otok asked while motioning brother Atertak to follow.

Remembering his muskox tale and how over eagerness weighted trouble down upon him, Unark revised the statement.

"I saw only seven *tuktu,* Father, but surely there must follow as many as the great white bird has feathers." Unark restated.

"Possibly, Son. Your uncle and I will see," Otok replied while smiling slightly at his son's revised tale.

Leaping atop the lookout rock, Otok's eyes scanned the southeast for movement at skyline. There, just visible at a high point where land and sky met, he saw a movement, then another and another. Unark had told a truth. *Tuktu* was on his way north. The spring migration had begun.

Otok and Atertak watched carefully. Grunting approval, each nodded acceptance of Unark's first sighting. Carefully, the band leaders counted.

First came seven, then a small band of eleven, then three large bulls. Excitement welled up in their eyes, and voices babbled rapidly. A hunt must be planned.

Since their arrival, the people had eaten only fish and a few small ground squirrels. The squirrels had been captured by Atertak using a "fallen-stone" rock trap. Flesh, heart, and liver of *tuktu* would do much to replenish the strength depleted on the journey north. Also, there would be the opportunity to devour the large, white grubs carried by *tutku* beneath its back hide. These grubs were established along the animal's backbone by Arctic warble flies when eggs were deposited within back hair the summer before. The resulting larvae burrowed beneath and through back skin and lodged along either side of the caribou backbones. They are considered a grand delicacy when found in an animal and immediately eaten with great delight.

> *Warble fly grubs (larva) were highly prized by all native cultures who traveled the barren regions during the 10,000 years man persisted there. Such grubs grew to thumb size, at times, and were excessively high in protein. They were eaten immediately and with great relish, much as candy would be today.*

The First Hunt

The hunt plan was simple. Otok and Atertak, armed with three quartz-headed, wood-shafted spears, would cross the first shallow rivulet to the low, jumbled, rock island. Here, once *tuktu* crossed the fast, much larger river, an ambush from hiding would take place. The first animals would be allowed to pass and enter the small rivulet nearest the esker. Here, they'd be met by Unark and Kayok, Atertak's oldest son. Confronted by the two boys, who would hold in hiding until the lead animals entered water, the lead caribou would turn back upon themselves and onto the island.

By this time, any animals following the lead seven, would be within striking distance of Otok and Atertak. In the confusion that would surely follow, the brothers certainly would be able to down two or more animals.

It was a good plan. The boys were delighted with their assignment. Each would receive a short-shafted spear to wave at *tuktu* when their time to leap from hiding was upon them.

The women and other three children, two girls and a boy child, were allowed to watch but only from high above, near the esker's highest point. It would be necessary that they remain absolutely quiet and frozen still while hiding behind the rocks. *Tuktu* was leery, and though poor of eyesight, his sense of another's presence and his sense of smell were very good.

Knowing "God of *Tuktu*" was more apt to reward the hunter who wore special hunting skins, Otok and Atertak donned their finest caribou skin capes. Each had been fitted with the long hump hair of *omingmak*, the muskox. *Omingmak's* strong hair would fall down over their arms, causing each hunter to gain in arm strength when engaging the mighty *tuktu*. Much strength would be needed to drive the long wooden spear shafts deep enough into the deer for a certain kill.

Next, each hunter's shoulder-length head hair was combed straight by using the bleached backbone and ribcage of a *siksik* (ground squirrel). Such action, before a hunt, would see god-of-the-hunt smile down upon them. This was so, for was not the ground squirrel the one who best hid from *tuktu* when he passed?

Readied, the hunters, followed by their sons, slowly crept down the esker's rock- and brush-covered southeastern slope. At the first stream the boys were assigned their hiding places. These consisted of animal-sized rocks, black in color, a short spear toss away from water's edge.

Sighting *tuktu* had been a step towards erasing Unark's previous mistake. A good showing in this assignment would do much to reaffirm faith lost in him by his father. This would be a big test.

Unark was left in charge of cousin Kayok. It would be Unark's decision as to when the boys should leap from hiding to drive *tuktu* back towards Otok and Atertak. It was an undertaking with much responsibility.

At this moment the lead caribou worked slowly over a gravel ridge three low hills away. Otok and Atertak had plenty of time to ready themselves.

At the island's center, a number of large, block-shaped stones sat as they had been mixed and tossed. Snaking between their bulk ran a narrow, well-worn, deep, trail. It was a path etched there by tens of thousands of animal hooves over hundreds of years. Along the island beaches, rocks lessened in size while numbers increased. No cloven-hoofed animal would dare go that way for fear of breaking a leg. Knowing these facts, the hunters stationed themselves behind a pair of huge boulders half way across the island. Otok would hide a spear length north of the trail while Atertak hid further on to the south on the trail.

Before crossing to the small island, Otok tested the wind. It blew right. Only a light breeze from the northeast-by-east could be felt. The migrating animals would be long past either hunter before discovering their presence. If luck held, the animals might even reach the hiding place of the two boys before scenting any trouble. And, with luck, *tuktu* might never smell the men who intended to kill them.

Time passed! The afternoon sun grew hot. Hunting skins caused heavy perspiration. Flies buzzed about. Wind died, allowing gnats to mass above and about the hunters. It was hard not to brush the hungry hordes aside. Both hunters knew success depended on their ability to hold undetected.

They held frozen, a spear length from the migration path.

Then came a sound of splashing. Animals had entered the water to their east. Several more sounds of splashing water, a grunt and then silence.

Both men readied themselves. They must now make their bodies a part of the hiding rock. *Tuktu* must pass by without knowing of their presence.

Within moments a new sound came from the east. It was as if someone softly beat the leg bone of *omingmak* rapidly on stone. Then, more sound, intermingled in a steady drumming noise. *Tuktu* rapidly approached his arch enemy, "the people."

Only the buzzing of gnats and the drumming of cloven hooves echoed in the hunters' ears. The sound increased in tempo until it became nearly deafening. The men held rigid.

Like a prancing god, the lead animal, an aging cow heavy with calf, trotted past the hidden hunters. Tucked close in behind her rump came last year's nubbin calf, now grown to better than half mother's size. Next, another followed by two young males. All passed within touching distance of the motionless hunters.

The first part of the ambush plan had worked. The hunters continued to hold frozen against rocks, eyes nearly closed and motionless while pointed down towards their feet. Scent from the passage of animals clotted their nostrils.

Moments later, more caribou trotted into view. These, a mixture of young and old cows, most burdened with unborn calves trotted along the ancient trail as if drawn by a magnet. Within the group, several yearling bulls jostled for lead position as they trotted along. This action caused one young male to dart to the left of Atertak's rock, and off the trail.

Startled by the animal's straying action, Atertak's hand and eyes moved ever so slightly. It was enough! Upwards reared the young buck, its front hooves leaving ground simultaneously, its nostrils snorting a grunt of warning, its eyes blinking a glaze of fear.

As if guided by the "god of lightning," Atertak's arms lunged forward and upward. The wooden shaft, so long held motionless in his hand, plunged deep into the animal's chest. Blood ruptured violently down the blade to cover Atertak's arms and hands. Only inches separated the two. Death had arrived. Animal and man thudded heavily to earth, bodies entangled as if one.

Unark watched the old cows cautiously enter the water yards away. Beside her trotted a splendid year-old calf. Unark remained hidden, without movement, his left hand restraining cousin Kayok at the shoulder. He must not fail his father. The cow must drip water from her belly hair before a move to drive her and the herd was made.

Steadily and cautiously the lead cow and her six companions forded the final waterway beneath Heronhead Esker. Time for action would come soon.

43

A hundred yards behind the seven leaders, Unark could see more heads pop into view above the island skyline. Hand pressure on his cousin's shoulder increased, breath came in short sips through clenched teeth.

"Kayok . . . it is time . . . drive them back!" yelped Unark while leaping forward from behind the rock.

Kayok, startled by his cousin's raspy yelp, froze momentarily before darting forward. It was enough of a pause to give Unark a six-spear-length head start.

 The lead cow had just placed her front feet on firm bank when Unark leapt towards her. Instantly, she reeled about, front hooves landing back in river water. Two leaps later she raced back across the island where now another action among the following herd was taking place.

Five of the lead cow's following animals managed equal mid-stream turns and headed back. But, the nubbin yearling, baffled by its mother's quick reverse of direction, hesitated for a moment before beginning his turn. That moment of hesitation would cost him his life.

44

Unark, short spear held high, was nearly on the lead cow's nose by the time it leapt into retreat. The boy had covered the ground so rapidly that his final steps catapulted his body past the lead animal to halt at her left flank. He stood a yard into the water. Spray from the retreating cow's hooves rained across Unark's face as she sped off.

What followed was never completely understood by the fourteen-year old but was clearly viewed by Kayok.

Kayok, some distance behind, was amazed to see the speed Unark managed to attain when dispatching himself at the lead cow. In only a moment his cousin was upon the animal. It had been Kayok's understanding that they were only to frighten the first animals back, not attack and engage them.

But, there, right before him, cousin Unark raced up beside the lead animal, turned to his right, raised his spear high and thrust it home into a somewhat bewildered yearling, again and again.

Kayok said that the attack on the yearling occurred a second after Unark risked his life as the lead cow wheeled high and about, front hooves nearly striking him on the head.

Only with the cow in full retreat did Unark's attention revert to the smaller animal on his right. Automatically, the youth's arms reached high, again and again, to thrust downward each time, driving the short spear into the yearling's backside. Rich red blood covered several inches of the quartz and wooden weapon.

The killing was over in moments. Kayok, feet planted at water's edge, watched in astonished admiration as his cousin, Unark, leapt upon the animal's back and, with a final thrust, drove the spear deep between its shoulder blades. The yearling's sturdy legs folded and its belly dropped beneath the water surface to rest on bottom.

Unark, shoulder muscles straining, held rigidly to the wooden shaft that now rested a finger above animal and the water surface. He remained there until all movement beneath his thighs ceased.

"Unark . . . Unark . . . have you killed him? Is he dead? Be sure before you get off! Can I help?" yelled Kayok while springing forward into the icy water.

"He is mine, Kayok. He moves no more. You can only help me drag him to shore, Cousin. He is mine! I have killed the mighty *tuktu* . . . you see?" proudly blustered the fourteen-year-old youth.

Pandemonium had broken out at mid-island. Atertak struggled to free himself from beneath the thrashing, dying two-year-old bull. Twice, flailing hooves struck the hunter on his thighs. Pain arched upwards into his back. Finally, with a wrenching lunge, the hunter freed his pinned leg and foot and regained an upright position. Two spears were yet to be used. Frightened caribou raced about, their movements without purpose, guided only by panic.

Four strides away, Otok thrust his spear deep into the chest of a large, brown-colored cow as it reared in an attempt to escape. As her body descended towards the ground, the hunter held firm to the spear's wooden shaft, causing the spear butt to engage the hard ground. Next, came a sharp snapping, created when the shaft broke under the weight of the animal as it pivoted past. Body weight caused the white quartz spearhead completely to penetrate the animal's chest cavity, exiting through the back next to the right shoulder.

As his spear broke, Otok fell backwards and rolled to his left. The smitten cow plummeted past him, stumbled to her front knees, regained an upward position, then floundered off. She would die moments later, her body semi-submerged in water at the island's edge.

By now, the lead cow, unaware of her loss, was rapidly retreating across the first water crossing. She would not become aware of the missing calf until a mile of ground was covered. Behind, all members of the herd trotted in panic. Even the three bulls who lagged behind in the northward migration now trotted south in panic.

Back on the island, Atertak had managed to propel spear number two into the flank of another two-year-old male. The wound created was enough to slow the animal down so the hunter might catch it at the water crossing. Then, howling at the top of his lungs, Atertak launched himself upon the animal's back. The third spear was then thrust down through its back just behind the shoulder blades. The young bull collapsed, smitten by Atertak's weight and a paralyzing pain in its chest. *Tuktu* died before stomach hair touched river water.

Otok had tried for another but failed when spear two ricocheted off the face of a large black rock. The animal he sought was young and provided a very small target.

High on the esker, women and children watched in delight and horror. Twice they'd seen their men fall beneath the hooves of *tuktu*. But, as fast as panic took hold, delight reoccurred when the hunters bounced to their feet in pursuit of another animal. And, there was that laughing pride all felt when the young boy, Unark, felled his nubbin buck. Before their eyes they'd seen a child become a man.

The sun had turned far to the west by the time Otok and his band finished their hunt by dragging four caribou carcasses up onto Heronhead esker. Unark, "the-boy-now-a-man," would accept no help in dragging his kill home. He bristled with pride, sinewy muscles straining with each lift and pull. Finally, completely exhausted, the youngster laid his prize beside the kills of his father and uncle. The feast could now begin.

Attago, a senior member of Otok's band, was given the honor of opening each animal's chest cavity. She'd done so hundreds of times before. Using a sharp-edged tool of clear white quartz, the aging matriarch quickly sliced open each animal's stomach. Smell from digestive gas and decomposing vegetation washed up and over those who'd crowded too close. Smiles and laughter accompanied the exposing of each caribou's entrails.

When Attago reached the fourth and final animal, she motioned to Unark to come close. Then, with aging eyes sparkling happiness, the old woman handed the boy her cutting tool. He would be given the honor of cutting on his first kill.

Gently, at first, Unark pressed the quartz implement against soft belly flesh. There came a sensation of hollow hair tearing beneath the sharp, erratic edge of stone. Then, pressing harder, a feel of ripping flesh pulsated up the young man's arm. A moment later Unark's hand jumped forward under pressure and descended into the beast's innards. Smell and steam erupted up into the boy's face. For a moment his stomach churned and sank, then intermingled with a moment of sadness for the animal's passing. The thought passed fleetingly, and Unark grinned broadly at his grandmother. There was no need to say anything. Truly, Unark had become a man. From this day forth he would join the band's hunts.

Finishing up her job, Attago now plunged hand and knife deep into the body cavity of the fourth animal. Extracting a hand-sized heart, still hot and steaming, she lifted it up and handed it to grandson, Unark. He must eat the raw heart of his first kill if the magic was to continue. Ancient tradition deemed it so.

Grinning broadly, Unark lifted the prize for all to see, then bit deeply. The boy, now a man, gleamed in pride as warm blood oozed down his chin. It took five more mouthfuls to see the heart disappear. The audience cheered and jumped about. The older members nodded in admiring approval.

With the first-kill ceremony completed, everyone got into the act. Otok and Atertak's wives opened the remaining carcasses and retrieved the hearts and livers. These were to be eaten raw within moments. Much power could be attained by such action.

The early summer sun fell below the skyline as the kill celebration came to an end. All lay stuffed with fresh raw meat. Sleep was in order. Tomorrow there would be plenty of time to prepare, or bury in ice storage, remaining portions of the kill.

Twilight descended. The people slept. All was quiet. Only an occasional buzz of mosquitoes, or mournful howl of a wolf, disturbed the tranquil scene. The world stilled its pace, then stopped.

Semi-darkness had fallen when the lead cow again approached the ancient crossing below Heronhead. Instinct, now stronger than any fear gained from the incident nearly half a day previously, drove her to return north once again. Cautiously, the first water crossing was approached. Head held high, nostrils breathed deep. Three times she entered the water, only to retreat again. Finally, with hesitation, she crossed. Behind the lead cow a herd, now grown to forty-seven members, followed obediently. Time could no longer wait. The unborn calf within her stirred, only days from birth.

At the point where the ambush previously occurred, the cow stopped, hesitated, stomped the ground several times, then continued on. The ambush would leave an instinctual impression during all the years to come. The ford below Heronhead would forever remain a place of fear.

Where her yearling calf met its fate, the cow tossed her head about, breathed deep several times, then snorted. There was no response. She passed on, stepped ashore, turned right and began to climb the northern slope of the esker. The lead cow and the small animal caravan passed two hundred yards north of Otok's encampment without incident. Full bellies and warm shelter do much to dampen alertness.

The Second Hunt

Otok woke to the warmth of morning sun penetrating shelter skin. Somewhere outside, he heard the yelping voice of Unark calling his name. It came from the east, near the esker's edge.

Sleep clouding his brain, Otok sat up to answer the call. What was the silly boy up to?

Without warning, Unark burst through the tent's doorway.

"*Tuktu . . . tuktu . . .* thousands of them, Father, thousands of them across river. This time I tell the truth," stammered the young man.

The boy must be believed this time for he had a first kill and was a man. Otok gathered his skin robe about himself and headed towards the rock outlook at the esker's edge.

It was so. There, a mile south of river crossing, a large herd of caribou milled in preparation to fording.

"You speak a truth, Son. There are a thousand, or more. They will cross, but so will thousands of others in days to come. Before we hunt again the kill of yesterday must be prepared and stored," Otok softly explained the law of the land to his over-anxious son.

"But, Father, this may be all that come. I must make a second kill to remain a man," Unark pleaded.

This day there would be no hunt. Instead, two large cooking fires were lit upon Heronhead, and a pair of caribou hindquarters were cooked. The remainder of the animals were stored beneath tundra mosses in the brown peat valley directly west of camp. Here, frozen ground was easily reached when the top layer of moss was peeled back. By storing the meat directly against the frozen ground, or in it, then relaying mosses over it, the cache would endure throughout hot summer months.

The cow Otok killed contained a special treat within its body. An unborn calf was discovered immediately when Attago opened the stomach cavity. Such meat was highly prized and a great delicacy. It, too, was stored beneath the moss in a frozen ground crevice. Here it would freeze solid within a matter of three days. Later the calf would be withdrawn to be eaten during the coming of the full moon. Tradition and superstition dictated that such action occur if the God of *Tuktu* was to continue to smile down upon the band.

Four days passed before Unark experienced a second chance to hunt *tuktu*. Thousands of animals had passed before the camp on Heronhead. Otok and Atertak had hunted on the second day, killing four more animals, but young Unark had been left back at camp, where it became his duty to fish for the family.

Day five saw a shift in the caribou migration. Instead of swimming across the narrows below Heronhead Esker, the herd had moved its water entry a half mile to the north. Here, at the end of a rocky point that jutted far out into the main lake, the lead animals were forced to swim nearly a half mile to the western shore. Hunting pressure and scent of man had forced the relocation of their crossing point.

This day would see young Unark get his first lesson in how caribou are harvested from a kayak. Prior to departing, Otok explained to his son how the thrust of the spear must be very accurate if *tuktu* was to be taken in the water crossing. The quartz-tipped spear must strike a soft spot directly behind the skull where vertebrae and skull connect. Here, the spinal cord was most vulnerable to being severed. The opening was no longer than the size of *tuktu*'s eye. The kill must be made with one thrust of the spear. If the spear point did its job and severed the spinal cord, the animal would die instantly. If it missed and engaged the neck on either side of this killing spot, the animal would thrash about, and a second chance for a killing thrust would be impossible to obtain.

Otok furthered explained to his young son that, once killed, *tuktu* could be left in the water due to the animal's hollow hair, which kept the carcass from sinking. This day, with a northeast wind blowing, the harvested carcasses would probably end up ashore, close to Heronhead.

The next lesson young Unark would learn was how two men in a kayak could intercept the swimming caribou. Placing Unark in the forward portion of the kayak, Otok pushed off. They would paddle about a quarter mile up the east shore, then hide among the maze of glacier stones that made up a small point halfway between Heronhead and the long, rocky point where the herd was entering lake water.

Once hidden, Otok told his son they'd have to wait until the targeted caribou had swum to the halfway point in the lake bay. Once there, if *tuktu* saw the kayak coming, they'd become confused, with some animals wanting to return, while others attempted to reach the far shore.

In the confusion, the hunters would have the animals at their mercy. The closer the hunters could paddle their kayak to the swimming herd without being detected, the better their chance at being able to come up alongside for a killing thrust of the spear.

Otok and Unark waited nearly two hours before a herd of twenty-five animals entered the lake. In the lead came a cautious old cow, heavy with unborn twin fawns. Three times she began to swim, only to turn back. The followers crowded close on the shore, their nervous prancing an indication that they wanted to cross. Then, finally making up her mind, she struck out across the bay. One by one, the others followed.

The herd had nearly reached midway when Unark, mouth all agrin, turned to his father and nodded the question, "Do we go now?"

Otok shook his head, "No." He wanted the animals far enough past the point of no return to ensure the best chance for his young, inexperienced son to make a kill.

Moments passed slowly. Then, with a thrust of his paddle, Otok indicated it was time to go. The herd had passed the midway point in the bay and were fighting a stiff shift in wind. The hunters must take advantage of this distraction.

Keeping as low a profile as possible, father and son drove their paddles hard, making the skin boat leap across the choppy water. Within a hundred strokes, they'd closed the gap between the prey and themselves down to a few yards. So far, so good. The herd had turned slightly more north to fight the wind. This placed the hunters behind them, coming up on their rear. Not until Otok instructed Unark to boat the paddle and ready the spear did any of the animals realize they were there.

Upon discovery, the herd split. Ten animals went to the right with the wind, bent on returning to the entry point. The others turned slightly left, headed across the bay but more toward Heronhead than towards the closest land to their left.

Otok would have to choose. Digging the paddle to the right, he aimed the kayak at a young bull that had chosen to follow the old cow to the left. Three strokes brought the kayak's bow in line with the young bull's head. Only a spear length separated animal and skin boat. One more paddle thrust closed the gap. As animal hair touched boat skin, Unark, spear already raised, marked his target and rammed the quartz spear head home.

As instructed by his father, he immediately pulled back on the spear. It took a second tug to withdraw the spear, which had penetrated the animal's neck up to the broadest portion of the white quartz head.

As his weapon came free, Unark was startled to see the animal he'd speared react with only a series of heavy shudders. There was no thrashing of legs or wild head swinging. It was as his father had told him. A single strike, if properly placed, rendered the mighty *tuktu* helpless and instantly dead. The carcass now lay, head down, its back barely breaching the water surface, as it gently drifted with the swells.

Otok, upon seeing the spear blade withdrawn, knew his son had made a clean kill. He was pleased beyond belief! Truly his son, Unark, had become a man during the migration of *tuktu* the spring of his fourteenth year.

Leaving the young bull to float ashore, Otok once again drove his paddle deep, taking a straight course for the last animal in the brown cow's small herd, now numbering fourteen. Laying his spear aside, Unark took up his paddle to help.

The brown cow was just wading ashore as the two hunters caught up with the last animal, a small cow. Once again Unark raised his spear and drove the point toward the vital spinal joint between skull and back vertebrae. Over-confidence from his first kill played a trick on the young hunter. He missed the spine this time and cut a long slice along the cow's neck instead. Immediately the animal threw her head backwards and thrashed frantically with her forelegs. Mass confusion erupted.

Two more thrusts of the spear failed to subdue the thrashing animal. One met the heavy skull structure and glanced. The second penetrated the right shoulder but failed to deal a killing blow.

Realizing his son's attempts were failing, Otok stroked the kayak forward, then raised his spear high and drove the weapon completely through the cow's upper ribs.

The quartz head pierced the heart and instantly killed the animal. It would be a lesson young Unark would remember his entire life. Never again would he not give forethought to where the thrust of his spear would strike a swimming *tuktu*.

The hunt ended with another celebration as the women of the band collected and cleaned the two animals. Once again Unark was praised for his hunting skills, but the young man could only shun the comments, remembering how badly he'd performed on animal number two.

Late June brought hordes of hungry mosquitoes and gnats. Most of Unark's time was spent gathering a short bushy plant that produced a greenish brown paste when boiled in a rock basin. Smeared over the body's exposed skin, this paste made an excellent bug repellent.

Note: The Arctic tundra produces a short, twelve- to eighteen-inch bush that smells heavily of oil of citronella. Some call it Labrador tea, a name given to it by early European explorers when they discovered it made a substitute for tea.

However, it does make an excellent mosquito repellent when smeared on the flesh. Natural oil of citronella is produced by this Arctic willow bush. Citronella is a natural mosquito repellent.

June faded into July, and July into August. Late August saw the reappearance of *tuktu* and the frosts of fall. The small band would soon leave their summer home to follow the migration of caribou south. Before this happened, several more animals must be harvested. From them, winter clothing would be made. Second-year cows would be selected because their skins were the softest and also were strongest for sewing.

Before Otok's band headed south, only enough time would be spent at the summer camp, after the hides were gathered, to allow the women of the band to flesh and soften the hides. Winter would be spent, as it always had been, at the treeline along the banks of the huge body of water now called Snowbird Lake. There, the family would enjoy the comforts of easy access to firewood and the shelter of trees during the long winter that followed. Here the women of the family would fit the recently gathered hides into winter clothing while the men continued to gather more caribou for winter. It would take five to ten caribou for each adult and three to five for each child for winter nourishment requirements to be met.

Once situated at their winter camp, it would be a month or more before the main herd of caribou would arrive. Today that would be around November 1, a date that the caribou of today still keep at the north end of Snowbird Lake.

With winter passed, spring begins in mid May. The family would once again repeat the process of the following of the migration of *tuktu*.

Tips and Bits
OF THE NORTHERN NATURAL WORLD

Along northern Hudson Bay, at posts such as that at Reversing Falls on Wager Bay, wood—in the form of building supplies or firewood—was one of the main trade goods bartered by the Hudson Bay Company with the natives.

Chapter 6

Kashechewan's Grassland Geese

Bobby Wynne, our native Cree guide, pointed northward, smiled slightly, then dropped the freshly cut bundles of six-foot-long willow brush. Less than a mile to our north, a huge flock of snow and blue geese mushroomed skyward, then settled back to earth. The yelping and jabbering of snow geese is unmistakable. Quickly Bobby began to thrust willow butts in an eight-foot circle. It took two minutes to create the makeshift blind for my hunting companions—"Bobber" Anne Orth and Waldo, my ancient yellow lab—and me.

A moment later, nineteen Hutchinson geese flared above us, jabbered a complaint as their bodies shifted backwards and upwards with the wind. Our intrusion into the grasslands of James Bay had been duly noted.

"Lots of new geese," our Cree guide muttered, as he hurried off upwind to place a set of eighteen windsock decoys.

Bobby's soft-spoken words had a great deal of support. During a mile-long trek across sparse grassy tideflats, flocks of geese, most of them Canadians, raised skyward at our passing, only to settle back to earth immediately. Except for one flock of a hundred, most were one- or two-family gatherings.

Once we were settled in our blind, we saw geese in every direction. Later, I learned they were trading back and forth between freshwater potholes and grassland feeding areas. Our blind sat two miles east of the timberline and two miles west of the mud flats. The setting was reminiscent of the vast wheatland of southern Manitoba.

Anne and I had come to the Albany River delta in search of a story on the area's immense variety of waterfowl. Nowhere else in North America can the waterfowler hunt birds from the eastern and central flyways at the same time. Here an immense variety of waterfowl species adds to the intrigue. In a single day a hunter may see four species of honkers, snow, and blue geese, Brant, a lost flock of speckle bellies, pintails, black ducks, mallards, widgeons, baldpate, two species of teal, plus a variety of divers, including scooter and Harlequin ducks. It is here, on the western edge of James Bay in Ontario, that two flyways divide, sending some birds migrating southeast, others southwest.

Anne and I had settled on the Albany River deltas and its native Cree village of Kashechewan for good reason. There is but one goose camp, run by my longtime friend, Charlie Wynne. Kashechewan has a small population, unlike Moosonee, one hundred miles to the south. Moosonsee hosts two goose camps but has five times the native hunters, thus heavy hunting pressure. Both villages are serviced by commercial air via Air Creebec Airlines. Since I prefer solitude when waterfowling, we've selected the Kashechewan camp.

NOTE: James and Hudson Bay goose camps once numbered more than two dozen. Due to mismanagement and a very short season, many have failed. Today, even though air transportation is less expensive, there are only six operating camps. The Hudson Bay camps have a shorter season, two and one-half weeks. The James Bay camps, farther south, have a month. Bookings are normally done four days of hunting to a trip.

Returning to the blind after setting decoys, Bobby began to create mouth music, as only the Crees can do.

"*Kee-uuk . . . kee-uk*" He pauses, then once again produced sounds, "*Kee-uk . . . keee-uuk . . . kee-uk.*"

Three hundred yards to our south, an east-bound flock of twelve blues and snows veered northward in response. Pitching left, then right, the birds began a noisy approach towards the eighteen false geese.

Encouraged by Bobby's pleading, the incoming flock increased its jabbering, then set wing. Two hundred feet existed between gun and goose.

Suddenly, forty feet over us, seven silent Hutchinson geese broke into cry, arched into the wind and began to settle toward the decoys. They'd come low from the northwest, undetected by our keen-eyed guide.

Unnerved, the question became, "Which birds?"

Anne made the decision for me. Her gun raised and she fired on the closest pure white snow. It collapsed, instantly hitting tide flat grass solidly. My first shot folded an adult blue that plunged to earth, dead. My second shot made another white-headed blue hesitate, fold, and plummet earthward.

There had only been a single report from my companion's pump. Why?

Turning towards Anne, it immediately became obvious why she'd hesitated. Following the direction of her gaze, just out of gun range, a hundred snows and blues flared upwards. Behind them fourteen inbound honkers, now honking alarm, beat heavy wing to gain altitude. To our west a thousand or more snows and blues mushroomed skyward, startled by the gun shots. No sooner did they raise than they settled back to earth.

Waldo, next to react, retrieved Anne's snow first. But before the old dog's retrieving style, retarded by arthritis, could bring the last blue to hand, another flock of honkers flared skyward.

Nine Hutchinsons came next, yapping all the way. Anne doubled, and my little over/under .20 gauge collected a trailing single as the flock floated past my partner's side.

A single honker came next, unable to resist Bobby's calls. At sight of the thirteen-pound bird, our guides changed mouth tone to a *"Kurr-aunk,"* giving his notes a lower pitch. (No one can call geese like the Cree Indians on James Bay.) It did the trick, and I collected goose number four with a single shot.

So far, neither of us had missed. This would change shortly as flock after flock of pintail, black duck, mallard, and green-wing teal tore by overhead, racing with the wind, headed for the salt flats.

The biggest surprise of the trip was the number of Hutchinson geese (miniature honkers) and pintail ducks holding at Kashechewan. They were there by the tens of thousands.

Note: Transportation to Charlie's camp at Kashechewan had been via car, an eighteen-hour drive from Minneapolis, Minnesota, to Timmons, Ontario. At Timmons, Waldo, Anne, and I boarded Air Creebec's flight #805 and headed north to the gravel strip at Kashechewan. Unlike forty years ago when I last hunted James Bay, the only way in was via float plane. Then it was a long, time-consuming process, which cost dearly. Today, landing strips are available at all native villages on the bay.

Those who wish to hunt James Bay or Hudson Bay can avoid the long drive to Timmons, Ontario, by flying commercial jet to that point. Once there, a connecting flight on Air Creebec Airlines is available. Air Creebec flies twenty-four-passenger, turbo props north. This eases travel time to less than a day.

I elected to take my yellow Labrador along. When questioned, Air Creebec said there would be no problem. All I needed was a kennel in which he must ride. In 1996 it cost me $253.00 Canadian dollars ($160.00 US) for Waldo's round-trip ride. If you love your old retriever as much as I do Waldo, the cost is well worth it. Waldo may not be the fastest retriever, being twelve years old at the time and burdened with arthritis, but the old dog got the job done.

All too soon we had our limits of ducks and geese. It had been a short half day, our first, with three and one-half more to come. There would be fresh fried goose and duck breast on the table tonight. I could hardly wait. Charlie's camp is run on the American plan, and Charlie's wife, Elsie, is one fantastic cook.

High tide was an hour past when our party began its return to camp. We raced hurriedly down the tide-created river to beat the receding tide. The sun was setting, and we were tired. Had we waited much longer, there was the chance of being stranded up the river, waiting for the next high tide, eleven hours away. Each day, the guides plan the hunting trips according to tide flow. At low tide two to four miles of barren mud flats are exposed on either side of the Albany River delta. Walking across this mud-covered sand and gravel can be tough.

Against a fire-orange sky, thousands and thousands of green-wing teal erupted at our passing. Their flushing created a muffled roar as they rose from the exposed mud flats. Blackbirds in an Iowa cornfield would be the comparison. Once we'd passed, they resettled instantly and began their skittish feeding pattern. Neither Anne or I had ever seen so many greenwings in one place. In all, we may have counted forty to fifty thousand. In among the teal, hundreds of black ducks, pintail, and widgeons silhouetted themselves against the sunset. It was an awesome site, one seen only once or twice in a lifetime.

Day two was a repeat of day one. Bobby's soft voice, "Shoot. Shoot!" urged Anne and me to fire on a flock of honkers, the first to set wing on our decoys. Three birds collapsed, thudding to the tideflat grasses. We were well on our way into another great day of gunning in a world created for waterfowlers.

As the day before, there wasn't any trouble collecting a limit. The only problem came when deciding which birds to take. During the eight-hour hunt, we must have allowed 500 birds to pass over the decoys without shooting. Why end such pleasure? Anne ended up choosing to shoot adult snows, her only exception being that first honker. Except for the double I made on the first honkers, I chose all adult blues. Ducks consisted of all male birds, pintails and mallards, and three black ducks which were collected without knowing the difference between drakes and hens.

It was a hunt such as no other I've had in years. All hunts are good, no matter what the take, but this one was special. I'd gone back to a waterfowl world where I'd spent days guiding tourists as a teenager. Very little had changed. The bay still smelled and tasted of salt. The marsh still glistened silver bright, and the waterfowl erupted in abundance over the bay's gray-brown mud flats. It was a step back in time, one that brought tears to my eye as I boarded the turbo prop for our return flight back into reality.

NOTE: For information on Charlie Wynne's goose camp, turn to the Information Pages at the end of the book.

Chapter 7

A Dog Named "Teto"

It was a scene every waterfowler hopes to see one day. A prized retriever stretched flat out in full flight, bent on running down a crippled Canadian honker. Amid clouds of flying mud and spraying water, the epic unfolded. It was classic—one never to be forgotten.

Slowly the distance between man's best friend and his adversary closed. One hundred feet . . . seventy . . . fifty . . . twenty-five . . . ten . . . and then only inches. As with action in a slow motion movie, the scene continues. In an explosion of feathers, mud, hair, and water, it came to an end. Man's best friend had finished what man hadn't been able to complete. Goose and dog became one.

But, alas, something was wrong! Who were those outsiders racing down on our stage in a muddied four-wheeler? Two humans, no less, clung desperately to the bucking, metal monster as it roared frantically along the path taken by goose and dog. Could they be the hunters who wounded our fleeing bird? No way . . . it was I, the writer of this chapter, who had wing-tipped Mr. Goose. How dare they interfere! Didn't that dog have everything under control? Certainly he did!

But, whose dog was it? He hadn't come with me. Maybe he belonged to the two interfering humans. All questions would soon be answered.

Far out on the saltwater mud flats of Hudson Bay, the dog, the goose, the four-wheeler, and two humans came together—each player in the act now etched in a darkened silhouette against the silver tidewater background. There would be no loss of cripples this day.

I now began a long trek across the boot-gripping tidewater mud. No matter what, that cripple was *my* goose!

Moments after I set out, the dirty, roaring metal monster headed toward me. It wasn't long before a smiling, mud-spattered pair of gunners slid to a stop at my side.

"Lose a goose, Gapen?" queried the mud-caked driver, John Hicks, owner of the Nanuk Goose Hunting Camp at which I had been staying.

Behind John, one hand clinging to the seat's rear handhold, the other hunter, and my goose, sat Verna Bartlett, Nanuk's booking agent. Verna was equally as dirtied by tidewater mud as John.

"Yeah . . . thanks a lot. That would have been a long run if you three hadn't come along," I responded, attention riveted on the dog now seated in the four-wheeler's attached trailer. John grinned as he saw my interest in the dog.

"Gapen, I want to introduce you to Teto. Not bad, huh? He's learning, isn't he?" John laughed back as my astonishment continued to show.

Before me, four legs planted in the trailer box, stood the funniest looking retriever I've ever seen. He looked like a Husky, a miniature Husky. He was small, too small to carry a goose the size of the one I'd just seen him carrying. He was ugly! There was no normal retriever lines gracing his body. His lines were those of a rejected runt from some distant police academy. Besides, the tail turned up in a corkscrew manner, which was more associated with those ugly, little, yapping lap dogs older women seem to like to own. And his color—what color? My gawd, this thing that grinned at me from within the box of that trailer might have been called the original Heinz 57 variety canine.

"John, I just saw that 'thing' retrieve a goose, didn't I? He doesn't even look as big as the goose!" I blurted out as my host prepared to take me aboard.

"Sure did! He belongs to one of our guides who got sick and had to return to Churchill two days after arriving. Would you believe Teto is just a little over a year old? George has had him hunting spring geese, but other than that, his only experience has been the past three weeks here at Nanuk," John further explained.

Sitting next to my new-found benefactor during our ride back to camp was a bit humbling, but Teto didn't press the advantage. I received several licks and a couple of snuggles to make things more tolerable.

So, that is how I became aquainted with one of the greatest little waterfowl retrievers I've ever know. In addition to this, Teto may well have been the weirdest looking dog with which I've hunted.

Teto became a close companion the remaining three days of our stay at Nanuk. He went everywhere with my two hunting companions and me. Albert, our native guide, wasn't completely enthralled with the idea, but noting our delight at Teto's antics, he could hardly squash the idea.

Time after time the bright-eyed, little cur made retrieves only a highly trained Labrador might accomplish. Each time, he was rewarded with words of praise and a few pats on the head—and, each time, Teto seems to shrug this flattery off, appearing to be more interested in distant geese or some unseen adversary. There was an aloofness about this mangy mutt that was almost irritating. Admittedly, Teto was good, but at the tender age of one-and-a-half years, you'd think he'd have a little humility! If he were old, like this writer, then he'd have a right to be self-important and self-righteous!

Even so, Teto wasn't all good. He had bad points. For one thing, Teto didn't care much for water. I never saw him make those curving dives out over a flooded ditch to retrieve a downed bird. No siree, not Teto! Instead, Nanuk's famous cur retriever would gingerly tiptoe up to water edge, stick right paw forward, then down, and eventually follow through by entering the water, Nope, Teto wasn't all perfect. He may have thought so at times, but I found out Mr. Perfect had faults.

Take the time my hunting party downed three snow geese at one time. Mr. Perfect ran first to the nearest, then to the farthest, picking neither to retrieve. Instead, he stood there looking after the departing flock and finally picked up the second bird and returned to the blind. One of those pedigreed, field trail retrievers would have known exactly which bird was to come first. However, even I'm not too sure which one was supposed to be retrieved first. No matter, I'm not the one with that self-important attitude problem.

Teto was the only dog at camp. There isn't much of a need for retrievers along the tideflats of Hudson Bay. Everything is so flat and low-bushed that it's hard to lose a wounded bird. Native guides do most of the retrieving.

Being the only dog in camp left Teto in an enviable position. Everyone poured all the affection normally given their own hunting dog on him. In other words, Teto was spoiled. At least that's how I saw it. Some would say my attitude was a bit envious—maybe with some basis.

There was one time when I missed three huge honkers that passed right over me within easy range. Anyone else might have cast a few looks of condolence. Not Teto! He just looked away disgusted and refused to respond to even the most tender of enticing words. The brat was spoiled and self-righteous—and arrogant to boot!

It's funny a dog like that can get to you so much. Teto was nothing. If I were to see him anywhere else, he'd not be noticed—just a cur to be ignored. But here things were different. Here, along the mud flats of world-famous Hudson Bay, the little mutt's natural skill made him king.

That doesn't finish my story of Teto! There's more! Do you know what else he could do? Teto had appointed himself guard dog at the camp. With polar bears always a problem, especially at night, the yappy little cur would set upon any white bear that happened into camp. I remember one incident in particular.

It began when camp was rudely awakened at 2:00 A.M. the night after Teto ran down my big honker. Continuous yapping came from the direction of the camp's goose-cleaning station. John, Verna, and I were elected to run down for a look-see. We'd traveled less than a third of the way when the four-wheelers' lights caught Teto trotting back our way—back hair stood rigidly erect, tail curved tightly into a corkscrew, pointed ears held high, and eyes glistening with excitement. He obviously was engaged in a game he much enjoyed.

Bolstered by our arrival, Teto reversed direction and bolted back down the trail. Whatever was out there better take care; "Mr. Mean" was on his way!

Instantly, Teto was lost in the darkness ahead, his whereabouts noted only by the constant yapping, which now began again. Rounding the last curve in the trail, there came a fleeting glimpse of what Mr. Mean was disturbed about. A huge, white male bear 100 times Teto's size ambled out of sight into the willow bush. Teto followed, jumping and jerking at its heels. The dog had to be crazy!

Willows swished back and forth, dog yaps sounded, grunts and snaps echoed from within the shrubs, and finally out came "Hero" Teto. The bear was gone, all 1,000 pounds of him.

Teto trotted back past us and up the trail toward camp. Not once, did he look at us or ask for any thanks. The only time he stopped was to glance back and see if we were coming. He did that in a somewhat disdainful manner, come to think about it.

Well, I'm still not too sure what to think of Teto. He's one of the best damn retrievers I've ever seen. He's ugly, arrogant, playful, talented, unafraid, cute, mean, but most of all too young to possess any of the great attributes associated with top-notch retrievers. Obviously he's not afraid of the meanest bear that walks, he retrieves geese nearly his own weight, and he possesses an air that commands respect and admiration from all who meet him.

Super dog, you say? Well, not quite, but John Hicks better keep that dog named Teto around for a while. One can only imagine the progress "Mr. Perfect" will attain in twelve months. At the age of two-and-a-half, Teto may have learned to walk on water, considering his dislike for it. I'm thinking of taking my three labs up next year to take lessons, no matter what the cost. Waldo, my fat, yellow lab who has great disdain for water, especially cold water, could learn much from Mr. Perfect. Come to think of it, he also might learn to walk on—Nawww!

Chapter 8

Manitoba Stew

Should she pull the trigger? Had it not been for the hoarse whispering insistence of her guide, Mike Reimer, maybe Anne wouldn't have. This wasn't the bull we'd been stalking. He seemed smaller, and his head was nearly pure white. The original bull had heavier horns and more of a brown cast to its forehead.

Several herd cows and calves ranged near. They seemed nervous, acting like they'd bolt any second. "Shoot, Anne!" came Mike's encouraging voice. But was this the right bull?

Questioning thoughts raced through Anne's head while she peered through the .270 Weatherby rifle scope. Softly the safety was eased off. The party had stalked this herd of nearly 125 for nearly thirty minutes. It contained one huge trophy-sized bull and several acceptable ones.

As the crack of Anne's .270 echoed across the tundra, a dark brown cow, which had wandered to within sixty-five feet of our hiding place, bolted directly at Anne. It was instantly obvious the cow had mistaken the returning echo as the spot from which the shot had come. Ten feet from Anne's hiding place, the cow turned right and trotted uphill. Excitement and panic exploded within all members of the party. The frenzied cow had unnerved everyone.

The trip to Commonwealth Lake had long been anticipated. Preparation for the six-day hunt included gathering hunting clothing and equipment for caribou, geese and the fast-flying snow partridge, the "ptarmigan." Both rifles and shotguns would be needed.

Anne and I were more than ready as we drove from my home in Minnesota to Winnipeg, Manitoba. There we'd meet Dennis Maksymetz, marketing director of Manitoba tourism. Dennis and Anne had licenses for all three game species sought. I would have to be content with shooting geese, ptarmigan, and photos.

The 700 miles between Winnipeg and Churchill, Manitoba, was accomplished via jet aircraft. At Churchill, our party was met by Doug Webber, owner of Dymond Lake Goose Camp, our first destination. It would be a twenty-five-minute flight across the Churchill River delta on Hudson Bay by float plane to Doug's main camp. Thirty minutes after arriving at the main camp, we headed northwest to Commonwealth Lake Outpost, 120 miles away. A hot meal of roast goose was consumed during the layover.

Landing at Commonwealth, all eyes lit up as the float plane taxied towards shore. Resting against the outpost wall were four huge caribou racks. On the cabin's meat rack hung four sets of front and hindquarters, along with four beautiful brown-and-white capes. The hunters in camp had done well. It was a good sign.

Shortly after arrival, the plane departed. It took with it four happy hunters, their trophy racks, capes, and meat. We were left to settle in, ready gear, and eat a supper of fresh caribou steaks as darkness descended. It was Dennis' and Anne's first taste of caribou meat. As always, it was tender and delightfully delicious, with a taste similar to that of a four-star cut of beef. The first caribou hunt would begin at sunrise.

7:00 A.M. September 16

Guide, Mike Reimer, drew a sharp breath as he gazed through the spotting scope. His intake of breath indicated a decent bull had been spotted. "Huge bull—take a look," Mike grunted as the scope was passed over.

"This is what we're going to have to do," Mike continued. "I figure they'll come down the opposite shoreline and head up that far slope. We can walk, undetected, along the lake shoreline to the other side of the bay and cut them off. There won't be much cover, but the sun and wind are in our favor."

Walking around the bay was much more easily said than done. Following Mike's six-foot-plus stride made all three of us happy that I'd stepped up our exercise program in the weeks prior to the hunt! At times, Arctic willow and sparse shoreline spruce were high enough to allow stalking in an upright position. However, much of the time we crept along in a crouch. Spongy, wet tundra moss and huge granite rocks confronted us at every step. Across the bay, the herd continued to migrate. The occasional animal wandering off towards lake shore for a drink or the flash of a sun-glanced horn above shoreline willow were our only indication of the herd's position.

One hundred yards from the spot where we would intercept, it became necessary to crawl our way through a heavy brush-filled bottom. Beyond this point, cover fell away. The crawl became a test of endurance. Waders, heavy blaze-orange coats, and ten pounds of rifle tend to impede one's ability to belly crawl.

The herd was moving, some already passing our point of ambush. It was vital we cover the last twenty-five yards as fast as possible. With one last effort, Mike and Anne reached a small, isolated clump of willow. To go further was impossible. From here an animal would have to be picked and shot. Dennis and I settled in ten yards to Mike and Anne's left and slightly behind them. Anne would take the first shot.

71

Guns ready, we watched as members of the herd broke through the gully willow into the clearing before us. Here, they spread out across the slope and began to feed. There were several nice bulls, but where was the big one? Minutes passed! Cows and calves ranged ever closer. Quiet though we were, the closest cows sensed our presence. Caribou may have poor eyesight, but this doesn't hinder a sixth sense they possess when it comes to impending danger.

Still, the prize bull failed to materialize. I could see Mike's nervousness as he and Anne took turns viewing the herd bulls through her rifle scope.

"I hope that trophy bull steps out soon, Anne. The closer females are getting nervous. If they bolt, they'll spook the whole herd over the hill," Mike whispered.

Where *was* that big bull? He was the one Anne wanted! One hundred and sixty yards up the slope stood a good-sized, white-faced bull. Mike now turned his attention to this animal. Slowly Anne's rifle was raised, but only to check out the rack and animal makeup. It was a nice rack with a head and cape that were nearly pure white.

"It's not the trophy bull, Mike!" Anne whispered.

"You're going to have to take him. The others are getting ready to bolt," Mike prodded.

Still Anne held off.

Finally, not wanting to second guess her guide, Anne settled in and softly pulled the trigger. The animal hunched over. It was a solid hit to the heart. Field dressing later showed the single shot had blown the lower part of the animal's heart away.

At that very moment, with the white-faced bull sagging slowly to tundra, I spotted the trophy bull as it stepped from behind a set of tall Arctic willow to our left.

"Dennis, on your left! The big one!" I whispered hoarsely. There, no more than a hundred feet away, stood a monster of an animal. The big ol' bull had been there all along, hidden from view by lake shore willow. Dennis calmly drew down and squeezed the trigger. The bull shuddered, then took a single step.

Dennis fired a second shot, making sure the huge bull stayed put, and as fast as it began, our caribou hunt ended. Two fine animals lay within 150 yards of each other. It would make cleaning and skinning simple.

Anne's first caribou hunt was one she'd never forget. The animal she collected wouldn't be a record, but it was better than average. He truly was beautiful. White forehead fur set behind a coal black nose and an elegant white cape made this bull worth mounting. However, Anne decided to be content with a set of horns for the wall.

The next few hours were spent photographing, skinning, quartering, and hauling the caribou back to the boat. None of the meat or hides were wasted.

Manitoba opened the season on barren-ground caribou hunting in 1995. The Kaminuriak herd, once numbering less than 100,000 animals, has grown to over 490,000.

Observation of caribou at Commonwealth Lake in 1996 and during numerous fishing trips to Canada's barrens has educated this writer into believing caribou cows and calves are the most suspicious and watchful animals in a herd. Unlike whitetail deer, where bucks are the wary ones, caribou bulls can be rather stupid.

For an example take the time a film crew, Anne, and I were producing a fishing film on the Dubawnt River in the Northwest Territories. A pair of large bulls were spotted on a hill above the river. I suggested Steve Childress, the cameraman, and Anne hold back just out of sight while I sneaked up on them and flagged the pair into camera range.

With a light wind over my shoulder, I began my sneak, crawling from rock to rock, up over the hill. Upon breaching the hill crest, two pairs of antlers could be seen behind a pair of large rocks. Slowly a white scarf was tied to the tip of the fishing rod I'd taken along to perform the art of flagging.

What is flagging? Flagging occurs when you attempt to entice wildlife into range when hunting by working on their sense of curiosity. You flag with something like a colorful rag on a stick. By waving the flag (rag) back over your head momentarily, then stopping after a couple of flips back and forth, you arouse the curiosity in animals with poor eyesight. In some cases, as long as the flagger lays hidden from his intended victim, flagging can even entice animals with keen vision.

Once the flagger has the animal's attention, waving the flag is only necessary when the animal shows disinterest. If the animal you intend to entice is making its way towards you, never flag more than a single wave to keep its interest up. Too much waving can frighten the animal off.

Slowly I crawled to the point where I could barely see one animal's nose. Settling in behind a large, moss-covered rock, I waved the white rag high above me three times back and forth. The nose turned towards me, nostrils flared slightly. I waited thirty seconds and waved the flag again. The nostrils flared once again. This time the nose tilted up.

After another minute, the flagging wave was repeated. Then, as if by magic, two sets of caribou horns emerged completely above the horizon. The horns stopped moving as the flag disappeared. Now the top half of the heads were visible, beady black eyes staring hard at the point where the flag had waved. One more flip of the flag did it. As if drawn by a magnet, the pair of magnificent animals emerged and trotted right at me. Every fifty feet they would stop, turn their heads sideways, as if to pay as little attention as possible to the flag. But, always the eyes would return to stare curiously in my direction. The next moment they would again prance and snort their way closer. Finally, with only a mere fifty feet separating us, the pair of caribou bulls trotted to the downwind side of me.

Now they trotted at a faster pace, but not without stopping every ten feet or so for a "look-see" at the flag, which would come and go.

I had predicted the bulls would come close to Anne and Steve. I placed them slightly downwind and to my left. What I had not predicted was that my two bulls would be so hypnotized by the flagging that my partners would have to scramble to prevent being run over. Steve kept the camera running to the very last moment. The lead animal was but twelve feet from the camera tripod when it sensed Steve and Anne's presence. I was told later, that it was I who should have had the camera at that moment.

Once past Anne and Steve, the two fell into a steady trot and soon disappeared over the western horizon. It was a lesson I'll never forget. It proved what I had always believed. Caribou have very poor eyesight. Because of this and their lack of human contact, caribou are extremely inquisitive when confronted with unfamiliar objects.

Manitoba's Kaminuriak herd winters in the sparsely treed regions of northern Manitoba and northeastern Saskatchewan. Migration to the herd's calving grounds is north along the west coast of Hudson Bay to Chesterfield Inlet. Here, between the native communities of Baker Lake and Rankin Inlet, the cows give birth to new generations of animals. Some, not many, are seen to swim the wide water breach created by Chesterfield Inlet and give birth along its northern shores. However, most of the herd summers south of Chesterfield.

Like all mainland herds, the Kaminuriak herd has been on a steady increase over the last ten years. Unlike the late 1970s and throughout the early 1980s, a new method of counting caribou populations has come into play today. Once counting was done via visual ground sighting. Today its done by grid photography from aircraft. Once aircraft photography came into play, the biologists conducting the surveys noted a near doubling of the numbers. What once may have been a herd thought to contain less than 100,000 animals may have really contained double that number. Even so, there has been a dramatic increase in all caribou herd populations in North America.

Once back at the Commonwealth Camp, racks, meat, and hides from our hunt were rapidly stored, and it was off to hunt the popular snow partridge, the ptarmigan. It was my time to shine. With a double, over/under .28 gauge slung over my arm and hunting buddy, Dennis, at my side, we began a two-mile walk across the peninsula behind camp. This time Anne tagged along to take pictures. Three hours later, with fourteen birds bagged, we returned just in time to consume another delicious meal of caribou steaks, mashed potatoes, and all the trimmings. Tomorrow morning we would be up early, board the float plane, and head back to the goose camp at Dymond Lake for three more days of goose and duck hunting.

The bull that instigated the stalk, the one Dennis shot, was going to rank in Manitoba's record book among the top ten.

Note: Manitoba caribou hunts not only provide the opportunity to hunt caribou but also to enjoy the thrill of working migrating geese and ducks, plus a bonus of shooting those little white partridges of the tundra.

6:00 A.M. September 18

A soft, hissing murmured throughout the salt flats as tidewater receded. The eastern horizon glowed bright orange as the fall sun crept skyward, its beauty broken only by immense flocks of moving waterfowl. They would be upon us soon, their yelping calls filling the air. Each day, at sunrise the geese of Hudson Bay migrate inland to feed on the tender eel grasses of the tide plains.

To my right, hidden by a large, moss-covered, tideflat rock, knelt my hunting partner, Anne, and our guide, Tom Brightnose. Dennis Maksymetz, recipient of the trophy caribou Anne had failed to see the day before, had elected to stay at willow line, 300 yards to our west. The coming hours would prove that Dennis was human, as a box and a half of magnum ammunition blew skyward with little results. Later, Dennis would laugh off my kidding in his natural, happy manner, letting me know, it was he who shot the *big bull*.

Thoughts of the caribou hunt were abruptly interrupted as Tom began a crescendo of yelping calls. To our east, seven honkers veered, steadied, then began a soft glide towards the tideflat pool directly in front of us.

"Ready? . . . Wait . . . Wait . . . Hold it . . . NOW, take 'em," came Tom's harsh whisper as the lead goose lowered its landing gear.

Etched by a golden morning glow, the two human forms emerged from behind the huge, black rock, gun barrels locked on the incoming targets. The gunners emerged as if sprung from a sunken trap door blind in a far away Arkansas rice field.

Four resounding peals of thunder echoed across the tideflats. There hadn't been time for the birds to turn or climb. Life ended at that moment for three giant honkers. They now lay only fifty feet from their adversaries. Only the expanding, rippling, surface rings on the water were left to tell the tale.

"Anne, great shot! Just like us Indians! Well . . . maybe better . . . huh?" came the giggling congratulations of our guide, Tom, who was not the greatest shotgun shot on the bay.

These three geese completed the roundup of ingredients needed for a Manitoba stew Anne had been contemplating putting together when we returned home. Caribou, ptarmigan and goose mixed together. What a recipe they would make when properly prepared in Anne's special wild game stew.

"Dan, was that last bird yours, or mine? I can't believe you doubled with that tiny .410 over/under!" Anne commented, while Tom retrieved the birds.

"Well, Anne, I'm not sure, but I know the juvenile on the left dropped on my first shot. I did pull on that back bird with my second shot, but I'm not sure if I hit it," I responded. Anne mumbled something like, "Sure! With a shotgun, you can produce miracles.

I had best leave the question of who shot what alone and be happy with the bird I know I shot."

There would be plenty of time back at Dymond Lake camp, during supper, to kid and attempt to sort out who shot what. Right now, another group of twenty honkers had veered our way, attracted by Tom's pleading calls.

Two hours later, with a limit of birds collected, the three of us stomped west towards camp. Dennis and his two geese were gathered up on the way. The only acknowledgment of his poor shooting performance came in the way of a big grin. There would be plenty to banter about later.

There was no problem collecting our limit of waterfowl during the next two days. With snow goose populations on a sharp increase during the later years in the 1990s, they have become as available as blackbirds in a fall cornfield. It actually became difficult not to shoot too soon at times. Juvenile birds were everywhere. Picking out the larger, mature adult birds was very difficult as the masses of snow geese came to the decoys, intrigued by the magic of Tom's mouth calling.

No one calls geese like the native Crees along the southern coast of Hudson Bay. As going to grade school is a pre-requisite for children in the United States, learning the art of calling waterfowl is mandatory for children of the Cree. It is a legacy passed on from generation to generation.

Will I go back? Nothing but death will keep me from it. Having hunted the Bay, experienced the smell of saltwater intermingled with the sound and sight of thousands of waterfowl, I'm compelled to return. Besides, Anne has a bigger and better caribou to collect than the one collected by her partner.

NOTE: For more information on the Kaminuriak caribou herd, link up to Manitoba's information pages on the web site at www.learner.org/content/k12/jnorth/1997/critters/caribou/862934195.html. Here you'll discover the

latest details on where the herd is, as well as the migra-
tion path they've covered during the last three years.
Manitoba biologists have rigged eight caribou with track-
ing collars which provide daily information on herd
movement.

This is a copy of a stew "Bobber" Anne concocted after her
Manitoba hunt. This recipe will appear in her second edition of
"Bobber" Anne's Fish/Fowl/Game Recipe Book

Three-Meat Manitoba Stew with Dumplings

Stew

    1 goose, skinned and cut up
    1 ptarmigan, skinned and cut up
    1 lb. caribou steak, cut into 3/4-inch cubes
    4 large potatoes, peeled and chunked
    6 carrots, cut into big cubes
    1 onion, cut into big cubes
    1 cup celery, cut into 1-inch pieces
    2 bay leaves
    1 tsp. onion salt
    1 tsp. pepper
    2 tsp. Kitchen Bouquet seasoning
    1¼ cups flour
    1¼ cups water

Dumplings

    3 tbls. shortening
    1½ cups flour
    2 tsp. baking powder
    ½ tsp. salt
    ¾ cup milk

Put goose pieces into large, heavy kettle, add bay leaves and water
to cover. Bring to a boil, lower heat and simmer 45 minutes. Add
ptarmigan, continue to simmer ½ hour or until all meat is done.

Remove meat, set aside. Skim any fat off top of remaining broth, remove bay leaves. Into the kettle, put caribou, vegetables, onion salt, pepper and Kitchen Bouquet. Add enough water to barely cover ingredients. Gently simmer 1 hour.

Meanwhile, take goose and ptarmigan meat off bones. Return meat to kettle. To thicken stew, shake the flour and water together. Quickly pour into boiling stew, stirring constantly. Lower heat. Mix together dumpling ingredients. Drop by tablespoonfuls onto stew. Simmer slowly 10 minutes uncovered, then 10 minutes covered. Test a dumpling for doneness—it should look dry inside. Stew is ready to serve.

Chapter 9

"No Problem"

Below, the mighty Churchill River roared and tore its way through granite walls of volcanic rock—rock covered with massive, rich, green spruce forests. Then, as if to quiet itself, it churned its way into the calm open water of an island-dotted lake. As the lake's eastern shoreline came into view, the river divided into three separate tributaries and continued to tear its way across central Saskatchewan.

Unlike the river's final exit into mammoth Hudson Bay, the Churchill River below rolled and lifted in a series of massive, white-cresting rapids. Downstream from each rapids lay an enormous churning eddy that hosted countless hundreds of hungry walleye, whitefish, and northern pike.

The Churchill, long used by natives and resorters for the gathering of food fish, is a very special waterway. Thousands of meandering weed-crowded bays provide the system excellent spawning grounds for northern pike. Gravel lifts, found at each twist and turn in the river's corridor, provide the necessary staging areas for walleye reproduction. Whitefish, a primary food source for these two gamefish, are found by the thousands in the Churchill's many connecting lakes. It is an ecosystem that provides and produces gamefish as fast as any in Canada.

Unlike any other river system in North America, the Churchill is split apart by thousands of glacier-carved ridges. On a topographical map, the Churchill system takes on the appearance of a southern strip pit mine operation gone amuck. There are so many fingers, bays, islands, and side tributaries that evaluating where the main river channel lies is all but impossible. Becoming lost on this massive jumble of rock and treed waterway could happen at the drop of a hat. It literally becomes a maze of confusion to the first-time travelers. The only salvation for those willing to travel the Churchill's 1,400-mile corridor is the current. Without the signal of the system's water-flow and some distinctive high granite hills, an angler would instant-ly become lost.

Such were my thoughts as the Twin Otter's engines slowed, and we began our descent into McIntosh Lake. My companion of twelve years, Laurie Dickhart, and I were about to be reunited with my lifelong friend, Ruffo Schindler. Many an old tale would cross the dinner table at Sportsman Lodge over the next four days.

Ruffo and I had fished together for nearly twenty years in about as many locations. My friend had become the manager of each location, new resort, or outpost camp. Ruffo is a man on the cutting edge when it comes to opening up new fishing grounds in the North. There are not many areas he has not fished.

Ruffo began guiding at the age of fourteen. His early clients were those who wanted to trek the small Pacific-bound streams along the western coast of British Columbia. If you were tough enough, and a dedicated enough steelheader, Ruffo was your man. His sister, Karen, once told me the family became worried about Ruffo at one time when in his room they found a book entitled *Fish to Live With*. From age ten, his interest was only fishing. Girls, a natural obsession for young men, had no place in Ruffo's life.

The winter of his fifteenth birthday, Ruffo began writing every northern Canadian resort that had placed a fishing ad in *Outdoor Life* magazine. He wanted to guide in the Far North!

Much to his delight, April 11, seven days after his fifteenth birthday, he received an answer from a Mr. Jack Jackson of Waterbury Lodge on Waterbury Lake in northern Saskatchewan. Waterbury lies directly west of Wollaston Lake along the southern border of the Northwest Territories.

Within thirty days, young Ruffo was off on the adventure of a lifetime—an adventure that would see this young man fish some of North America's premier trophy northern pike and lake trout waters in their early years.

Ruffo lasted three years at Waterbury. These were years that taught the young student of the north a great deal. During his second year he became head guide and began bringing in more fish than the lodge's native guides. Ruffo's gentle manner, smiling face, and his favorite reply, "No problem!" became his trademark. Fishermen loved Ruffo and, when returning to Waterbury, would have no other guide.

But, after three years, the restless eighteen-year old got "the itch" once again. It was time to move on. Newer, bigger, and better water lay to the north. Rumors persisted about a lake called Snowbird, north and east of Waterbury. World-class record lake trout by the hundreds were thought to swim beneath Snowbird's surface. Migrating natives who had cast food nets in Snowbird brought tales of huge fish that destroyed their nets or were so large they refused to be hauled to the surface. Armed with only rumors, Ruffo began to inquire. He would leave Waterbury. He had to move on!

In Minneapolis, Minnesota, Ruffo found a group of investors building a lodge on the western shores of Snowbird. The project had begun in 1969. Ruffo appeared on the scene in 1972. The group of corporate investors had been having trouble getting their project off the ground. Upon interviewing Ruffo, they found a solution for their troubles. He was hired on the spot and soon became camp manager. Snowbird was not a lodge for just anyone. It was a fishing prize only a select few and their friends got to fish—in other words, a closed fishing club.

The Snowbird camp was finished in the fall of 1973. During the first three years, Ruffo acted as assistant manager and head guide. During his fourth year, he became camp manager, a job cast aside by one of the corporate investors who admitted he was not the man for the job—but the young British Columbian was.

During his seven years at Snowbird, Ruffo experienced his happiest years in the North. He became an expert at catching monster lake trout. Ruffo discovered spots that are still considered the lake's best trout producers. Some of them he has never divulged. They remain his secret, even today.

At age twenty-five, Ruffo saw the corporation that built Snowbird Lodge fall apart. Too many big fish had been killed, and those who created the lake trout Shangri-La tired of their prize. Fishing was not what it was when they first arrived. The fall of 1980 saw the Quonset-style cabins visited for the last time. The once highly prized corporate sanctuary lay dead and deserted, its buildings the visiting sites for seagulls and wandering bears. Ruffo was forced to move on.

Obtaining another position in the North wasn't hard. The young man was instantly hired by Brian McIntosh of Sickle Lake Lodge in northern Manitoba. It was here I met Ruffo and became acquainted with his fishing world-famous "No Problem!" attitude. Carl Malz, editor of *Fishing Facts* magazine, and I first met Ruffo while testing one of Sickle's many outpost camps.

We soon became friends with the smiling, cheerful, young man, while he guided us to some of the finest trophy pike fishing either of us had ever experienced.

At a time when catch and release was not part of the angling repertoire, Ruffo began a catch-and-release program on the lakes on which the Sickle operation had outposts. Educated by his experience at Snowbird, Ruffo made the decision that in northern lakes, where fish growth was less than half a pound per year, the heavy killing of its largest breeding game fish had to stop. Many anglers objected, but it became known that if you wanted to fish with Ruffo Schindler, you would have to release most of your big fish. Only one could be kept for mounting.

I remember one instance when a lady friend and I were fishing one of Ruffo's managed Sickle Lodge outpost camps, a lake called Kasmere. That summer Ruffo decided he would manage the new Kasmere outpost himself rather than hire someone for the job.

Kasmere Lake had an unusually high population of trophy lake trout and northern pike. The new catch-and-release program must be strictly enforced if the fishery was to survive.

Upon our arrival, Ruffo insisted he guide the two of us for our first four days. We caught and released dozens of trout and pike over twenty pounds.

One day, after an unusually good morning of trout angling in the rain, Donna, my fishing companion, became soaked to the knees when attempting to jump ashore for shore lunch. It was cold and miserable out. We debated returning to the outpost twelve miles downlake. Instead Ruffo suggested we continue to have shore lunch of fresh lake trout fillets. He would solve Donna's cold and wet foot problem after lunch.

The fire dried her bluejeans, but we both wondered what our guide would do to solve the problem of her cold feet and wet boots.

With shore lunch over, Ruffo asked from what spot in the aluminum boat Donna would like to fish. Upon learning she wanted to fish from the middle seat, he picked up two very large stones he had placed beside and beneath the shore lunch fire. They were carried to the boat and placed on the bottom where Donna's feet would rest. We departed for more fishing.

The result became instantly apparent. The stones were well heated during shore lunch, and by placing her wet boots on the hot stones, Donna not only dried her boots, but warmed her feet as well. To my surprise, the stones held their heat for hours. It was a very good solution to a problem that might have ruined a great day of fishing. Looking back at the hot-stone solution, I now realize that my friend, Ruffo, has bestowed on me, and others, many simple outdoor remedies.

Ruffo lasted twelve months at the Sickle Lake operation, then went on to try a year with Mercury Marine in Winnipeg. They attempted to make him into a salesman. That was not for him. The North continued to call. The tourist business by now was embedded deeply in his blood.

He had married just prior to his stint with Mercury. Settling down and becoming a family man seemed the right thing to do, but Maxine and he both realized his heart was in the Far North. If their marriage was going to work, she would have to travel with him.

Soon, with Maxine in tow and pregnant, they hired on to manage Mike Dyste's outpost camp on Monroe Lake. A year later the two began a three-year stint at Nejaleni Lake Lodge. Once again I fished with my old friend at this sub-Arctic lake trout lake.

Nejaleni proved to be another challenge for Ruffo. Though the camp had gained a reputation as a northern pike fishery, Ruffo soon learned that was not the case. Outdoor writers had falsified their stories about large pike readily available at Nej. Pike fishing was good only a couple weeks a year.

However, lake trout trophy fish in the twenty- to thirty-pound size were constantly available throughout the resort's entire season. Ruffo, a man to always tell the truth about what fishing is like in the lakes he works, turned Nejaleni's reputation back to what it was supposed to be.

From there, Ruffo went on to manage North of Sixty's Obre Lake camp when it was in its last days under the Fredricksons' management. Try as he would, the owners failed to take his advice, and the camp failed financially in the fall of 1991. I was there that last year and remember some of the problems Ruffo faced. He handled them as always with his 'No Problem' attitude, but when financing failed, Ruffo moved on.

In 1992, Maxine and he began a completely new adventure. They became co-owners of Sportsman Lodge in northern Saskatchewan. Ike Enns, a well-known resort owner in Manitoba and Ontario, needed a partner or manager for Sportsman. Knowing the sturdy reputation Ruffo had achieved in the North, he jumped at the chance when Ruffo departed the failing Fredrickson operation.

Note: The North of Sixty operation, including the outpost on Snowbird Lake, were taken over by Clark Jenney of Wayzata, Minnesota, and is now running successfully.

I reunited with my friend, Ruffo, at Sportsman Lodge in 1997. It had been five years since we'd fished together at Obre.

Upon my arriving at Sportsman Lodge on McIntosh Lake, my friend quickly informed me that I'd take plenty of fat walleye and a goodly number of pike up to forty inches. But, though the lake has a good population of lake trout, August wasn't the time to catch them. They had become short-period feeders during the hot month and would be a real challenge.

During our short stay, Ruffo's honest analysis of his operation proved to be right on. Laurie and I caught a number of fat walleye from two-and-a-half to seven-and-a-half pounds, as well as a goodly number of pike from thirty-five to thirty-nine-and-a-half inches. Only one ten-pound lake trout was taken and released. Once again my old friend had called it in his honest, straight-forward manner. Honesty is a rare quality in those who operate fishing camps. Fish weights often double, and numbers certainly do when the angler asks, "How's fishing at your place, Mr. Resorter?"

Maybe that's why I decided to tell the true tale of a very special man whose heart is securely entrenched in the land of northern pine, lake trout, granite rock, and trophy pike. He is one in a million—an honest, knowledgeable man of the North. He's one you can count on to tell you the truth and get you through the rough spots when you're traveling the northern land.

One last story he likes to tell; he tells it with a dreamy look in his eye. It must be *the* truth because it's told by a truthful friend of mine.

Back in 1976, when Ruffo was managing Snowbird Lodge, he guided a special friend, Al Olson of Minneapolis, Minnesota, to a rather large lake trout. Once landed, it weighed in at thirty-eight pounds. What happened during the fight to land that big fish is the tale.

It seems the trophy fish was caught on a large, #10 flatfish plug, one of Ruffo's favorites for lakers. During the battle, near its end, another much larger fish attempted to take the flatfish from the engaged fish.

The second fish, according to Ruffo, was at least twice the size of the hooked trout. Snowbird's water is crystal clear, so there was no mistaking what the huge trout was attempting to do. She wanted that silver flatfish.

Twice Al brought the thirty-eight pounder to boat. Twice the monster trout came in close, continuously attempting to engage and devour the flatfish hanging from the hooked fish's mouth.

On the second pass, Ruffo attempted to net, not the hooked 38 pounder, but the monster fish! He missed, then instructing Al to hold the hooked trout close, Ruffo cast his silver flatfish past the engaged fish.

Anyone knowing the makeup of a flatfish can imagine what happened next. At each attempt, the silver lure failed to attain enough depth to hold the position of the engaged trout and its hungry companion. Try as he would, Ruffo could not get the floating flatfish reeled deeply enough to attract the trout.

At this point in the story, my friend's eyes cloud up a little. "Never again," he laments, "will I fail to have another rigged rod and reel in the boat—one rigged with a heavy jig would be best."

When asked how much he thought the monster trout weighed, he sighed and said, "Eighty pounds, at least. You know, I believe Snowbird holds the world-record lake trout. Out there, in one of those many hidden, deep holes, there has to be a trout over seventy pounds . . . maybe more than one. Who knows?"

You know what? I believe him. He's never told me an untruth. Ruffo Schindler is one of a kind and deserving of a chapter in my book on the Far North.

For information on Sportsman Lodge, see the information pages at the end of the book.

Tips and Bits

OF THE NORTHERN NATURAL WORLD

Taddy or Tatty?

John Hicks, Dan Gapen's host on the polar bear foray in the Wager Bay chapter (see Chapter 21) is a direct descendant of Dick Tatty. John's mother was a Tutu, daughter of Dick Tatty's second oldest daughter. You can learn more about John's remarkable mother by referring to Chapter 18 in Dan Gapen's hardback book, *Fishing Rivers of the Far North.*

Chapter 10

Trophy Pike on the Fly

Carefully, guide Chester Tuck eased our boat into position. It would be a cast of about eighty feet. With a final stroke, Chester's paddle dug deep, then held fast.

"There she lies, Dan; it's up to you now," said the round-faced guide.

Chester was right. Just ahead, lying beneath two-and-a-half feet of crystal-clear water, rested a huge northern pike, its red gill rakers pulsating with each breath. She sat at a slight right angle to the boat. Enticing this lady into "strike" could be a problem.

Water temperature on Wollaston Lake had dropped dramatically two days before when a heavy Arctic cold front came rampaging across the land. Surface temperature had dropped from sixty-one degrees to a mere forty-three degrees in the shallow bays as the cold front rolled in. Pike had instantly deserted the shallows and headed into deep lake water. It left my partner, Carl Malz, and me with little to do but wait.

Two days after the cold front descended, as a late afternoon sun warmed the water, we found our first pike "up shallow" once again. Sixty hours had passed since the storm front had descended.

91

Carl and I had beaten the shallow waters all morning with little success. The pike had come back into the bays, but they just weren't taking. Bucktails, spoons, and spinner baits, normally excellent producers of shallow-water pike, had enticed only three fish over eight pounds, none over twelve. A number of shaker pike had been boated, but the trophy fish wouldn't have anything to do with us.

Frustrated by our lack of success, I'd drawn back into my fishing memory and honed in on a trip years ago when a friend and I had enticed dormant northerns into striking by using giant streamer flies on a fly rod. Conditions had been similar, and it was in desperation that we'd turned to fly rods. The switch produced excellent results that day. Why not now?

When I mentioned my idea to Carl, he grinned, laid back a bit, and suggested I show him. Carl had neglected to take a fly rod along, and I had but one, an eight-and-a-half-foot, medium-action rod which would do a number of jobs on such a trip. Everything from whitefish to lake trout and northern pike could be worked with such equipment.

Holding the boat fast, Chester grinned and nodded toward the waiting fish. It took four false casts to propel the huge streamer fly out past the waiting fish. On the fifth try, it settled to the water and sank slowly toward bottom, six feet beyond the northern's mouth. At a point one foot off the bottom, I began a twitching retrieve. Foot by foot the fly was jerked toward the target. Then, just as it was about to pass over the pike's nose, I hesitated and allowed the eight-inch long fly to drop head first to bottom just six inches in front of the waiting teeth. I allowed it to rest about six seconds, twitched, then let the fly settle back once again. The fish's gills flared, but she refused to strike. Two more times the fly was twitched and allowed to rest head down on the mossy bottom.

That was it! With a forward surge and a flare of gills, the trophy fish engulfed the colorful prize. I set hard, and the battle began.

And a battle it was! That pike's first run tore off nearly a hundred feet of line. Backing showed in rod guides as it ended. Next, she turned back and surged another fifty feet to our right. This fish was all I could handle.

Ten minutes passed while my stubborn foe darted back and forth across the shallow, short-weed-infested mud flats. With each surge, a cloud of bottom silt rose and spread across the water surface. During the fight, several other fish were dislodged from their resting places, a fact noted by fishermen and guide alike. There would be time for them a bit later.

Finally the nineteen-pound trophy was lifted into the boat, unhooked, photographed, and gently released. The battle had lasted just over fifteen minutes, according to my partner, Carl.

"Okay, Gapen; prove it again," prodded Carl as we watched the exhausted lady swim off.

Four hours later Carl had all the proof he needed. I had managed to boat some dozen and a half pike on the brilliantly colored Tantalizer Steamer Fly while my partner, Carl, had succeeded, with a variety of spoons and plugs, in bringing to boat gunnel only three fish

Why was this possible? I'm not sure! But, over the years, it has been my experience that dormant pike, when you can spot them, cannot resist a furry streamer fly twitched directly in front of their nose. This is especially true when the fly contains some type of mylar material that glitters.

Eight years ago, on a lake called Flett, in northern Canada, Bob Vos and I managed to catch and release twelve pike over twenty pounds in one day using the Tantalizer Fly. The largest fish tipped the scales at twenty-seven-and-a-half pounds. That day with Carl Malz on Wollaston, my largest fish was just over twenty pounds. In both cases, we were coming off a cold front, and pike weren't taking anything, even though they had come back up into shallower water.

If you've not tried northern pike on a fly, it's a sport not to be missed. To me, it's part hunting and part fishing—a very exciting experience!

To prepare one's self for such an outing the following is a "must" list of things the angler should select before heading out. Take along a fly rod in the nine- or ten-pound weight class. Flyline should be a weight forward model in the nine- or ten-gauge class. Heavy leader material in sizes thirty-,twenty-five-, twenty-, fifteen-, and twelve-pound size is a must to form tapered leaders heavy enough to support the large streamer flies. A coil of fifteen- or twenty-pound monel wire (braided), which forms the final nine inches of the tapered leader, must also be part of your equipment. There are those who recommend one hundred-pound mono for this last nine to fourteen inches of leader, but it has been my experience that pike teeth can cut even this thickness of material, and flies fail to work properly under the duress created by this heavy mono.

Besides, that heavy one hundred-pound mono at leader's end has a tendency to create malfunctions in how the leader works. The final item on the list must be a selection of brilliantly colored six-to-eight-inch long streamer flies. Since I have always tied my own, this item has never been a problem to find. However, few sport shops carry such items, and the angler may have to hunt to find just what he's after.

The Tantalizer, as I named my favorite fly, comes in eight colors and two styles, in a streamer fly pattern and six colors as a floating popper fly. Depending on weather conditions, the colors that work best are yellow/black, orange/black, chartreuse/white, and red/white. If clouds and bad weather prevail, try using black/white or blue/white.

No matter what color fly you select, retrieve action can make or break you. Always get the fly well out past the targeted fish. Strip line in a slow, deliberate, two-foot-long stroke, bringing the fly toward the fish's head. Once your fly is within inches of the target, allow it to settle, then twitch repeatedly, allowing the fly to hold just ahead of the pike's face. You may have to repeat the process, but it's been my experience that's only necessary in one out of five cases.

Fly fishing for northern pike is not solely confined to shallow water. Late one year, while fishing with Dennis Maksymetz of Manitoba Travel at God's Lake, the large streamer flies produced several trophy pike off cabbage beds, along the outer deep-water edges. Here, retrieve remained similar, but the hesitation and twitching were restricted by allowing the fly to drop three to four feet into the open pockets between weed stems.

What's nice about using the Tantalizer Streamer Fly is that you seldom miss a strike, even when the fly is on a drop. Why? The material in this large fly acts like Velcro. Once entangled in the pike's teeth, it is nearly impossible to disengage, even when the barb is not set.

Those who hunt the mighty Muskie—take note of this artificial lure. You have not lived until you feel the thrill experienced as your first muskie on a fly takes that first leap skyward.

There it is—another tip on how to improve the thrill of summer fishing. No matter where you go north this coming summer, it's my advice that you tote along the fly equipment suggested in this chapter. It could make the difference between a great vacation and just the same old thing.

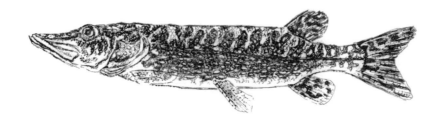

Tips and Bits
OF THE NORTHERN NATURAL WORLD

The "clicking" noise heard as caribou prance across the tundra is not their hooves striking stone. Instead, the clicking comes from a loose cartilage in their foot as it snaps back and forth each time the hoof is extended. For the most part, the caribou foot is made up of soft meat and cartilage. The muted clicking noise made as they walk is remindful of two stones being tapped together under water.

Chapter 11

After the Tourists Have Gone

The last of the summer fishermen, a group of six from Chicago, Illinois, had departed but twenty-four hours prior to arrival of the huge boar black bear. Our first inkling that company had arrived came when the rattling of kitchen utensils drew Anne Orth and me to investigate.

"Maybe John's in the kitchen cabin cleaning up? Let's go over and help," Anne suggested while stepping outside our sleeping cabin and heading out towards the cooking cabin eighty feet away.

Anne entered the cabin first.

"John, that's our mess; we'll clean . . ." Her voice fell off.

There had been no response. No response, that is, except for an unidentified soft shuffling sound that came from somewhere behind the kitchen table. In the shadows between the table and sink a huge darkened body shifted slightly.

"It's a bear . . . it's a bear!" Anne whispered hoarsely while side-stepping backwards past me out the door.

Sure enough, there he was, rooting gently among the disrupted groceries now scattered upon the kitchen floor. Slowly the head raised, beady black eyes fixed upon the intruders not more than eight feet away.

What followed in the next twenty seconds is hard to recall, so fast did it occur. With lightening speed, the bear raised upwards, placed his left front paw on the counter and began an exit through a torn window screen through which he'd entered.

As with any good photographer and conveyer of tales, I raced out the door and around back. My hopes were to catch the intruder as he exited the kitchen window. It would be a once in a lifetime photo. Imagine, to catch an intruding black bear in the act of exiting his crime. And, to make it better, the window through which he traveled was barely large enough to accommodate his immense bulk.

Rounding the cabin corner, camera ready, it was already too late. Our intruder had exited the too-small window and was racing 100 feet away into scattered timber. Did this mean I'd missed my "once-in-a-lifetime" chance to photograph the intruder? Not on your life. The bear would come back.

Anne and I hurried off to inform John Andrews, camp manager, of the new guest. Surely, John would not be too happy about the newcomer. A quick damage survey had disclosed the bear not only ripped up the kitchen insides, but had torn open all four screen windows on the cabin.

John was found happily bagging garbage to be flown out with the same float plane that would transfer Anne and me to our final destination, the Wholdaia Lake Outpost. Here, we'd end our stay in the north with an additional week of wilderness fishing.

Seeing that the Anaunathad Camp was built on the mainland, John preferred that the camp garbage be sent back to main camp at Obre Lake where it could be properly disposed. Today, the garbage gathering would prove to be a bit too little, too late.

Upon hearing our report, John raced to the kitchen cabin for a damage survey of his own. Behind, he left a nearly finished project exposed. This was to prove unwise.

Inspection complete, John mumbled a few bitter words, then returned to the beach to complete his chore.

Anne and I chose to guard the cabin, hoping for a photo of the vandal, should he return to the scene of the crime. Suddenly, from down on the beach, came a sharp whistle. Quickly the two of us ran back to where John now stood frozen.

While the three of us were up in the kitchen, the bear had circled camp and immediately smelled the newly bagged garbage. Without hesitation, he trotted up to the free meal and tore into John's neatly stored prize. The bear must have done it with great gusto for several of the bags lay scattered between beach and bushes.

John's return had interrupted the intruder's frolic for free food. Three sharp whistles was all it took to force the large black bear back into the bushes some distance up the beach. At this point, all involved realized this was a very bold bear. Knowing this, the three of us elected to stay on the beach, John and Anne on the dock, while I selected a spot directly behind the garbage bags.

Moments later the bear reappeared, sauntering down the beach as if he owned it. Three times he disappeared into shoreline vegetation. Each time the intruder reappeared closer. His gait increased in speed. There seemed to be no fear of the human scent.

Eventually, after a final disappearance, his huge head and shoulders emerged from behind the gas barrels just off the beach next to the dock. Here, he hesitated a moment, only long enough to have his picture taken, then headed directly at the stacked garbage and this writer. His pace was rapid. The final approach began only seventy feet from the garbage bags.

A gusty wind blew directly from behind me towards the oncoming bear. Forward progress was startling, so fast was his pace. Obviously, heavy garbage scent covered my human odor.

With twitching nose searching, the bear came forward. Through my telephoto lens the bear's head grew ominous. Rapidly the camera's shutter clicked. I could no longer focus the lens as a final shot was pressed off.

A startling reality hit. The lens I was using would only draw down to a mere eleven-and-a-half feet. At the moment my final photo was taken all that could be seen in the viewfinder was huge 'out-of-focus' bear head. Most noticeable was the shiny wet nose, gray-sided muzzle and reddish brown nose bridge hair. All these rested astride a deathly pair of black beady eyes.

The bear was close, maybe too close!

A thought raced through my mind. If only I could change lenses to a wide angle—it was a crazy thought!

To my left, a loud yell erupted. John, unable to control his anticipation, saw fit to repel the animal the only way he knew how.

At the very moment John yelled, I was in the process of pushing backwards with my knees. No longer able to shoot photos, I began to retreat. My intent, though it reads dim and blurred now, was to step backwards into the lake. After all, wasn't it the garbage Mr. Bear was after?

At the sound of John's yell and the raising of his arms, Mr. Bear wheeled about and raced back into shoreline vegetation.

How close had the bear come to the garbage and the photographer hiding behind it? Less than ten feet, according to Anne when she stepped it off moments later. Nine short feet could have been covered by the intruder in two steps.

Was that the end of our bear story? Not in your life!

Moments after being driven from the beach garbage, the bear circled camp and attempted to enter a second cooking cabin. Again, driven by the need to get that "once-in-a-lifetime" photo, Anne and I sneaked up on the uninvited guest. Almost immediately he sensed that we were there and sped off in retreat.

Moments later, John's whistle indicated the persistent bear had returned to the beach garbage. Once again, frantic yelling, arm waving and whistling drove the animal back into the woods. This time he elected to stay gone.

Thirty minutes later our plane arrived. It would take Anne and me to Wholdaia Lake where we'd fish without company of any kind during the final late days of fall. Much to John's relief, it would be this same plane that would transport the seven sacks of garbage to Obre Lake Lodge for disposal.

Is it here the tale ends? Maybe so, maybe not!

Dawn came late the first day at Wholdaia. Southwest winds blew a heavy layer of low clouds and with them, rain. Not heavy hard rain—instead, drizzling intermittent rain that soaked everything. It was a morning to wait the weather out, relax, meditate, and catch up on sleep. In the northern world, it's best not to fight Mother Nature. Things will always change shortly. After all, it was the last day of August, and northern travelers must expect some turbulent weather, at least a day or two. Besides, there's a special comfort in warming one's self beside a puffing aerotight stove with the glow it gives off.

Outside, a gathering of Lapland Longspurs, bent on early migration, eagerly accepted handfuls of oatmeal tossed their way. Sleep came easy as wind and rain battered the tiny plywood outpost cabin. Wind speed increased, its moaning about the cabin walls the tranquilizer needed to induce a retreat deeper into sleeping bags.

Hours passed! Then, there came a sound within the blustery wind. It came from the north, passed overhead and departed south. The migration of Canadian geese had begun.

Wind direction had changed. It now blew from the north. In two short hours, a 140-degree shift in direction had occurred. Honkers only migrate south on favorable winds.

Sleep forgotten, Anne and I exited the cabin door to watch the overhead passage. Pressed by hard blowing northern winds, intermingled with sudden downdrafts, Canadian geese sideslipped their way past, a mere 200 feet above us.

They came by the hundreds, yelping their delight at the new-found freedom felt as migration instincts drew them southward.

They came in families of five, in bunches of twenty, and in flocks of hundreds. The geese continued to pass overhead as the two humans gazed in awe and wonder. The first geese of the migration always bring a thrill to those who marvel at the world of nature. It leaves humans humbled by a lack of knowing and an ineptness to follow these royal birds of the north.

Rain continued, the north wind blew stronger, and an intermittent sprinkle of sleet beat earthward. Honkers by the thousands followed those who came before. The two humans continued to feed the puffing wood stove and listened to the northern world outside the frail cabin. There would be no angling for the giant pike of Wholdaia this day. That would have to wait.

It was 3:00 P.M. and the migrating geese had gained altitude, the rain and wind had lessened—all signs of better weather to follow.

Slowly, conditions improved until the southbound geese were but waving specks in the gray skies. After 8:00 P.M., the sun broke through. Clear blue skies could be seen along the northern horizon. A cooling chill descended. Clear weather was on its way. Anne and I would gaze upon a rose-red sunset. Tomorrow, we would go in search of the giant fish of Wholdaia Lake.

To the south of the plywood outpost camp, a wolf howled as a golden moon broke from beneath the departing clouds of darkened gray. All lay quiet except for the distant honking of migrating geese. They would continue to pass overhead throughout the moonlit night, their wilderness voices soothing those who slept below.

Dogrib

A tale is told by the aged men among the Dené part of the Chippewa nation about the time a single Dené warrior defeated the entire Dogrib tribe. It is a tale told with bravado and pride, and it's always told when the moon is full and the campfire coals blaze fiery red and orange. It is a tale for the young, to create pride in who they are.

Years ago, before the coming of "White Father," the Dogrib nation had encamped upon Dené land near the eastern waters of the lake known as Athabasca—"lake with reeds in shallow water." They had come in force, so many were they that Dené leaders feared an attack on them could bring the death of many Dené warriors and maybe the defeat of the entire Dené nation. It was a dark time in Dené history.

For three summer moons, Dené leaders sent their best scouts out to spy on the dreaded Dogrib. As each returned, the reports became more ominous. The Dogrib were working their way west, further into the heart of Dené land. By October, the Dogrib had entered the Grease River valley. Here, within the deep valleys and high, rocky hills, they were gathering up all the fish and game that rightfully belonged to the Dené. Something must be done, but what?

The Dogrib were fierce fighters. Tales of their killing ways had been known to the wise Dené leaders for countless turnings of the summer season. A council must be formed and a decision made. To allow the westward advance of the feared Dogrib would soon bring them across the northern half of Athabasca, to the area where the southern river entered and the great river exited the lake of reeds. It would then be too late, for the Dené's stronghold would surely be discovered on the western shores between the great rivers.

Late into the night the elders discussed their plight. Three were for war; three were for retreat. Finally a decision was reached. They would send one last scout out, their very best. He would be Hono, the man who tracked caribou on rock. He must go. He was wise and had fought many successful battles against the Cree. He was the oldest of the scouts, and his decision would bring the right way.

Before dawn, that very night, Hono left, clad only in his hunting buckskins, carrying a bow, ten arrows, and a hunting ax. If he traveled fast, he would return before the coming of the next full moon. The leaders would prepare their warriors during Hono's absence, but the final decision would only come with his return.

Hono discovered the first hunting Dogrib at the Little Grease River falls where it entered the big lake. Since the last report, the Dogrib had come south a matter of two days' walk from where the Big Grease River entered at the long bay's eastern end.

Hono watched in horror as fourteen Dogrib braves speared dozens of fish, some as long as a child's body, from the Denés' favorite fishing place. He lay undetected, high above the Dogrib, on a rocky hill.

Two days passed. More Dogrib joined those at the Little Grease River falls. Soon there were a hundred or more. Several smoking fires were lit, and now the women of the Dogrib began to smoke the meat of the fish taken from the land and the waters of the Dené. This was not good. It appeared that the dreaded Dogrib were planning to stay the winter.

At night, far to the east among the countless hills and valleys along the lake, Hono counted many more smoking fires. There must be more than a thousand Dogrib. Hono's report would not be good. Yet, he must return tomorrow, for winter would soon be upon the land. The great lake had already iced over. Only the bays, where the rivers entered, held patches of open water.

It was the fires that gave Hono an idea. What if, atop the hills above the Dogrib encampments, he were to light as many fires as the coming of two moons? Would that not show the Dogrib that many more Dené braves lived to the east than there were Dogrib? Surely the Dogrib had sent scouts west and knew they were in Dené land. Would their scouts not have seen that the Dené nation lay in small bands to the west? Knowing that must have given the Dogrib courage to advance upon Dené land.

But what if the Dogrib were to think they were outnumbered by Dené gathered in the hills above them? Maybe they could be made to believe war and death were about to come down upon them. Would they not become fearful and leave the land to the Dené?

It took Hono two days to place sixty stacks of firewood high upon the Grease River's highest and longest hill. Then, as darkness fell, he began to light them, starting at the westernmost pile of dead wood and green spruce boughs. One by one the fires roared skyward, sending smoke and a bright firelight into the night. Hono raced as hard as he could, and as the deep night hour passed, all piles were blazing high, each a signal to those below that many braves were waiting for the dawn to bring war upon the intruders.

Below, the Dogrib braves laughed as the first fire was seen to brighten the night sky, but as the numbers of fires increased to as many fingers as on their two hands, concern crossed their faces.

There were more Dené than previously scouted. When the fires reached as many days as it takes for the moon to return, the Dogrib elders gathered in council. This they had not expected. So many Dené gathered against them.

As the last fire was lit on the western hill above them, a decision was made. They must leave the land of the Dené for surely there must be fifty braves at each of these big night fires. They would be outnumbered three to one, and even the Dogrib braves, as fierce as they were, could not withstand those odds.

Late the next day the Dogrib tribe gathered on the ice of Athabasca. Would they travel east where more Dené and the fierce-fighting Cree lived? Northward travel would be tough through the high, rocky hills and deep valleys. West across the ice would be easiest, but they had to travel fast to avoid the hoard of Denépewa warriors that now held on the high hill above the Grease River.

The decision was made. They would travel fast, day and night, to the west. They would pass the western home of the Dené nation by the cover of night, and once on the great river that ran north, they'd be free. They must hurry for it would take only a day for the Dené warriors to discover their disappearance. Dragging canoes and travois with all their worldly goods, they departed.

High above them, Hono watched the retreat. At first he thought the Dogrib were gathering for war, but as the tribe began to rapidly walk west, family after family, he knew his trick had worked.

During the next day and a half, Hono spied on the retreating Dogrib. Once satisfied that their intent was departure, he raced as fast as his legs would carry him to tell his elders the news. The Dené must not think the Dogrib were coming to attack. They must be allowed to pass by.

Seven days after the trek began, the Dogrib slipped past the last Dené campsite under the darkness of a new moon. Hours later canoes were launched at the great river's first fast-water area, and the Dogrib headed north. It would be a hard journey with the loss of many people. Numerous times the canoes had to be portaged when solid ice blocked passage. By late December, the Dogrib band settled into a wooded area near the point where the great river entered the lake known as Slave.

So it is that the Dogrib nation came to rest upon the shores of Great Slave Lake many moons ago.

Hono became a folk hero, and even today the Dené on the shores of Lake Athabasca tell the tale of how just one Dené scout defeated a nation of 1,000 Dogrib.

Tips and Bits
OF THE NORTHERN NATURAL WORLD

The sight of a crazed caribou leaping about in all directions on a hot summer day most likely results from a large insect called the warble fly.

This fly is a blood sucker and hosts a vicious bite. However, the main objection caribou have is this insect's reproductive process. Warble flies reproduce by laying eggs on a caribou's back. Once hatched, the larva buries itself beneath the animal's skin. Under the skin, they dig down and settle in. Once situated, the grub continues to grow until it reaches the size of a human's index finger.

Note: These grubs were relished as a great delicacy by the Inuits. The grub is made up of ninety-five percent protein.

Once mature, the white grub emerges into adulthood after eating its way out through the caribou's skin. As it reaches the outside world, it sheds its larva stage and becomes an adult warble fly, which will repeat the process.

No wonder caribou instinctively panic in the very presence of this insect.

Chapter 13

Russian Bar

On the commercial fishing barge at Russian Bar, five days of heavy blow from the southwest had the five fisherman weary. Dozens of untended gill nets were last pulled six days before. With heavy seas, cold winds, and a barometer falling and rising every twelve hours, the huge lake trout of Athabasca would have been active. Active trout meant full nets. Full nets meant heavy, back-breaking labor awaited the five.

Rubin Sernoff, a ruddy-faced, overweight man in his late sixties, suddenly slammed his fist down on the crude, plywood table.

"'Tis 'nuff uff this damn weather. I must get off this damn barge or go all bot nutty," the huge, six-foot-four-inch Rubin pro-claimed in guttural English, heavily toned by his native Russian tongue.

It was obvious that cramped quarters and confinement were taking their toll on the four Russians. Only the native Denépewa, Joe Martin, seemed relaxed and able to withstand the boring, long-term confinement. Possibly Joe, through nineteen years of frigid winters, long nights, and the cramped quarters of a twelve by eighteen-foot log cabin, had programmed the young native to withstand such environment.

"Yuh, sum kond uff storm. Gutto loose lots of trout if du storm lusts too much longer," commented Pete Kabolik, expert net repairer and launch pilot.

Pete, a tall, raw-boned Russian immigrant from Moscow, had recently immigrated to Canada. Back home, he'd been an officer in the Russian army and had seen most of his comrades killed during the Germans' western march into Russia.

Pete had been badly wounded in his right leg during the winter of 1944 at about the time the German drive stalled. He walked with a bad limp because of the wound but never complained. Often, Pete, a man in his late fifties, would compensate for the bad leg by doing more work than his designated job demanded. Such effort was a point of pride with the raw-boned six footer.

Joe Stenko, the seventy-two-year-old leader, and John Kaskik, sixty-three-year-old mechanic, both of Russian descent, made up the balance of the crew. All had fished commercially in Russia during their earlier years—Joe and Pete in the Baltic Sea area, John and Rubin in the Bering Sea. All were highly qualified in the art of harvesting fish for the commercial market.

Coal lamps flickered as wisps of wind pushed their way through the cracks in the barge's wood walls. The barge's bow raised and lowered as rollers off the big lake managed to force their way through a pair of islands that protected the barge from the wind's main force. A moaning sound ebbed and flowed as the southwesterner forced the wind around the barge's roof edges.

Tied to the barge's downwind side, a thirty-two-foot wooden net tender rolled and pitched, straining to their limits the one-and-a-half-inch hemp ropes that held her. The tender had been constructed in Ft. McMurray, Alberta, 400 miles south, near the headwaters of the Pease River.

It was a hardy ship, but even the Vodka, as its Russian crew had named it, would be hard pressed to withstand the fifteen-foot high seas now rolling down Lake Athabasca.

Long into the night, the rough-and-tumble crew of the Vodka played cards, smoked cigarettes, and drank the white juice of their homeland. Joe, the native Dené, unable to stand the game his companions played, slipped out of the dimly lit main room and stood silently watching the storm from the barge's rear deck.

Nearly forty years separated young Joe from the youngest Russian, Pete. Add to this the fact that the four Russians always spoke in their own language when drinking and playing cards; it was natural for Joe to withdraw at such times.

Also, the outside air was fresh and remindful of the winter days to come. It was better here, outside, away from the smell of human bodies and the loud sound of their arguing. He hoped this night would not bring a fight between Rubin and John, as had happened many times before. Sometimes the fight because so violent that both men ended up with a bloody mouth and nose, not to mention the broken furniture that had to be fixed afterwards. It was Joe who always had to clean up after them.

Not wanting to be involved with or be around the Russians, the young Dené softly walked down the wood plank and onto the island. Hard drops of icy rain pelted his face. Making his way to the tent where the fish cleaners lived, he slipped inside. Several of his native friends were asleep, but old Ambrose sat in the far corner, smoking his ancient tar-blackened pipe.

"What's wrong, Joe? Those Russians fighting again?" questioned the old native.

"Naw, but I'm sure they will before the night's over. Rather sleep in here on the dirt floor then out there on a bed anyway. No telling what will happen this time if Rubin and John get into it again. Rubin has been mumbling about putting a knife to that old bastard the next time they get into it. And I don't want to be around if that happens," commented the young man as he sat down in the corner and leaned back against the tent's wooden corner brace.

Ambrose nodded and relaxed, thoughts once again slipping back to the days before Athabasca saw the likes of the Russians or the white miners who now blasted their land apart.

Hours later, Joe awakened to the sound of wood breaking and cussing humans engaged in battle. He had fallen asleep sitting up. Quietly he lay down, turned on his side, and drifted back to sleep. Minutes later, only the sound of waves crashing upon shore rocks could be heard. The wind had subsided. The storm would pass this night, and he would have to work hard the next day as the first nets off Russian Bar were pulled.

Note: The Crackingstone Point commercial fishing operation lasted from 1946 till the early 1950s. During that time, one and a half million pounds of fish a year were harvested.

The Russians were not the first to commercially fish Athabasca. Several men from Edmonton, Alberta, who also happened to be of Russian and Slovakian descent, began a commercial operation in the late 1930s. However, the high costs of transportation and a lack of interest in the product drove them into bankruptcy as World War II started.

Athabasca lake trout are rich in fat and produce a product not well received in the North American market. However, after the war, the immigrant Russians found a way to process these fatty fish and created an overseas market in which to sell them.

Most of the trout taken from Athabasca were caught in seven- or eight-inch gill nets. The weights of the fish harvested ran from near thirty pounds up to seventy-five pounds.

After the war, fishermen froze their catch on the spot at Crackingstone Point and shipped them via barge down the lake, up the Athabasca River, to Fort McMurray (the old town waterways), then on to Edmonton by rail.

From Edmonton they were overnighted by air to the Japanese and Russian marketplace. But, in the end, the cost of transportation, coupled with the cost of doing business, and they, too, went out of business.

Commercial fishing of all kinds, even by the native people, was halted in the mid sixties.

Morning dawned sunny, with blue skies. The squawking of seagulls and the rushing gurgle of heavy waves crashing on the rocks of Crackingstone Point brought young Joe to his feet. Hurriedly he left the tent and crossed the plank into the barge's main room. A broken chair nearly tripped him, but he gracefully sidestepped it, only to bump against a wooden table that lay tipped, its right side resting against the floor. To the table's left, a dark red stain, nearly a foot across, indicated that there had been a brutal fight. Joe wondered if Rubin's threat had come to pass.

Looking toward the sleeping quarters, Joe noted a pair of woolen-sock-clad feet protruding from behind the pull curtain that acted as a door. Fearing what he'd find, he cautiously pulled the curtain aside. There before him, lying face cocked sideways on the floor was Rubin. His face, what could be seen, was bloody and swollen. But, much to Joe's relief, Rubin was breathing.

Suddenly the swollen eye opened and a crude grunt and a gruff question ensued, "What da hell you lookin' at, kud?"

It was obvious Rubin was alive but a bit worse off for his fight. Where was old John? The question was immediately answered as the seventy-two-year-old brute of a man leaped from an upper bunk.

"Dammit, Joe! Why da hull didn't you wake us?" John admonished while striding across the room, stepping over Rubin in the process.

"Dot Rubin thought ha could take me, but yo see ha couldn't," laughed the old man, glancing down at his victim as he passed.

Slowly Rubin gained his knees, then his feet. His expression was ugly, not only on the side where he'd sustained a heavy blow to the ear and cheek by a weapon large and heavy enough to open a large wound and pulverize the facial flesh.

The young Dené could only imagine old Joe's ham-size fist hammering down upon flesh. He shuddered at the thought and rapidly departed.

An hour later the five men left Crackingstone Point and headed west against six-foot swells created by the week-long storm. Instead of heading south to Russian Bar, the wooden tender went west. It would take four hours of pounding through the heavy water before they reached the first of thirty-nine nets laid on the western bank.

All nets would have to be pulled by hand. With such a long delay since they were last lifted, each net would be a special challenge of heavy, back-breaking labor.

Reaching the first net flag, Pete gathered in the flag float and pulled heavily on the net rope. Feeling the heavy thrashing of fish below, he summoned Joe to give a hand. It took all their strength to drag the first forty-five-pound trout on board. Right behind it, six feet down the net, a thirty-two-pounder thrashed its way aboard. Ten feet further along, a sixty-one-pounder thrashed hard, resisting the attempt to drag it above surface.

Old Joe, his heavy face smiling broadly, joined in. With the passing of twenty minutes, the 100-yard-long net was completely on board. Total take was fifty-three trout ranging from twenty-seven to sixty-nine pounds. Total weight: 2,067 pounds. At this rate, they would only be able to lift ten of the thirty-nine nets this day.

Note: Commercial netting by the Russians in the late 1940s and early 1950s saw the use of eight-inch gill netting. Smaller fish, those under twenty pounds, would swim right through the larger netting, unhurt. The intent was to take larger, fatter fish that contained heavier amounts of oil. When processed, the oily fat was extracted and barreled. Then the body was frozen and stored for shipment, minus its head and tail. Even though the head was considered waste, it was not discarded until its cheeks were cut away. Cheeks were considered a delicacy. Many were eaten by the crew. The rest were barreled and sold separately at a higher price.

It took three days to gather all thirty-nine nets and reset them. Pete was kept busy each day mending nets as they came aboard. Before resetting, each net had to be restrung where larger fish had torn loose or twisted the light cotton mesh into a tangled, tattered mess.

Note: The largest fish recorded, caught in a commercial net in the early 1960s before commercial fishing was shut down on Athabasca, weighed 102 pounds. It was taken from the lake's deepest hole fifty miles west of the old Dunnar mine at Crackingstone Point. The hole reaches 407 feet in depth.

Once the thirty-nine western nets had been lifted, the tender and its crew headed south to work the eleven nets placed on Russian Bar. Here they encountered fewer fish than taken in the western nets. The thirty-nine western nets had been placed from a depth of thirty feet down to 120 feet. Those on Russian Bar had been set across the Bar, which holds an average depth of thirty feet. It was obvious that big trout had avoided this shallow water during the storm.

Two nets had completely disappeared, victims of settings that were too shallow. These nets set in the fifteen- to twenty-five-foot depths on Russian Bar, had been torn from their moorings, rolled into a tangled ball of twine, and deposited in a deep hole on the eastern side of the Bar. They would continue to kill fish for three or four yeas before finally rotting away.

Note: During the 1940s and 1950s and early 1960s, cotton mesh was used. It is a material that, given time, rots away. Nets lost during that period of commercial netting have long since rotted and are no longer a threat to the fishery.

However, today nylon mesh is used. It's a material that does not disintegrate. Once lost, a nylon gill net can kill fish for forty to sixty years. Not until the rotting bodies of fish, bottom weeds, or lake scum force them into lake bottom does the killing stop.

The harvest of trout continued that season. The loss of two nets didn't hinder the total take of 1,200,000 pounds. Only the coming of winter could accomplish cessation of the harvesting. On September 24, the Russians loaded a final load of frozen trout on the old barge, attached the wooden tender to its rear and headed west.

Joe Martin and the 122 other Denés who had worked at cleaning, preparing, and freezing the catch, headed back to Fond du Lac. Here they would spend the next nine months under the extreme harsh winter for which Athabasca is noted. Another season would begin in mid May when the Russians returned.

Payment for their labor came in the form of credit at the Hudson Bay post in Fond du Lac. In the end, sad but true, the native workers of the Russian fishermen would only receive half of what they had been promised. Once again the misuse of native people came about. Not only the Russians cheated the workers, but the Hudson Bay post, famous for its misuse of native populations, got their cut.

Postnote: Today, Lake Athabasca still shows the effects of the Russian netting. From the point of Uranium City (midway down the lake), west to the shallow, marshy waters of its western basin, few lake trout over forty pounds are caught.

The western region of Athabasca hosts thousands of lake trout over twenty pounds, but almost always they are under forty pounds. Oh, there's an occasional fifty pounder taken, but these are few and far between.

However, the eastern basin is famous for its trophy trout. During the summer of 1997, nine trout over fifty pounds were caught and released by anglers, with one a sixty-one pounder, taken from a 120-foot-deep hole south of Poplar Point.

Today the Fond du Lac band of Indians controls all the commercial fishing rights to the huge lake. It has been their choice to cease netting in exchange for the lucrative tourist trade. Anglers seeking that once-in-a-lifetime lake trout trophy are descending on Athabasca in goodly numbers.

Some feel the next world-record lake trout will come from Lake Athabasca. They could be correct. So far, up until 1998, four fish over sixty pounds have been caught and released, the largest a sixty-four pounder.

For more information on where to fish on Lake Athabasca, turn to the information section in the book's last chapter.

Tips and Bits
OF THE NORTHERN NATURAL WORLD

Walruses are called "Tooth Walkers" by the northern natives . . . with good reason. To obtain footing on an iceberg, the northern walrus pulls itself up on the icebergs with its tusks. Contrary to belief, walrus tusks are not used for digging clams. Instead, the tusks are used like a sleigh runner while the walrus are propelling their bodies across the ocean floor. While sleighing across the bottom surface, walruses actually dislodge clams from the bottom by blowing a stream of water at them.

Walrus mothers are particularly nurturing to their young. They may nurse and care for their young for more than two years.

Chapter 14

"Inuit" Hidden Rumors

The "People," as they were called, roamed free across the inner barrens of Northwest Territory for as long as historians can recall. Official Canadian records testify to their existence as early as 1917. Explorers came in contact with them in the late 1890s, fur traders in the 1920s. They were a people who roamed the northern wastelands of the Kazan, Thelon, and Dubawnt River basins.

Farley Mowat tells of their life, existence, and plight in his books, *The Forgotten People* and *People of the Deer*. Some say Mowat's books over dramatized and told a false tale about the Inuits. Whether or not this is true may never be resolved.

The fact that no Canadian government officials cried "Wolf!" when the books were published may give us a clue. The Canadian Parliament in Ottawa was, at one time, going to vote on a bill to outlaw Mowat's *People of the Deer,* but eventually they decided against the idea. This, in itself, should be a clue that there had to be a great deal of truth in Mowat's words. Politicians never cry fowl unless guilty of the crimes of which they are accused.

119

Note: In the book, River of the Far North *by Dan Gapen, Sr., the basic problems faced by the inland Inuits is laid out and explained. See Chapter 3. Similar information can be found in Gapen's one-hour, thirty-five-minute video, "The Forgotten Land."*

To update the reader, the following information is available in a multitude of official records and historical documents.

The Inuit were a human population that migrated across the land bridge between the eastern continent of Russia and the western land known today as Alaska. Their passage occurred shortly after the melting of North America's glacier ice cap.

They were an extremely primitive race, small in stature, and Asian in eye and skin appearance. It is thought that these people are of the same native race that populated Central and South America.

What made the Inuit of the central Arctic barren different was the stagnation of their race. As late as 1910, records show they harvested game, mainly caribou, with the primitive weapon of their ancestors—the stone-tipped spear. The bow and arrow, normally thought to be the weapon of the original native North American, was never part of their hunting paraphernalia. Some claim that certain factions of the Inuit, mainly those who inhabited the eastern Great Slave Lake and north area, shot some type of crossbow, but, that has never really been documented.

As best as historians can determine, the population of barren Inuits never exceeded 10,000 and possibly hovered nearer the 5,000 mark at the turn of the century.

Today the Inuits no longer exist. Their story is simple. During the early 1900s, these people came in contact with whiteman. And, as often is the case, whiteman's diseases and social ways became their downfall.

The Inuits lived entirely off the land and its migrating caribou herds. Where the caribou went, so went the Inuit. Their clothing was made from caribou skins, their utensils from the bone and horns of the caribou, their shelters also from the skins and antlers. The caribou were life itself to these people.

Only when white man came to trade for fur with these people did their demise begin. Records show a great many Inuit died from measles, whooping cough, dysentery, and the common cold after their first contact with whites. But, disease alone didn't seal their fate. Another more deadly force, greed for the dollars, spelled doom to this primitive race.

During the 1920s and 1930s, there was flourishing trade between white trappers and the Inuit. White fox skins, much in demand in Europe, were traded for whiteman's food staples such as flour, sugar, tea, and salt. The Inuit culture changed. No longer did they depend on the ways of old. An easier, better way came into being. Then as history would have it, the second world war broke out in Europe. The need for white fox vanished overnight.

Having become dependent on whiteman's goods, the main population of Inuits waited patiently during the spring and summer of 1941 for the fur traders to return. Not until too late did they realize their fox furs would go unsold that season.

Winter descended! The caribou migration had long since gone south. The trout had left the streams, concentrating in Arctic lakes. Little food was available. Thus, by the winter of 1942, many starved. Some hung on, especially those with elders who knew the old way. It is estimated that more than half the population of people of the barrens perished during the winter of 1941-1942.

The next season saw some of the Inuit attempt to return to the ways of the past. Most once again waited for the coming of the white trader. A native culture, such as the Inuit had, never doubted the word of their fellow man. When the traders told them to gather fox furs, that they would return to trade in the spring, it was believed to be the truth. There was no word for untruth in the Inuit language.

Weakened by a year and a half of starvation, those Inuit who remained became even more susceptible to whiteman's disease, and, by the spring of 1944, eighty-five percent of the original population had disappeared.

At that point, our story becomes fuzzy. History and governmental records tell us that only fifty-two remaining Inuit were transferred by air from a trading post on Negilinia Lake in 1952 to the small Hudson Bay community of Eskimo Point.

This starving, dirty, unhealthy, and bewildered group contained a mere three women of child-bearing age. The fate of the inland people had been sealed. They would be no more. Evolution would melt them into the salty peoples' culture, their barrenland ways lost forever.

It is those years between the end of World War II and the final exodus of the people in 1952 that are so unclear. This period is flawed in rumor, innuendo, and lies. This period politicians and government agencies in Canada do not talk about. This period shows a loss of records and documents.

Rumor has it that the Canadian government, through its native affairs department, began a program of economic reclamation of the barrenland peoples; that float plane after float plane load of the Inuit were dispensed far to the south to participate in a fish-harvesting venture that would move them into the modern world and give them economic stability.

Rumor has it that fish harvesting and processing operations were set up on Nueltin, Wholdaia, Scott, and Wollaston Lakes. The Inuit would be the labor force in this venture. It became a massive welfare program that saw entire families displaced and relocated. At the least, those who were transferred became the tools of this new government experiment.

What the government failed to figure into their equation was the Inuit culture. These were people of the open barrens. Tall, massive forests had never been part of their life. Add to this the hate that existed between the Denépewa and Cree Indians on whose land these fish operations were placed, and the project was surely doomed for failure.

Two and a half years after it began, again as rumor would have it, the operations were shut down. It had become economically unfeasible to harvest fish in this isolated land and see any profit derived from it. The government had spent millions, and had nothing to show for it. The Inuits, a nomadic people, had failed to bend to the ways of whiteman. Twelve hours of daily hard labor, cleaning and collecting fish they'd never see used by their own, was, at best, incomprehensible.

Some failed to work; others tried but were unfamiliar with the work habits required of them. A few vanished, presumably in an attempt to return home. The ones who did attempt to work and change became discouraged when the promises bestowed upon them by government agents failed to come about.

One day, without notice, the government advisors just left, never to be seen again. Hundreds of Inuit were left to attempt a return to their homeland, hundreds of miles to the north. It became a case of genocide. Without proper clothing, hunting gear, or a mode of transportation, the people became victims of winter's wrath.

No one knows how they died for there were no witnesses to tell the story. One can only imagine the horrors of that trek north.

Rumor has it that some government officials simply washed their hands of the dollar-losing operations, closed the books, and cut their losses. So gross was the stupidity in government that those involved actually believed the people they deserted at the fish-harvesting operations would be able to return home on their own without government help.

Rumor is the key word. Why? Because today no records exist in Ottawa that it ever happened. Politicians will emphatically deny that such operations ever existed. Only the tales of the Cree and Denépewa elders remain to feed the rumors.

There is one concrete fact that even the government fails to deny. In the early 1970s, an unknown author published a book on the genocide of the barrenland people and the government fish-cleaning operations. So damaging were its contents that hard-liners within the governmental legal system chose to stop the publication. They did so . . . but not before several hundred copies leaked into the public forum. The book names politicians, government agents, dates, and places.

Rumor? Maybe . . . but with a twisted sort of truth that can only be part of the north's history.

Does the author of this book believe the rumor? Yes, he has seen the sites, looked for the missing documents, listened to the old Indian tales, and interviewed the bush pilots who flew the people south.

It must be so.

Chapter 15

Arctic Night Song

A low, morbid cry wafted gently across the hidden tundra draw. Unseen, the singer, a creature of obvious mystery, held momentarily, awaiting a response that never came. Moments later, dissatisfied with the results, it sent forth its tune again, this time even more pleadingly. Time held. The world slowed. The night stopped. Still no answer!

Near the draw's eastern end, where an Arctic stream danced and departed the narrow valley, a huge rock lay etched against the star-filled sky. From here, as if from the stone itself, the night song seemed to come.

Once again the morbid song erupted skyward, this time high pitched and more demanding. Moments passed; a night star burst into a glittering brilliance, then plunged towards earth, burning itself into obscurity and final death.

Suddenly, as if a hidden appendage on the huge stone had come to life, an outcrop slowly formed atop the blackened stone. It rose hairy and humped, with front shoulder bones arched skyward.

Once again the dark world within the draw stopped, while only time moved on.

Long moments drifted by before the low, throaty moan sounded again. It came muffled at first, as if smothered by some unseen shroud of cloth, then increased in volume until the wailing consumed the world. The tiny, darkened tundra draw had become a part of something bigger than itself, a hub from which the moaning call connected all living things within its range.

Then, atop the rock, the black hairy form began to lift higher until a gracious head held as far skyward as one might imagine possible. Rugged, thinly sculptured jaws parted wide as the rich melody continued. At that very moment it became a song that consumed earth and sky alike.

Above, there came a crackling of light that ripped across the sky, then abruptly faded away. Once again the dancing light reappeared, this time in pale colors of pink and green. It was as if the morbid call had wakened the god of the night sky.

Far to the west another calling moan came. The new song seemed somewhat higher pitched and femalelike. The new tune seemed to roll down upon the darkened tundra draw as if it were the gentle washing waves of water upon a sandy beach.

Time held still once again, with only night stars and the god of light responding to the moment.

Then, as before, the blackened form upon the rock raised skyward and sang its tune. This time the song became a pleading cry that wailed a path westward across the tundra.

Moments later the response, a cry of happiness formed in a series of short moans and yelps, returned.

As the blackened hairy form had appeared upon the rock, it now disappeared in silence, headed west. Darkness enveloped the departure.

The world held silent once again. The tiny tundra draw and its happy brook lay blanketed beneath a dark sky filled with a million flickering stars and the colorful dancing lights of the night god.

Chapter 16

Night of the Banjo

Crystal spears of illuminating light heightened, then faded only to illuminate once again as aurora borealis danced high atop the sub-Arctic scene below. A million glittering stars held base for the dazzling show. It was as it had been ten thousand nights before . . . yet somehow different.

Across the bay waters of Wholdaia Lake, banjo pickin' music came and went, as if tuned to the lights above. In harmony, they ebbed and flowed. It was a peaceful scene, a place of togetherness for all involved.

Four small, plywood shanties, the final result of an outpost fishing camp, were seen to hold firmly to a sandy esker overlooking the bay. From the windows of one shanty, there wafted light . . . a single propane lamp buzzed and sputtered warmth within, then pierced out into a darkened night.

Periodically, soft fading laughter and an intermingling of human voices came and went. These were strange sounds, a mix of multiple languages, murmuring short and choppy one moment, then soft and guttural the next . . . sounds which always faded into the harmony of the twanging banjo.

127

It was obvious a gathering was taking place. It was a friendly gathering, one which held firm as the marriage of multiple languages tattooed approval in time to the banjo's drifting melodies. Intermittently a muffled clapping of hands would signal a new tune be played, and more gentle pickin' would commence.

High atop an outcropping of glacial rock to the west, a lone, shaggy Arctic wolf stopped his search for fuzzy lemming. Slowly he tilted his head and paused. It was not a pause of disturbance, but one of curiosity and wonder. The coming and going of banjo music and the accompanying fluctuating sounds of voices had reached his ears. It was a sound unlike this place and yet one that seemed to belong. Holding, the wolf listened for a while. Then, as if satisfied, he lowered his nose, sniffed a tiny rut in the lichen stems below, and moved off in pursuit of dinner.

More muffled laughter floated skyward. The dancing lights, now pastel green, pale red, and glittering silver blue, continued to roll across the sky. As if some magical painter wielded a mystic brush on a star-filled, blackened pallet, the art scene came and went. Up and down, across and through, the crystal etchings pulsated on and off. The night sky lived.

A strange gathering of culture, tradition, and human beings, had come to Wholdaia Lake this night. A party of twelve men, four anglos, five Japanese, and three native Indians, had come in search of the mighty great trout and colorful Arctic grayling. The day had been successful. A celebration party was in order.

Ingredients for such an event were comprised of one banjo, a dimly lit plywood cabin, tales of the day past, mosquitoes, Labatts Blue Beer, mountain music, an Arctic lake, oriental saki, the soft-bearded voice of Bob Ecker, a million stars, tundra moss, and a primitive wilderness setting.

Bob Ecker, native of Humbolt, Saskatchewan, picked gently at his most prized possession. One need not ask him if he loved banjo music and the instrument from which it came. Evidence of such could be seen in the glowing face and caressing touch, as fingers plucked across the banjo strings. The banjo's leather strap, worn and dirtied with time, arched easily to Ecker's back. A long-ago-trapped fox tail fluttered downward from its tie as each note sounded. Seated atop the shanty's cold, airtight stove, body hunched around his instrument of music, the soft-faced Dutchman was easily recognized as an integral part of this far wilderness place.

As each melody ended, there came a humming of "aaaahs" and "ooohs," knowing approval voiced by Japanese members of the party. A more quiet appreciation crossed the faces of the three native guides, while the four whites clapped and jabbered their acceptance. Midnight came and went. The cabin glowed as over-head, the propane light blazed brightly, sputtered periodically, then glowed on. No one wished to be the first to leave. Conversations and laughter continued. Another tune, this one a bit faster, was heard to dance across the room. Grunts and nods of approval greeted the change in pace. Faces lit up, and laughter came. A toast with spirits was in order. Japanese saki, Canadian beer, and Scotch whisky were raised in tribute—to a wilderness, a banjo picker, companionship, and most of all, fellowship between men.

Two o'clock in the morning came and went; time moved on, and still melodic sounds drifted out and across night sky. And then it was time for a Japanese man to salute his companions, old and new, in tradi-tional song. Face aglow, Kazuo Asami, resident of Tokyo, rose and began to sing. It was a deep-throated, festive song of hope and happi-ness for the future. Instantly Kazuo's countrymen joined in. Voices strengthened, and a rhythmic clapping echo escaped from between the loose fitting plywood walls, out into the night and across the bay waters of Wholdaia Lake. The song ended, and approval echoed in hand claps and vocal "bravos." Banjo music began again.

The coming and going of picking music and old songs would affect all who walked the tundra this night—an effect not unpleasant—and even somewhat soothing; a sound which somehow belonged to this far wilderness place. These men, their laughter and music, belonged. Somehow, those who listened knew they had come, not to destroy, but to cherish and treat with respect a land which would always remain a part of their soul.

It was 3:00 A.M., and notes from the gentle banjo had all but disappeared when a curious red fox tiptoed into the golden light of the shanty window. Drawn by the muffled music, this curious animal sniffed, his long nose reaching out. There were no smells of food. Stealthily, he moved off toward a clump of dwarfed spruce. Maybe a foolish ptarmigan slept within.

Slowly the sputtering lamp faded. Overhead the night sky painter continued to work his magic. Across bay waters, the lonesome cry of a loon wavered off into the darkness. All became quiet.

Chapter 17

Cree Myths

The Cree Nation believes "Weesayjac" to be the creature of earth, or at least, the first human form to walk the earth. It was Weesayjac who created so many of the ways the Cree Nation hunts and fishes its natural world. It was Weesayjac who created the shapes and coloring of so much of the North's wildlife.

Consider the tale of the Common Loon (*moca* in Cree) and how it got its flat shape and the positioning of its legs . . . legs that protrude directly behind the body instead of from beneath its body like other swimming birds.

The Myth

Late one fall day Weesayjac needed to gather food for the winter. Being somewhat of a trickster, he came up with the idea of inviting all his bird friends over for supper and a night of games. For dinner Weesayjac offered only the best berries, seeds, and fishy morsels for his feathered friends.

Then he suggested they play a game where all must cover their eyes with their wingtips. No one would be allowed to peek once the game started, no matter what they heard. The game was to guess who was touching you, but to start, only Weesayjac was allowed to have his eyes uncovered.

As the game began, those covering their eyes could hear the strangest sounds, but no one peeked. There was the honk of a goose, the squawk of a duck, and the cluck of a grouse, but nary a soul looked.

About halfway through the game, there came the loud trumpet of a swan, followed by the flapping of heavy wings and a loud snap. Moca, the loon, could stand it no longer, so, as carefully as he could, he peeked.

Much to his horror, there across the tent stood Weesayjac, his hands wrapped around the swan's neck, which he had just snapped. Behind him in the tent's corner lay the bodies of many of Moca's friends.

"He's killing us! He's killing us!" cried Moca as he bolted for the tent's open end.

Alerted by Moca, the raven, seagull, ptarmigan, spruce hen, eagle, and hawk broke for the door at the same time. Being faster of wing, they all reached the doorway ahead of Moca and escaped. As Moca passed Weesayjac, who had run to the door of the tent to block the escapes, the creature's foot stomped down on Moca with such force that his body was flattened and his legs pushed to the back of his body.

But, being a strong bird, Moca managed to twist his way from under Weesayjac's heavy foot and escape. The escape was not without consequences. His body would remain flattened, and his legs would never again go back to their original position.

And that's the story of why the common loon is structured the way it is. Even in his trickery, Weesayjac was able to enhance the animal life around him. If it were not for his flat body and trailing legs, the loon could not dive as deep as he does and swim as fast as he does today.

Myth Two

Then there's the tale of Wapikano, the snow owl, and why the male bird has those dark spots on its breast, while the female is pure white.

It seems that one winter a large, male white owl took to robbing Weesayjac's rabbit snares. Each time Weesayjac would set a snare and manage to catch a rabbit, Wapicano would follow Weesayjac's track in the snow and eat his rabbit. This continued for two moons in the coldest part of the winter.

Weesayjac became angry and vowed to kill the white owl, no matter what it took. One day, shortly after the new moon, Weesayjac set out across the swamps, setting snares wherever the rabbit trails were best. Of course, Wapikano, the male snow owl, followed.

Knowing this would happen, after he'd set a dozen traps, Weesayjac doubled back, and at the sixth snare he'd set, he watched. By the time he'd doubled back, that sixth snare had already captured a rabbit. This was good, for surely Wapikano would come to rob the snare of Weesayjac's winter food.

There was one problem! Near the sixth snare Weesayjac could not find a good enough hiding place from which to jump on Wapikano. He elected to hide behind a large spruce tree trunk several yards away. Maybe, if he was fast enough, and Wapikano had eaten enough of the snared rabbit, Weesayjac could catch him before he got off the ground.

Weesayjac didn't have long to wait. Shortly after he got settled, the silent coming of Wapikano could be felt, and the huge, white bird glided down on the struggling, snared rabbit. With one mighty thrust of his beak, the owl killed the rabbit and began to eat.

Weesayjac waited until Wapikano had eaten half the rabbit, but because anger overwhelmed him, he chose not to wait any longer and jumped at the startled owl.

It was a miss, and the attempt to kill Wapikano failed as Weesayjac landed in the snow, on top of the half-eaten rabbit.

Wapikano flapped upwards and landed on the top branches of the very tree behind which Weesayjac had hidden.

That was insulting! Weesayjac shook his fist at the arrogant snow owl whose yellow eyes now laughed down at him. Without a weapon, the frustrated Weesayjac dug deep in the snow in an attempt to find a rock. He clawed out a brownish-black gob of swamp mud and quickly formed it into a hard ball. This would be as good as a stone if he could hit the thieving white owl.

Rearing back and pitching the compacted ball as hard as he could, Weesayjac made his attempt to knock the owl from its perch in the tree.

The throw was true, but just as the ball was about to hit Wapikano, it broke into dozens of tiny pieces which splattered the chest of the pure white owl.

Wapikano was horrified. His bright, white coat had been splattered full of dark spots. Those dark spots remain today on the chest of every male member of the snowy owl family.

So ashamed was Wapikano of his dress that he didn't fly again for two moons. No more did he rob others of their food. His self starving caused him to shrink in size and forever become smaller than his mate.

And that's the story of why the male white owl is smaller and why his coat is dotted with dark specks, even today. Without knowing it, Weesayjac had 'gifted' the male snow owl so it attracts predators with its coloring, while its pure white mate sets undetected on the nest.

Chapter 18

Athabasca's Desert

Two days of walking had brought the old, brown cow no closer
to her destination, the McFarlane River basin. Her tracks wandered aimlessly across the tan sands of Athabasca's southern
shoreline area. As the crow flies, she'd covered a mere twenty-five
miles. Actual walking distance was more like eighty miles.

Food had been scarce. Most of the grasses were bitter and unap-
pealing in taste. Leaves of the sparce stands of wind-worn birch
were often too high to reach. For most of the way, willow brush had
made up her sole food source.

Near the end of the second day, a strong wind from the north
whipped stinging sand pellets against her flanks and hairless
underside. To guard against this irritation, the old caribou stuck
to low ground as much as possible. Though these low areas protected her from direct contact with the winds, there were draw-
backs. Soft, steel-edged sand pellets had blown into deep drifts
along the shallow draws and valleys.

Continuous walking across these one- to two-foot-deep beds of
sand had worn at her hooves' outer skin. In places where a hot,

late-day sun had heated these beds to an excess of 100 degrees, the burning sand caused the old cow to shuffle her feet as they engaged the sand. The soft, weblike portions of her hooves were becoming raw and painful.

Less than a mile from where she walked, the heavy rollers of Lake Athabasca exploded upon the sand and stone beaches of the lake's southern shore. Were she to change course and continue her trek along the lake shore, relief from the blistering sands of the desertlike dunes could easily be attained. However, getting to the Williams River was all her instincts allowed. That meant that as straight a course as possible must be followed. Veering north would only create a loss of time.

Reaching the western edge of the Archibald River, the old cow looked down from a thirty-foot-high dune, expecting to see the fast-flowing, clear waters of the Williams. Instead, more miles of sands rolled to the east of the small, narrow river below.

The sun had all but disappeared when the aged woodland caribou attempted to descend the nearly sheer face of the Archibald River dune. As soon as she placed her front feet over the dune's lip, she knew a mistake had been made. Desperately she attempted to withdraw her forward legs, but a commitment had been made. The weight of her hind quarters broke the edge of the dune away, and she began a slide and tumble, which would end her life.

Her body wrenched to the right as front legs dug deep into the soft lip sand. In slow motion she tumbled . . . first hindquarters over head, then legs over back. The right front leg had been badly dislocated on that first head-over-heels tumble. As she attempted to regain balance, the injured leg flopped wildly back under her body, useless and unresponsive. Six times her body cartwheeled down the face of the dune to lodge itself across a huge, black rock. There it held as shifting sand began to cover the hindquarters, then the mid section.

Finally, just minutes after the accident, the final grains slipped across the mound of sand under which all but the old cow's neck and head lay. Dazed by the fall and the smothering effect of the shifting sand, the old cow lie quietly, her breathing labored.

Her breaths came in short, heavy snorts. Each intake carried with it multiple grains of sand, which eventually began to clog her airway.

Struggle as she might, breaking lose from the heavy blanket of sand was impossible. Maybe if her front leg had not been disabled, she would have succeeded, but without its use, the struggle became fruitless. The harder she tried, the deeper she breathed. The deeper she breathed, the more sand she took into her nose and lungs.

Finally, completely exhausted, she gave up and allowed life to slip from her body. She would die, six hours after the accident, under a northern sky full of glittering stars while the northern wind, now a soft breeze, dislodged more dune sand to completely cover her body. Her race to join the balance of the small herd of woodland caribou on the eastern shores of the Williams River had been her undoing.

Weeks later, a strong southeastern wind would slowly dislodge the blanket of sand that covered the old cow's body. Once it was discovered, ravens, a pair of silver fox, and a myriad of wood mice and shrews would pick clean the bones of the old cow. Her inner body cavity would be ripped open and eaten by a starving, old black bear. All that would be left was a pile of bleached bones sticking up through the crust of dislodged sands.

Two years later, a pair of wandering fishermen discovered the weathered bones, looked them over, and wondered what fate had been dealt to their owner.

"Anne, maybe it's an old wolf kill. These dunes have a couple of packs that prey on the barrenland caribou that winter here," said the male human as they carefully examined the remains.

"What kind of animal is this, Dan?" questioned Anne.

"Not sure . . . maybe moose or caribou," came his response.

The pair of humans stayed only a few minutes, then moved on. It was a long walk back to Lake Athabasca where their native guide and the fishing boat that had carried them across giant Lake Athabasca waited.

Saskatchewan's sand dunes consist of a series of dune fields that stretch sixty miles along the southern shore of Lake Athabasca in the province's northernmost region. They are the largest active sand surface in Canada and the northernmost desert in the world.

Humans have lived in or about the Athabasca sand dunes intermittently for the past 8,000 years. Archeologists established that prehistoric hunters have used the sand dunes to harvest the barrenland and woodland caribou for thousands of years.

Five hundred years ago, the inland Inuit harvested winter caribou here. Not till the southern Denépewa moved north, driving the Inuits out, did culture change.

Peter Pond and Peter Fidler, fur traders and explorers, first worked the sand dune area in the late 1700s. Pond came first, arriving via the McFarlane River in 1778. A Hudson Bay post was established on Athabasca's northern shore in 1851 at the site of Fond du Lac, a thriving native community today.

Science tells us the dunes were formed 8,000 years ago by the retreating ice-age glaciers. The spillways coming off the glaciers deposited millions of tons of crushed sand along the shores of what today is Lake Athabasca.

Two major spillways were created by the melting glacier. Today, one of the spillway paths is the MacFarlane River. The other is the Williams River. It is between these two rivers that sand dunes were created.

As prehistoric Lake Athabasca shrank in size, its southern shores and bottom were exposed. Heavy northern winds then did the rest, blowing tons of the fine lake-bottom sand into what today is called Canada's only sub-Arctic desert.

The dunes have managed to hold their own against the passing of time by revitalizing themselves when heavy winds push the exposed sand back and forth across the area between the two rivers.

In some regions, such as the MacFarlane River, the sands slowly smother trees on the forest edge, while in others, the wind exhumes the ghostly skeletons of trees buried hundreds of years before.

This continuous action of burying and exposing the natural vegetation goes on today as it has for 8,000 years. It is possible to see clumps of birch trees, the root system exposed as much as six feet beneath where the trunk once began to grow. In other spots, maybe just over the hill, another birch clump may be buried with its trunk as deep as ten feet beneath the sand surface. Here, the upper foliage may be the only sign that a tree grows, its leaves touching the drifting sand surface.

In other areas the loose sand may have completely disappeared, leaving a hard desert pavement of rock permeated with course grains of wind-driven sand. Often the stones atop the desert pavement appear to be highly polished as if sand blasted by an unseen polishing machine.

These stones, called "Ventifacts," have many sides. Many are cube-shaped while others may be perfectly round. The one thing they all have in common is their highly polished look, a product of thousands of years of sand blasting.

Within the Athabasca sand dunes are ten separate classifications of vegetation that grow nowhere else in the world. The dunes also support the vegetation normally found in the Saskatchewan forests. Plants such as blueberries, black spruce, teallerleaf, lichens, Arctic willows, Labrador tea, and jack pine can be found attempting to eke out an existence in the harsh environment. What is so different is not the species so much as the few numbers of these plants and trees existing within the dunes.

Outsiders entering the region of the dunes are immediately struck by the odd out-of-place feeling of the area. It is like stepping through a door into the world of the Arabian knights, where at any moment one might see camel caravans crossing as on the Sahara Desert of northern Africa.

For more information, see information index at the end of the book.

Chapter 19

The Trapper

There had been bear signs around the camp at High Hill Lake for better than ten days, unusual bear signs. A rather large animal with a grotesque abnormality to its right front paw had been snooping around.

Twice Mervin Mackey had seen signs beneath the cabin's rear window. Claw marks on the window sill showed the animal's intent had been to enter the cabin by dislodging its window. Each time the intruder had come during the night when Mervin and his dogs were away at a trapping outpost thirty miles to the northwest.

It was late fall. Snow had come twice, only to vanish at the touch of the high-noon autumn sun. This was not a time for black bears. They should already be bedding down for their long winter hibernation.

Having seen the signs, Mackey wasn't a bit surprised when the very night he returned to his High Hill camp, the dogs roared into thunderous outcry shortly after dark. The bear had returned!

Outside, a rising half moon had begun to light up the ground beneath the black skeletons of spruce. The western sky still held its blood-red fading light close to the horizon.

Mackey's loaded .30-06 rifle rested to the right of the cabin's outside door. It was easily reached as the trapper stepped away from the wooden table where a late dinner had just been consumed.

Cautiously he opened the door. For a moment, he stared into a setting of semi-darkness. He held to the doorstep a moment, slightly blinded from the effect of the yellow glare of the gasoline lantern that hung behind him, directly above the table.

Eyes focused. There . . . only feet from the tethered dogs, a tall, gaunt animal loomed high above the barking animals. The bear stood on hind legs, head tilted back, front legs making menacing gestures of battle.

Fear gripped the trapper . . . fear not for himself but for his dogs. With his right hand he gripped the rifle barrel, thrusting it forward into his left hand. The stock had just risen above beltline when a sharp, thudding blow struck him at the point where the rifle butt and ribs joined. The powerful blow threw Mackey backwards into the cabin where he landed under the table, rifle still in hand.

Somehow the bear had diverted its aggressive intent from the dogs to the trapper and managed, in a second, to cover the twenty feet between them. The bear had been so fast that Mackey had completely failed to react. Had it not been for the bear's hesitation in the doorway, this tale might have ended right here.

Instinct took over! Without aiming, Mackey pointed his rifle toward the menacing, black silhouette in the cabin's doorway and pulled the trigger. Momentarily the cabin was aglow in orange as the muzzle blast echoed. Luckily the shot hit home, sending the intruder back onto the cabin's log step.

Scrambling forward, Mackey injected a second shell, and from his knees, placed a killing shot into the bear's skull. The intruder shuddered, then lay still, one forepaw gripping the lower door frame. Outside the dogs continued their noisy uproar.

Careful examination of the bear showed the reason for his intruding ways and his unwillingness to hibernate. The left front foot was missing, lost to a trap or maybe a fight earlier in life. For reasons unexplained, the remaining stump had become infected and now lay open and swollen, greenish discharge oozing from the opening. Obviously the bear had been in a great deal of pain.

Further inspection showed a bear that carried no fat . . . so gaunt and skinny that its ribs showed prominently through a coat of thin side hair. This was a bear that should have weighed in excess of 500 pounds but now carried less than 250. Hibernation for this creature had been out of the question. It would have starved to death before the new year came to pass.

Mervin Mackey suffered three broken ribs in his encounter with the three-legged bear. Since it was early November and the outside world lay 150 miles to the south, Mackey decided to wrap his ribs tightly with strips of moosehide and let nature do its thing. Today he's no worse for wear. However, when asked, he did admit there were some painful moments for the first six weeks after the encounter with the bear.

I interviewed Mervin Mackey during July in the summer of 1992 at a lake called Silsby. Silsby Lake lies ninety air miles east of the town of Thompson in north central Manitoba. Mervin was still trapping at the ripe old age of sixty-nine. However, along with his wintertime activities, Mackey had gone into summer guiding of fishing tourists as well as commercial fishing to supplement his income.

This tough, old bushman had many tales to tell. Take the time he shot a large bull moose with nothing but a .22 rifle.

As so often is the case in the Far North, the men who make their living off the land, only carry .22-caliber rifles. Such firearms weigh less, and the ammunition they fire is small and virtually weightless. When every ounce has to be backpacked in, this becomes not only important, but lifesaving at times.

Late one winter, with meat supplies virtually depleted, Mackey came across a rather large bull moose. The bull stood chest deep in snow that had nearly covered a red willow grove. Moose consume the tender willow tips as one of their nutritious winter food supplements.

With light snow falling and the promise of a harder snow to come, heavy clouds in the northwest were rapidly descending. Mackey made the decision to shoot the animal where he was. Retrieving the meat from this location would be hard, but to wait might mean the complete loss of the animal as heavy snows obscured its whereabouts.

Mackey managed to get within eighty feet of the bull by using gusting snow as his cover. At this point, everything between the animal and him was open. Raising his rifle, he fired once, then again, and finally, a third time. Not until the third shot solidly hit home did the moose flinch. Seemingly irritated by the soft pop of the .22-caliber rifle and the stinging burn it created, the old bull began to slowly walk off.

Mackey knew he'd hit the animal each time he fired. Try as he might, there wasn't enough visibility to get a fourth shot off. Snow squalls, driven by an increasing wind, obscured his vision.

He did the only thing he could. Digging a hole deep in the snow with a snow shoe, he laid out his sleeping bag and settled in for a night's sleep. It made no sense to chase the wounded animal. It would only continue to walk if pursued. If left alone, the animal would eventually settle down to rest. The snow was falling steadily, but not enough to completely cover the imprints made by the walking moose. It takes a great deal of blowing snow to obliterate the body tracks made by this horse-sized animal.

Clear, blue skies greeted Mackey the next morning as he thrust his head from the sleeping bag. The hole had filled with a foot of fresh snow. It covered him completely. No wonder he'd slept so warmly. Snow makes an excellent insulator.

Picking up the moose's trail was easy. Even though the trail was all but filled in, a deep, soft impression remained where each stride had been taken. Twenty minutes into the trailing, Mackey spotted his bull beneath a large jackpine. It lay, legs beneath it, still alive but unable to get up. Walking up to the animal, the trapper killed him with a single .22 shot to the back of the head.

At the moment of death, the animal's hind foot lashed out, nearly hitting Mackey's right leg. The thrusting leg struck a four-inch spruce with its hoof, hitting so hard that the tree trunk snapped in half. Mervin Mackey never forgot that incident and recognized with great respect, the moose's ability to fight back with its hooves.

Another time, Mervin saw four caribou crossing a frozen lake. Once again he was able to sneak close enough to use his .22 rifle. He shot one animal between the eyes, an action that caused it to sit backwards on its haunches, then settle down on the ice as if asleep.

The other three caribou then trotted over to the downed animal and laid down beside it. Mackey commenced to kill them one by one with a .22 caliber lead bullet behind the ear. Not one of the animals attempted to rise. Those four caribou produced enough meat to get Mackey through the winter of 1988. It also proved to Mervin just how curiously stupid caribou can be.

Mervin Mackey, a man of Scotch-Irish and Cree Indian blood, left home when he was thirteen years old to work in the lumber camps of northern Ontario. There he learned the skills of a lumberjack, including the operation of heavy equipment such as bulldozers and log skidders. But, it was a life not to his liking. Spending four months at a time in a camp with a bunch of rough-and-tumble ax men, only to get drunk in town at the end, was not for him.

Eventually a drunken brawl got him in enough trouble that he headed west and north forever. At the age of twenty-two, he began trapping and never returned to the old ways.

Mervin's travels took him as far north as Uranium City in the Northwest Territories when the famous town was made up of but three tents. Here, he trapped Arctic wolves as an assigned trapper for the territorial government.

Mackey even spent seven months in Mexico after a relapse into drinking while in his mid thirties. With only $1,000 to his name, he wandered across Mexico's back country, ending up finally 500 miles south of Mexico City. Here he showed the locals how to trap bobcats and ferrets.

Why or how Mackey went to Mexico was never divulged. Possibly it had something to do with the two-and-one-half-year marriage to a half Mexican woman he had met in northern Saskatchewan on one of his few re-entries into society as we know it.

Mervin Mackey finally settled down near Blind River, Ontario, where he trapped for sixteen years. From there, he traveled into Manitoba's northern region where I first met the gnarled and weathered outdoorsman.

Interesting Trapping Facts as Related by Mervin Mackey in Our Last Meeting

1. A trapper must consume, each day, one pound of grease, three pounds of meat, and bannock to maintain life during the cold winter days in the north. This diet is followed if no other foods are available.

2. To maintain one's self, a trapper must collect three caribou or one three-year-old moose to enable him to spend five months of winter in the north.

3. During some winters, Mackey would enter the trapline in the fall at a weight of 215 pounds and depart in the spring at 185 pounds.

4. Scent pole: To attract fox, place a red rag on a four-foot pole. Then place the pole on a clump of marsh grass where it can be

Migration

Yesterday's Home

Tideflats

Ptarmigan

Innocence

Nanook

Kitchen 1500 B.C.

Casimir Island

Avoiding Bugs

Muskox "Bad Boy"

Gorge-of-Death

St. Mary's "Inuksuk"

Today's Inuit

Food Cache 1500 B.C.

What's Up?

The Trophy

O'Shaughnessy

Serenity

Winisk Super

Charlie Wynns

The Goose Man

Waldo's Buddy

Treeline Pike

Arctic Prize

Who Are You?

Live Iceberg

The Dubawnt

Heaven

Lonesome Brood

Life Begins

Arctic Shore Lunch

readily seen from any direction. Next urinate or spit snuff on it. The flag movement will attract the animal into smelling distance. Then the smell takes over, causing the curious animal to come in and rescent the pole. Your trap is placed below the grass by the pole. This trick isn't just for fox. Wolverine and wolves will also be attracted by this trick.

5. One of the best scented attractors is created when whitefish are set out to ferment. The oil is drained off and used.

6. To attract marten, use strawberry jam. They love it! The more, the better.

7. Boiled fish is always better than raw fish when baiting traps for mink.

8. Canned tuna, salmon, or sardines make a great bait for ermine or mink.

9. Otter fat or fat oil doesn't freeze and will make an excellent attractor, once boiled down in a frying pan. Place the thick oil in a bottle to be used later when willow sticks are dipped in it to cover other scents around the set trap.

Note: To make the oil even better, burn it a bit in the frying pan. This oil is a wonderful attractor for fisher, mink, and marten.

10. To feed sleigh dogs, a trapper must gather six pounds of fish per day for each dog. Successful trappers house ten dogs, running only five at a time while resting the other five. The sixty pounds of raw fish a day is always supplemented with any beaver carcasses that are left after skinning, once the choice meat cuts are taken off for the trapper.

11. Otters love to harass beaver. This includes going into the beaver house and dragging the beaver young into open water. Once clear of the house, the otter will rough handle the young beaver until they kill it. It is an action similar to how a housecat plays with a mouse. The otter may be cute, but his play antics can be very cruel.

12. To entice elusive wolves, fishers, or foxes, try freezing fermented whitefish in a tube of bark when water makes up forty to fifty percent of the frozen mass. Next, take bark off the frozen cylinder and place it in an open-watered hole on lake ice. Allow seventy-five percent of the cylinder to protrude above the surface ice. Frozen in, the animals can't carry it off and are forced to gnaw on it there. Traps are then placed strategically around the cylinder.

13. The average trapper can cover eighteen miles a day on foot. With a team of five dogs, this distance is increased to thirty-five miles a day. The modern trapper, equipped with a snowmobile, can cover seventy-five miles a day and attend traps properly.

Mervin Mackey is a man unto himself. He takes no partners, fearing they may lack the ability to fare well in the woods. His life revolves around animals.

"To trap an animal successfully, you must first learn to catch it with your hands," he said to me one day. I believe Mervin Mackey could do just that. As far as I know, he still walks the wintry wilds northeast of Thompson, Manitoba. And if he doesn't, I don't want to know. In my mind, I would rather let some things be as they've always been.

> *Note: Mervin Mackey enjoys eating spring geese. Maybe it's his native blood that creates the urge. His answer to those who argue against spring hunting goes like this:*
>
> *"Why not eat them in the spring when they taste good? In the fall they taste bad and have less nutrients and fat.*
>
> *"What's the difference? Kill 'em in the spring and lose a few young or kill 'em in the fall so they can't have young the next spring?"*

Mervin laughs. One time the Department of Natural Resources sent a helicopter to catch him hunting in spring. A three-man crew flew around for four days chasing Mackey, never catching him. At

$450.00 an hour for chopper time, plus crew pay, the bill was enormous. All that for six geese he ate and enjoyed. Mackey has a hard time understanding the modern man.

Tips and Bits

OF THE NORTHERN NATURAL WORLD

On spring ice floes, mother seals often continue to use their winter blow holes after the birth of their kits. Seldom will the kit dive with the mother on her hunts for food below. Instead, the kit is covered with snow by the mother's flippers before she dives. Since the seal kit gives off *no* scent and is colored pure white at birth, hunting polar bears often miss the kit when attacking the mother.

Chapter 20

Whitefish
Gamefish in the 2000s

A late June moon radiated Gapen's pool as Jim Ferrell, my fishing partner, dropped anchor across the bow of our freighter canoe. Jim and I, for the past two summers, guided tourists from the United States who came to my parents' lodge in search of Lake Nipigon's record brook trout. This night, however, brook trout were not our target. Lake Superior whitefish, which migrate up river at this time of year, were what we sought.

It was midnight, and millions of hatching mayflies filled the air, littering the big river eddy's surface. It was this "once-a-year" hatch, which caused the whitefish to migrate and enjoy a surface-feeding binge. No one knew how whitefish knew the fly hatch was on; they seemed to appear magically.

With anchor set and canoe settled, we eyed the surrounding water for the telltale glimmer of surface disturbances, which would be our indication that whitefish were rising.

Finally, to our left, near an eddy break, three dark fins gracefully arched above the surface, then disappeared with only a glittering of disturbed water to reveal that they had come and gone.

Silence prevailed . . . broken only by the soft tinkling of surface currents.

There! Several more fins were sighted, an obvious sign that whitefish had gathered in numbers! Fishing would be good this night. Flies were cast in an upstream angle, allowed to drift quietly, then recast. On cast two, I set hook gently and was rewarded with a streaking line and a glittering silver fish catapulting into the moonlight. It would be the beginning of a fun-filled night of fishing.

In the end, Jim and I landed and released a pair of flashy, fresh-run rainbow trout and thirteen fat, four-to-ten-pound whitefish. Losses totalled three rainbows and nearly thirty whitefish. Whitefish are very difficult to land due to a paper thin mouth wall.

Eventually our fly lines became waterlogged, and the usable dry flies were all sinking. Jim and I returned to the lodge around 3:30 A.M., exhausted but happy.

Even today, almost fifty years later, I remember that night as if it were yesterday. The thrill remains! Nothing excites this angler more than whitefish rolling their way across a serene lake surface as twilight approaches.

Whitefish as a species does not receive the credit it deserves. Known mainly as a deep, cold-water table fish, the whitefish remains undiscovered. Many believe this fish can only be harvested via commercial netting. Nothing could be farther from the truth.

Where Whitefish Are Found

Whitefish exist in most of the states bordering Canada, as well as all of the Canadian provinces up to, and in many cases, above the sixtieth parallel. They exist in both lakes and rivers, sizes small and large. They can be found in Alaska, as well as the far reaches of Labrador. In all, there aren't many waters where this scrappy fish cannot be found north of the Canadian border.

There are eight species of whitefish in North America. Most common is the lake whitefish. All spawn in late fall, but eggs do not hatch until early spring, one of the longest incubation periods for freshwater species. It should also be noted that this fish can spawn in water temperatures as low as thirty-three degrees but fail to reproduce in water over forty-six degrees.

Feeding Habits

Whitefish are primarily insect feeders but, on occasion, will take small minnows or bottom critters such as a small crawfish or hell-grammite. Anglers targeting this species must use lures of equivalent size, color and shape to imitate these food items. Thus, fly fishermen have a distinct advantage over those equipped with spinning gear.

Yes, occasionally one can catch a whitefish on French spinners, bottom-walking rigs loaded with a leech, or even a Dardevle spoon. I remember, during my guiding years back in Ontario, when tourists would go nearly insane as hundreds of these finning fish came to the surface just prior to nightfall. Try as they might, failure was absolute as huge Dardevle spoons raced through surface water, time after time.

Though whitefish are a cold-water species, preferring water temperatures in the forties and low fifties, hatching flies will bring them up, even when surface temperatures hit the seventies. Once on the surface, they begin a special pattern of feeding. The pattern usually will cover a seventy-five-to-one-hundred-fifty-yard path along the shoreline or across a bay. Once they reach the end of the feeding zone, the school reverses itself and travels back over the path just taken.

School size depends on the quantity of flies hatching. The more flies on the water, the larger the whitefish school. Very seldom do schooling whitefish number less than eight or ten, with schools numbering forty to seventy fish common. An average school size numbers twenty-five to thirty-five fish. The feeding pattern width is seldom wider than twelve feet. Once a feeding school of whitefish is spotted, the angler must position himself to intercept them. *Never* attempt to follow the school. Sit and wait; the school is certain to return, time after time. Following them will only cause the feeding school to flush and reappear some distance away. Whitefish have keen senses and eyesight.

In rivers, feeding patterns are much shorter. Some only encompass a small eddy beneath a waterfall, others a short seventy-five-foot stretch of slick water along a riverbank.

No matter where whitefish feed, their graceful arching pattern of feeding is applied.

In lakes, the distance between the initial surface strike and reappearing to ingest another insect may be as much as twenty-five to thirty feet apart. In a river system, it will be far less. Whitefish in river eddys may arch to the surface, settle, then arch to the surface again in nearly the exact position.

No matter where you fish whitefish, one rule always applies. When fly hatches are massive, never attempt to compete with an over abundance of natural flies. Look for an opening in the surface, and place your offering in its middle. For reasons unknown to this angler, whitefish prefer to target solitary flies. Maybe it's easier for their eyes to focus on a single insect set off by itself.

> *Note: Do not move your fly once it has settled to the surface. Whitefish shy away from a fly that is moved or twitched. The slightest movement will see them select another target. Possibly, years of instinct has taught this species to avoid insects that move on the surface. Movement may be followed by flight as the hatching insect launches into the air to breed and reproduce its species.*

Remember, do not attempt to bring your fly to the fish. Always allow the fish to come to your fly. Whitefish angling is a sit-and-wait game. This same rule applies when working weighted nymphs for this fish.

Equipment

Standard fly rod and reels, such as a #7 system work best. Fly leaders with 4X or 5X tippets are preferred, and in some cases you may have to taper down to 6X.

Old reliable fly patterns work as well as anything. Muddlers in #14 or #12, dry flies in size #12 in patterns such as March Browns, Adams, Goddard Caddis, Henderickson, Gray and Grizzly Wulffs, and Female Adams work best.

In the far north, where shad fly hatches fail to occur, miniature insect species such as blackflies, mosquitos, and a wide variety of duns become the staple diet of whitefish. Here, dry fly patterns consist of black gnats, mosquitos, Adams, coachmans, and white millers (sizes #14 and #16 are preferred). A peacock hurl on the coachman dry or wet fly has a special attraction to far northern whitefish. It is my conclusion that the iridescent colors of peacock hurl presents a color pattern similar to that found on the Arctic blackfly larva.

Anglers not skilled in the art of fly fishing can join in by using a five-foot, ultralight spinning rod loaded with four-pound test line. To attain enough weight to cast a fly on an ultralight rod and reel, place a casting bubble twenty-four inches above the fly at the line's end. Purchase the style of casting bubble that allows water to be added (inside) for casting weight. Filling such a float to half full allows the float to remain on surface with the fly floating behind it.

When whitefish are seen arching near the surface, but failing to break the surface, they are then feeding on nymphs. This being the case, try using a Hare's Ear, stone fly, or March Brown nymph. The best nymph, day in day out, is a Hare's Ear in size #10.

Special Gear

When whitefish are working fast, foaming water beneath a waterfalls or fast rapids, an angler can use very small jigs such as a Jiget in the 1/64-ounce size. Another jig that will work well is a 1/32-ounce or 1/16-ounce Ugly Bug. Color selection can be anything from white, black, brown, or orange and depends on the insect nymph present in the system. Under these same conditions very small Eppinger "No-Tangle" French-style spinners in series #40 and #41 (small blades) squirrel tail models will also work. Possibly, it's the flash of a spinner blade that attracts the fish and the natural look of a squirrel tail that causes them to strike.

In the fast water of rivers, below waterfalls and within deep channel currents, the angler is able to catch this delicious table-fare throughout the summer months and on into the fall season. In lakes the availability time is somewhat restricted.

In northern states, mayfly hatches determine the prime feeding time slot. Mid-June through the first week of July is considered best. In southern regions of northern Ontario, Quebec, Saskatchewan and Manitoba, the time slot is confined to the fourth week of June on through the first three weeks of July. In northern portions of the Canadian provinces and the Northwest Territories, whitefish come to surface during the last week of July and the first three weeks of August.

These feeding time zones may vary slightly—everything depends on the whim of Mother Nature and her fly hatches. The time of day may vary in each region, but for best results, fish early and late daylight hours. Watch for the hatch to begin. Normal elapsed time of most insect life on which whitefish feed, is two to three hours.

Other Important Facts

Being a deep-water fish—forty to eighty feet in most inland lakes—whitefish are seldom taken in their natural habitat. At times they can be caught, but an angler who has the knowledge to meet this challenge must also have endless patience. Along with patience, he or she must be equipped with electronics capable of identifying the target. Whitefish show up on a graph as a solid, rather thin line, suspended over deep water. In northern states such as Minnesota, Michigan, or Maine, this layer of fish is generally found somewhere between sixty and sixty-eight feet deep. Don't confuse whitefish with ciscos, which are often found between thirty-six and thirty-eight feet.

The approach is easy. Rig an ultralight rod and reel with four-pound test line and a small, sensitive slip float. The recommended lures and baits are restricted to worm larvae, tiny jigs tipped with Mousies or a bit of worm, 1/32-ounce Ugly Bug jigs, and weighted flies, such as a Hare's Ear nymph. As in all lure presentations, there shouldn't be any movement of the lure once it has reached the depth at which the whitefish are suspended. The calmer the water, the better your chances.

Tip: On light, sensitive lines, slip floats are easily moved. To prevent improper positioning of the slip knot and float, mark your line with a permanent black felt tip marker at the proper spot. Should the knot move, the mark is easily detected, and knot placement can be properly corrected.

The best time of day to fish deep-water whitefish is 8:30 to 10:30 A.M. or 4:00 to 6:00 P.M. Deep-water light refractions, low and high, will turn feeding fish off.

The fish of my youth can be a difficult prey to capture. With a mouth small in size and paper thin in texture, a strong hook-set will result in failure. An angler must learn to set the hook lightly and fight this fish with soft hand pressure.

Whitefish fight harder than a brook trout, leap (at times) as much as a rainbow trout, and make runs longer than a salmon. Pound for pound, this fish has few equals. Yet, the whitefish continues to be ignored by most anglers. This missed opportunity is due to many anglers' lack of knowledge.

Today, things are changing. Many Canadian provinces have placed the once lowly whitefish on its game fish list. Maybe the day will soon come when the fish I've loved to catch for fifty-five years will gain its day in the sun.

Chapter 21

Ukkusikalik

Wager Bay

Cautiously, John Hicks began his ascent, stepping from one broken stone to another. The island's western end had been ground and re-ground for thousands of years by the bay's onslaught of ice. Thousands of tons of ice had descended upon the island's rocky shore, forcing up deep-water rock to be cracked, broken, and left behind as the melting days of summer came.

Each step had to be cautiously tested before placing one's weight upon it. Failure to do so could see an ankle twisted, or even worse, a leg broken. Such a happening, this far into the Arctic, could spell disaster for the recipient.

Fifty feet above and one hundred fifty feet in front of us, a huge, white bear lazily gazed down on the four of us. Laurie Dickhart, my adventure partner, and Roger Pilakapse of Rankin Inlet, Northwest Territories, made up the balance of our party. Roger had been guiding Laurie and me while we were fishing for Arctic Char.

Presently, fishing was the farthest thing from our minds. Fifty yards ahead of us was 2,000 pounds of ferocious, white Arctic bear.

"Folks, I think we can get really close to her if we're quiet. Don't dislodge any of those rocks, and we'll be all right," whispered our host and Arctic bear expert.

Roger giggled a bit and just smiled at John's instructions. Maybe he thought it was funny, but Laurie and I didn't. Laurie's face tensed a little at John's remark, and we both walked as if on broken glass.

An hour before, we'd come upon the bear while she had been devouring a freshly killed seal. From the looks of the carcass, she had consumed more than enough to fill her needs. Spooked by our intrusion, the bear had trotted up the coast a mile or so, then swam offshore to the small rock island where she now rested.

Twice she had tried to swim away to the next island but became discouraged at the approach of our boat. Not caring for our rodeo roundup tactics, and full of seal meat, she'd elected to saunter to the highest spot on the island and rest. At this point John decided we should have a closer look-see.

"Keep in single file, gang. Polar bears don't have such good eyesight. We'll be a lesser threat if she sees only one of us," instructed John as we hid behind a large boulder on the island's right side.

Slowly, step by step, in single file, we edged our way closer to the bear. Much to my surprise, John led us up the slope with a light wind at our backs. Later he explained that an approach that kept our scent away from the bear could create an aggressive response if the wind were to shift or the bear suddenly became aware of our presence. This way she knew we were there all the time, and it left her in control of the situation, both visually and in a scenting way.

My head bumped into John's backside about the same time I saw his hand lower and signal, "Stop." Slowly my head moved to the left, past John's left shoulder. There, no more than thirty-five feet away, snoozed a huge, white animal. She breathed slowly, ears flicking every so often, as a pesky blowfly buzzed about her head. The black nostrils, shiny and wet, flared as air came and went.

John signaled for us to spread out side by side. It was obvious he knew Laurie and I couldn't shoot pictures from the single-line staging. Ever so slowly, I edged to John's left while Laurie did the same on his right. We moved in extra slow motion. Hearts pounded, and breath shortened.

Halfway through a roll of film, the bear's eyes opened, and she slowly raised her head. John indicated that we should freeze. That wasn't necessary. At the first flick of her eye, I'd become mummified.

As if to show us she was queen of her domain, she lazily opened her massive mouth and yawned. Mesmerized, I watched an eighteen-inch, coal-black tongue roll up from the lower jaw and moisten her black nose. Then, as if we didn't exist, she settled back to snooze.

I could hear Laurie's breath expel, as mine did likewise. Talk about a heart-stopping situation! Never before had I felt such a rush when photographing wildlife.

As the camera shutter fell on the last of thirty-six photos, the bear's eye closest to us opened and seemed to rotate our way. It must have been a sign, for a moment later, John indicated by motioning his hand backwards that we should leave.

It took us ten minutes to retreat. We left as slowly as we had come. John would later explain that this was necessary because any sudden movement could set the bear into an aggressive posture. And, it doesn't take a white bear but a couple of seconds to cover distance between itself and an intruder headed for a boat.

Back in the boat, John had these reassuring words: "I wasn't worried; if she had attacked, Roger would have been the one she caught!" It was an obvious reference to the native's roly-poly, five-foot two-inch body .

The encounter with the mature, female polar bear on Wager Bay off Roes Welcome Sound at the north end of Hudson Bay would be one not soon forgotten. Our party would go on to explore the remainder of Wager. We would encounter walrus, seals, caribou, and more white bears, but none would carry the thrill we felt when four steps from 2,000 pounds of living, breathing, female white bear.

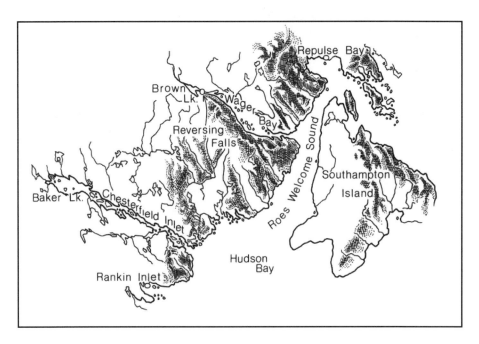

Latitude 66.45°
Longitude 90.85°

Wager Bay was named after the Right Honorable Charles Wager, who was first to discover the sixty-by-forty-mile fjord in 1742. At first, Charles Wager thought he'd discovered the Northwest Passage. But, after sailing halfway across the inlet, he discovered the heavy ebb and flow of the bay's sea-pulsating tide. At certain times, tide rise and fall on Wager measures twenty feet.

In 1747 William Moos and Francis Smith traveled the entire length of Wager Bay to Reversing Falls and Ford Lake. They confirmed Wager's earlier suspicions that no northwest passage to China would be found on this waterway.

Both the Moss and Wager parties had been commissioned in England to find a shorter route to China. The person able to find this shorter route would become rich beyond his wildest dreams. Britain, in the 1800s, was heavily into trading with the Chinese for spices and jewels.

Modern history tells of an American whaling station established at the mouth of Wager in 1900 by Thomas Luce & Sons out of Boston, Massachusetts. Within six years, weather (shortness of season), isolation, and remoteness forced the Luce family to abandon the station. Though thousands of whales were rendered, the venture lost money. Ships and crews were lost; cargo spoiled, and sickness took those who dared to stay more than one season.

The Royal Canadian Mounted Police established a post at Wager in 1910. It stayed active until the 1950s when a more modern post was established at Repulse Bay to the north and Rankin Inlet to the south.

In 1925 the famous Hudson Bay Company established a trading post on Ford Lake, just above Reversing Falls. It was called the Tascuyuk Post, named after the unique area on which it rested.

Reversing Falls is an oddity of nature that sees incoming tides force a rush of water west through the narrow, shallow, rocky shoal at Wager's western end. Twelve hours after the incoming rush, the ebbing tide causes water to race east across the same shallow rocky shoal. This coming and going of tide-forced waters creates deadly rapids with crushing waves that reach fifteen feet high. Passage through the narrows called Reversing Falls is best accomplished between tides. Many a careless native and trapper have perished when attempting to run the narrows during tide rush.

Not until the early twentieth century did a modern native population of humans exist in and about Wager Bay. Prior to that time, there had been a migrant population of native people who moved with the ebb and flow of the availability of food.

Prior to the establishment of the port at Reversing Falls in 1925, the area had been populated by the Aivilingmiut (people) from Repulse Bay and Roes Welcome Sound.

> *Note: In 1961, the remaining migrant people from Wager Bay moved into Repulse Bay permanently, never to live again under the old ways. The new ways of the "white eyes" prevailed, and a native culture that had existed for thousand of years vanished.*

Thus, the only permanent settlement on Wager existed between 1925 and 1961 . . . other than Thule Inuit natives who overran the primitive Dorsetman a thousand years before (late 800s and early 900s).

Thuleman are the ancestors of the present day Inuit people who currently exist along the ocean coastline of North America's Arctic Keewatin district.

> *History Note: Dorse men were a shy and timid people who survived the Arctic's seasons with a very limited number of stone tools. They were excellent hunters; so much so that, when necessary, they could toss a stone-bladed spear with their feet. Spears and stone knives were their only weapons, with the one exception of large stones, which they used to kill caribou under certain conditions.*
>
> *The Dorsetman culture existed for better than 3,000 years in the Wager Bay region of the Arctic. Not until the coming of Thuleman, who advanced across the Arctic from Alaska, starting 1,000 years ago, did Dorsetman cease to exist. By*

the year 1300, the final remaining Dorset people were swal-
lowed up by the advancing progress of the more aggressive
Thuleman.

Though sad, the highly spiritual culture of the Dorset
people could not withstand the intrusion of a more high-
ly developed crossbow-shooting tribe.

Final Note: Though believed to be the most primitive of
humans to inhabit northern North America, Dorsetman
was talented enough to make artificial teeth out of animal
teeth and jaws. These he placed in his mouth to help chew
food when his natural teeth rotted away or were lost.

Wager Bay is the only area in the Keewatin District of Northwest Territories where the people hunted seals while living in
snow houses and camping on the floating sea ice. They were
known to camp on the ice floes from as far south as the Paliak
Islands on Wager to the northeast shore of the Savage Islands.

Once the ice floes began to drift toward the open seas of Roes
Welcome Sound, they'd abandon their floating houses and gather
near the Tikiavjualaag Peninsula on Tinittuktag flats. Here the
largest gathering of these nomadic people took place each year
during the summer season.

To better understand the life and sense of the hardships of these
ancestors of the modern Eskimos (Inuit), it is necessary to examine a typical year's activities. Keep in mind they were a migrating
race, dependent on the availability of food.

Summer

Departing the gathering at Tinittuktag flats, the families would
spread out along the coastline of Wager. They now began to gather eggs and trap red char as it migrated up the small, ice-water
streams entering Wager.

To successfully trap the red fish, stone dams would be built
across the streams, stopping the fishes' downstream passage. Spears

made from driftwood and fishbone were used to impale and harvest the trapped fish. Some, using a trick from the past, would throw large, heavy stones down upon the barricaded fish, crushing their skulls.

Note: Char migration in early summer is to the sea from the inland lakes, not up the stream, but down.

The people also hunted the white whales that sought the nutrient-rich waters of Wager Bay. Both ringed and bearded seals were hunted to provide skins for their kayaks. Occasionally a walrus was harvested, but because these enormous sea creatures inhabited the entrance of Wager where the bay waters merged with Roes William Sound, few were taken. Venturing into such treacherous open water was too dangerous. Many who tried never came back.

Autumn

Fall was the time to hunt caribou. From this animal, the people gathered clothing material as well as meat. Much of the fall caribou hunting was done inland. Once the animals were harvested, they'd be placed in stone caches to be retrieved later when ice was thick enough to support the dog teams and sleighs sent to gather the cache meat.

Some ice fishing was done during the fall, when ice thickness permitted. The peoples' fish nets were made from caribou sinew during countless hours of tedious, hard labor.

Fall was also a time to make new, warm clothing, a necessity if the family was to survive the evil Arctic winter. Fall days in the Arctic are often sunny, warm and bug-free—an excellent time for the women of the family to gather outside their skin tents and sew.

Winter

Winter was a time for the people to move inland, away from the harshness of the bay's open shoreline. But, the move was never so far that a hunter from the family couldn't return to Wager to hunt seal in their breathing holes.

During winter, the people abandoned the skin tents in exchange for snow houses. Snow provided the best insulation for the sixty-degree-below-zero weather encountered in this region.

Many of the outer bay area families relied on the caribou caches left behind on the fall hunts. Some even planned the cache location with their winter homestead in mind.

However, there were several families that lived mainly on fresh seal during the harsh winter. These families always gathered near and around Reversing Falls. Because of this oddity in nature, the reversing tide flows kept water open year round at Reversing Falls. In this open water, hundreds of seals gathered each winter to feed on the abundant fish, which also gathered there during winter.

The seals provided a rich food supplement not found by those families who chose to live off the caribou caches inland. No family ever starved to death at Reversing Falls. The same cannot be said for those who chose to live off caribou.

After 1925, some families trapped during winter. Those who did trap and trade with the Hudson Bay Company covered the land as far south as Lorelland River and as far north as Douglas Harbor.

Note: Few families wintered inland after the Hudson Bay post was established in 1925. By 1932, no family was seen to winter inland off Wager Bay.

Spring

The yearly seal hunt began in earnest in the spring, with the newborn kits the main target. From the seal kits the people obtained a soft, fluffy, highly insulating skin that was used to keep their newly born children warm and comfortable.

Spring was also the time to collect newly lain eggs from the migratory and sea birds that nested inland. These egg-gathering jaunts were especially productive along the north shore of Ford Lake, above Reversing Falls and among the islands at the head of Wager Bay.

Note: Spring was also a very dangerous time for the people who gathered eggs laid by sea birds along the high rock cliffs of Wager. Dozens of polar bear would also descend on Wager to gather the delicately delicious morsels of spring. Encounters between the white bear and the people were numerous. In most cases, it was the people who lost the battle over eggs. Polar bears are astute climbers and have been seen to climb nearly vertical rock walls to harvests a single clutch of Puffin eggs.

Up until the publication of this book, no archeological survey had been done on Wager Bay. It remains a land of primitive beauty and Inuit law.

The John Tatty family has lived on or about Wager Bay for a long time. All Tatty descendants have open-water rights to hunt at all times. They are currently the only descendants of the original nomadic family who hunted Wager.

The Tattys also have all-winter rights to hunt the caribou that migrate in and about Wager. Once killed, by whomever, the cache of caribou meat becomes property of the Tatty family. The same is true of open-water fishing rights.

The one exception is when Wager Bay freezes over. During that time of year, all who pass are able to gather any style of food they may come upon.

The Tatty common law has existed since the abandonment of the Hudson Bay Traders post at Reversing Falls in the 1950s. It was John Tatty's grandfather, Dick Tatty (Wager Dick), who first established the post at Ford Lake (Taseuyuk) near Reversing Falls in 1925.

Upon arriving, Dick Tatty took to himself an Inuit woman, with whom he had a number of children. Dick Tatty was a tall, muscular, blond-haired Englishman. His descendants, two generations hence, are all dark-eyed, dark-skinned, and dark-haired.

Dick Tatty originally departed England via a sailing schooner in 1909 to establish a trading post at Chesterfield Inlet. Completing his mission in 1910, he stayed on to operate the post until his superiors in England requested he open another post at Wager.

Thus the story goes, and from the Tatty tale, that common law came to be on Wager Bay. The British government gave what they really didn't own.

Today the Tatty descendants own the animals that walk the land and sea of Wager Bay but do not own the land on which they roam. The land belongs to no one. It is the "people" who own the land, a law that has lasted 10,000 years through the coming and going of several tribes of people.

Roger Pilakapse

Tips and Bits
OF THE NORTHERN NATURAL WORLD

Though most Inuit hunters used fish bones as spear heads, the best spear head was made from a muskox horn. When split, the muskox horn produces barb-like appendages along its outer edges. Once a char is impaled, it seldom is able to shake loose.

Chapter 22

Boissevain

At the southern edge of the treeline, in the southwestern corner of Manitoba province, lies the small, friendly town of Boissevain. It is a community founded through a necessity to support the area's farming economy, 1,500 friendly, hard working, kind-hearted, happy people. It is a community and area in which I spend four weeks each fall relaxing, hunting, writing, and photographing the natural world.

In thirty-eight years of visiting Boissevain, this writer has come to know the surrounding area for its harvest of nature. Not only does the farmland, which rests in visual site of the town's TV tower, produce an abundance of human food products, but also there's an abundant natural bounty. Millions of waterfowl migrate within miles of the town each year.

Whitewater Lake, an eleven-mile-long body of marsh and water four miles west of town, is the resting magnet for much of the central waterfowl flyway. In 1996, one and one-half million geese and ducks sought refuge on Whitewater at the peak of the fall season.

To the south, six miles away, lie the game-filled Turtle Mountains. Thousands of whitetail deer, hundreds of giant moose, and a herd of magnificent elk walk this world of birch, willow, and aspen. Dozens of swampy lakes host tundra swans, muskrat, beaver, otter, and ducks. The land between the lakes teems with brush wolves, porcupine, ruffed grouse, wild turkey, and sharp-tailed grouse. Locals claim the Turtle Mountains are the prairie's Noah's Ark for wildlife.

Describing the world that surrounds and encompasses the quaint community of Boissevain may best be done by one of its own, a young writer by the name of Bonnie Champion.

The Treeline's Prairie

The entire existence of nature is a remarkable thing. Each part coexists with the other, completing the circle of life, each link depending on the other, like those in a chain. Sequestered in southern Manitoba, at the southern edge of treeline, is a vast part of Canada's prairies. The prairies contain a rugged beauty and wonder like none other. Life on the prairies is equally balanced.

The word "prairie" means "sea of grass." Many years ago, before the days of pioneers and settlement, that is what the prairies looked like. Flat lands covered with cascades of green grass as far as the eye could see. Gentle summer winds blowing over the thick carpet of grass, and flowers swaying and dancing to the silent song of the wind.

Long before gates and fences, street lights, and sidewalks, creatures like the prairie wolf (coyote) and fox roamed across the lands in search of food and peaceful existence.

Overhead, the hawk sailed ever so lightly and delicately in the prairie's blue sky. The only skyscrapers scattered along this land were the great oaks, cottonwoods, and willows which grew along the prairie river valleys . . . back in another time and another place where the only scents that filled the air were those of goldenrod, asters, wild indigo, and sprigs of clover.

Believe it or not, the prairies still hold some of the beauty they did once long ago. Those who have grown up in the captivity of cities or towns might not know of the beauty that still exists on the prairies today.

For those of us born and raised on a prairie farm, part of our "education" was learning about the past and the area in which we grew up, respecting the land, and learning about the various types of wildflowers and animals in the area.

Everything about the prairies is beautiful. The wide-open spaces between towns in the rural setting has a hidden beauty to those who know how to look. It comes in the way a prairie wind caresses tall grass in virgin fields or the way a river sings its song of life in the spring.

During the fall season, the prairie is filled with vibrant colors of red, yellow, brown, and orange. From the smoke gray color of its sky to the brown grass and brilliant colors of the tree leaves, beauty is everywhere.

There is a place from my childhood, a wonderful and peaceful place that, to me, is one of sincere beauty and rarity. Eight miles south of the little town of Melita is a piece of land called Nellie's. It is owned by my father and grandfather and is a section of land of true virginity. The Souris River, the valley, its animals and vegetation are all untouched by the hands of man. No matter what season— fall, winter, summer, spring—the beauty of it is like no other.

I remember late one fall, the air was cold and the sky a dark gray. Most of the colorful leaves had fallen, and frost was in the air. Straddled across a fallen oak, I watched the river eco system. Then I saw, standing alone and watchful, a buck. I could see his breath on the air and feel the heat of his eyes as he stood watching me. I made no sudden movement for fear of frightening him and denying myself the pleasure of his company. As I watched him, I thought I could see a sadness in his eyes. Winter would soon be here, and with it, almost certain death. Either from the weather, the lack of food, or via man, the struggle for survival would be hard.

He was old and very thin, his coat, a beautiful brown, showing balding spots. The cold grip of winter would surely take this beautiful creature. As I sat there watching him watching me, I remember how sad I felt for him. At some point I realized his death would be a part of life, and his death would be a means of survival for the coyotes that inhabit this prairie world. For one to survive, another must perish. That is the law of the wild—survival of the fittest.

I turned and fixed my gaze at a nearby tree. Here, a little squirrel was busy harvesting the remaining nuts that had fallen. He never noticed I was there, or if he did, he didn't care. He had work to do.

I turned back to look at the buck, but he was gone. The air had gotten cooler, and I realized that I, too, must go. As I stood to leave, I looked over once more. The buck was back and stood in the same place as before. I smiled briefly and raised a hand as if to say good-bye. He blinked once, twice, then slowly turned and walked away. That was the last I saw of him.

The winter months on the prairies are harsh. Cold winds blow fiercely, dropping wind chill. The air is so crisp that lungs feel as if they are on fire each time one inhales. Eyes water and burn. Snow covers the ground like a thick blanket of soft cotton. The land appears to no longer live, but not so. Deep in the prairie's wooded areas, there is life. Deer roam the bushes in search of food; white rabbits romp in the snow, leaving tracks for all to see. The fox, coyote, skunks, and badgers leave their burrows and scout the local farm yards in search of chickens, eggs, and the small rodents that inhabit cattle yards.

Wild birds, those capable of withstanding the crippling effects of winter, flitter in the treetops. Yes, the prairies are alive during the bitter winter months, months that seem to last forever. But, before long, the snow and the cruelty of winter are gone, and the effervescence of spring descends on the prairies.

Spring on the prairies brings the burst of new life. The air is filled with a pungent essence of budding flowers and trees, damp soil, and fresh grass. Life that slowly crept along its journey during winter, now leaps forth with great speed and determination, proving to the world that it didn't disappear.

Miniature leaf buds peek from naked branches; tiny bugs fill the air with their buzzing sounds and activities. Flowers burst into bloom, giving off sweet perfume. Spring's warm air and the bustling activity give clear indication that the prairies have awakened from their cumbersome sleep. Everywhere, fields of black earth are being worked by farmers, men and women alike.

Rivers and creeks burst forth with life. The sound of running water, pleasant and comforting is yet another indication of spring's resurgent life. Inhabitants come forth and make their presence known. Fish swim the rivers, lakes, and streams; turtles dig out of muddy beds; pond weed and plankton begin to grow. Beaver, otter, and mink are seen to frolic along creek beds. Birds are singing; the grass is green; and everything is back in its place.

Upon a willow branch, in the thicket near Boissevain's water reservoir, a lowly caterpillar drew its new body from a cocoon and became a beautiful butterfly with striking colors of orange, yellow, and black. The metamorphosis—something soft and fuzzy becoming a creature of enormous beauty—signals the coming of summer.

Spring departs just as quickly as it arrived, and the tree-line prairies are greeted by the heat and humidity of summer. It is amazing how different one area of the prairie can be from the next. Some places go without rain or any form of moisture for up to six weeks, while others can receive moisture every tenth day. It all depends on the geography of the area. A region such as Killarney, Manitoba, can receive rain three times a week because of the many lakes in the area, while an area such as Melita, Manitoba, is lucky if it receives rain three times a month. The only body of water in that area is the Souris River. Melita is only one and one-half hours west of Killarney on Highway 3.

In spite of what people think, prairies are not completely geographically the same. It is possible for prairies to have mountains. South of Boissevain on Highway 10 and south of Deloraine, Manitoba, are the Turtle Mountains. Further north in the Dauphin, Manitoba, region, the Duck Mountains are found (part of Riding Mountain National Park). Yes, it is possible for prairies to have mountains.

Summer has a beauty all its own. Golden wheat fields sway in hot summer breezes, dancing back and forth, a golden sea surrounded by gravel roads. Green hills on the horizon, crystal-clear blue skies above, and the scent of something sweet in the air. And at dusk, beautiful red sunsets deep within the horizon.

Summer nights bring inner peace, tranquillity, and that feeling that all is right with the world. Stars shine bright and clear. Cricket chirping fills the air, and the night owl's call can be heard throughout the farmland thickets.

Soon comes a time to harvest the golden fields of grain. Fall arrives with cold northwest winds and millions of waterfowl. Geese—snows, blue, white fronts, and Canadian honkers—descend on Boissevain's Whitewater Lake's resting areas. The town of Boissevain comes alive with hunters from the south.

The fourteen rooms of the Garden Motel are full of camo-clad hunters and their variety of dogs, some gold, others black, some blended in color. Fields surrounding the prairie town are filled with feeding geese and dozens of sets of artificial enticers.

The treeline prairies become a world of gold, white, grays, and blacks. Smoke billows high in columns as the aftermath of burning wheat stubble reaches skyward. It is a sky filled with the waving lines of migrating snow geese. The night sky over the small prairie town rings with the cries of geese passing south. Many will stay, held by the abundance of food and the natural obstruction of the Turtle Mountains. The prairies give off a duel harvest, one of grain, the other, waterfowl. The prairies become a land of plenty.

Soon the passage ends, and the winds of winter return. A yellow school bus travels the gravel roads once again, and the soft, rubbing sound of prairie grasses rustled by northern wind is all that remains.

* * *

The mention of southwestern Manitoba, for most of my readers, brings to mind waterfowling. The area around the small prairie community teems in ducks, geese, and sandhill cranes during spring and summer migrations.

Because of its being a leading waterfowl area, the town has its list of characters. One of these is Bert Barwick, local sports shop owner and goose guide. I've known Bert for thirty years.

Bert Barwick is one of those rough-and-tumble waterfowlers, rough in appearance and gruff of voice. He works a goose or duck call in an offbeat manner. The tune Bert plays to an incoming flock of mallards wouldn't win him any duck-calling contests, but it does entice ducks.

To best describe Bert, let me describe two hunts I witnessed in which the goose guide of Boissevain participated. Late one fall, while

I was driving a gravel road a couple miles south of Boissevain, I noted Bert's battered old blue pickup at the end of a quarter section. Seeing the truck meant Bert was guiding gunners somewhere nearby.

Three blocks past the pickup, in the ditch on the edge of the road that a friend, Dan Stewart, and I were driving, we spied a pair of popup blinds. They were no more than ten feet off the roadway. Pulling up alongside with the window down, I yelled for my friend to show himself.

Bert and the gunner he was guiding raised up, their heads emerging through slits cut in the popup blinds.

"What the hell are you doing, Bert? Guiding in a ditch?" I questioned while looking over his spread of decoys. It was the most unusual setup of decoys I'd ever seen. At its head, nearest the blind, was a lone drake pintail decoy. Behind it were six huge, jumbo honker decoys, mixed with a dozen windsock blue and snow decoys and several hard shell snow geese decoys. Behind these were twelve mallard decoys.

"Gapen, get the hell outta here! Can't you see we've got birds working?" Burt instructed with a smile. The only geese Dan and I could see were sitting in the middle of the section.

"My gawd, Bert; that's the oddest decoy set I've ever seen. You don't mix snows and honkers. And what the hell good is that lone drake pintail decoy?" I questioned my friend, ignoring his request that we leave.

"Gapen, that's my lucky duck. He's the one that makes the wary ones come in. You ought to know that by now," continued Bert as I began driving away.

Geese were coming north over the field a half section away. As much as I wanted to stay, I felt, for his guests' sake, I should move.

Well, you guessed it. Bert's three gunners nearly shot their limits of geese that day. Later, Bert told me if they'd been able to hit anything, they'd have killed their limits twice over.

As to the odd decoy set, my friend just laughed. He wouldn't commit to its validity one way or the other.

Bert Barwick is like that . . . a strange old character.

The second incident occurred the fall of 1997 on the day before Thanksgiving, November 27. I'd returned to Boissevain, after leaving

November 2, when the deadly winter storm drove me and all the remaining waterfowl south. I'd come back for peace and quiet in which to write. Arriving in town, I stopped at Bert's Sports Shop on Highway 10.

"Gapen, you bring your shotgun?" came the greeting from my friend. "Whitewater still has 5,000 mallards, mostly greenheads, and about 500 honkers. The Souris is holding birds, too," Bert continued.

I was dumbfounded. My friend had to be kidding. An hour later I would confirm the fact when Bill Ludgate, another hunting buddy from Boissevain, came by the motel and offered his gun and hunting clothes. Writing set aside, I'd spend the next two afternoons hunting the frozen surface of Whitewater.

Bert picked me up at 2:30 P.M. on the day before Thanksgiving. Shortly, the ancient old pickup bounced to a stop on a frozen field a couple hundred yards from the lake's north side. The lake was frozen solid with the exception of one patch of open water created by a 100-yard-long ice heave. The pressure ridge had split open an area about twenty-five by fifty yards. Ducks did the rest. They'd been keeping it open since freeze-up three weeks before.

"Look at the birds, Dan. Lots of 'em! There's a flock coming off, headed for the north shore," Bert commented as the old truck was shut down.

Sure enough, there they came, 300 yards to our west, about 150 green heads low to the ice, winging north. Reaching the frozen rushes, the mallards began to climb, and shortly they disappeared in the northern sky, headed for some distant pea field.

Fall harvesting of the pinto bean and pea fields in this area leaves enough leftover product to sustain a heavy waterfowl population well after the ice freezes. Beans and peas hold enough protein to allow ducks to live in below-zero habitat.

Behind that first flock came another, then another, and another. Bert and I hurried as best we could, but, by the time we'd walked far enough west to intercept the departing birds, the migration to food stopped.

Twenty minutes after we arrived, birds began to come in from the east, their target the open water a half mile off shore. Bert and I debated, then finally decided to try hunting them on the open ice. We'd left our white clothing back in town. We'd be very visible out in the open with the closest cover 400 yards away.

Reaching the open water, after carefully traversing the pressure ridge, the two of us spread out and lay flat on the ice. Maybe the incoming birds would take us for a couple of muskrat houses. The open water birds that hadn't departed did so as we neared their resting area.

Five minutes after settling on the ice, I heard Bert yell, "Mark!" and a moment later, two shots sounded and something thudded behind me.

"Sorry, Dan; didn't mean to hit you with that duck, but they surprised me by coming in from the north," said Bert, explaining the two shots.

The duck hadn't hit me, but after slamming into the ice, it had slid to within two feet of where I lay. A second duck had hit the ice twenty feet to the west of where my head lay. Looking around, I noted both ducks were bluebills. That seemed strange, seeing neither of us had noted any divers in the hordes of ducks that left the open water hole.

"Dan Stewart won't believe this, Bert," I commented as I became retriever for Bert. It was a subject both of us had discussed previously in the day. My buddy, Dan, is a dedicated waterfowler, and when he left on November 2, he had believed he and I were the last to shoot a duck in the Boissevain area. As a matter of fact, he was rather proud of that fact.

Five minutes after the two bluebills hit ice, a flock of seventy-five to 100 mallards headed our way, across the ice from the east. They bucked a west wind and had chosen a position ten to twenty feet above the ice.

Time seemed to stand still. Closer, ever closer, they beat their way toward us. Then, reaching gun range, the lead birds noted the pair of strange mounds on the water hole edge.

Three shots sounded as 150 wings beat hard to reach skyward. Two fat green head mallards folded, dropped, and smacked the ice surface hard. I'd missed my first bird, then cleanly killed a second with shot number two. Bert had fired once, collecting a single three and one-half pound green head.

In the southeast two more waves of mallards beat their way towards us. No time to retrieve birds. This time Bert collected a pair, and I failed miserably as my elbow slipped on the ice when I lifted to fire. Much to my surprise, one of the two Bert downed was a hen. I hadn't seen any hens in the birds we had viewed.

The next flock shied off before coming in to range, but a flock of twelve tried sneaking in from my south, and I managed to collect a pair.

The sun had settled below the western skyline when Bert and I decided to call it a day. We had collected ten mallards and two bluebills. The cold had taken its toll, and it would be nice to get back to a hot bath. Tomorrow, Thanksgiving Day in the States, would see us come back. We'd best let the ducks settle for the night. Someone had to keep the water open.

On Thanksgiving Day Bert and I returned in our whites. They worked better, and once again, we collected a dozen fat winter mallards. It was going to be a tale I'd relish telling my friend in Michigan. I took pictures. Without them, Dan Stewart would never believe Bert and I had shot ducks that late in the year in the land of southwestern Manitoba at the small prairie town of Boissevain.

To obtain more information on southwestern Manitoba's waterfowl gunning, turn to the information chapter at the end of the book.

181

Tips and Bits
of the Northern Natural World

The environment we leave behind is the only environment our children know. If what we leave is less than what we received, the outcome of the natural world, in the end, will be complete destruction. Is it now too late?

Chapter 23

The Goose Man

A fire-red October sunset blazed brightly across the western sky. Beneath its glow, miles of golden wheat stubble lit up, red and a little eerie. Etched in black, against the red wheat stubble, walked a man and dog, silhouetted as if painted on some Ducks Unlimited calendar. Both suffered from leg problems. Neither complained. Both were reaching a time in life when every hunt they shared might be their last.

One would have thought *this* hunt was their last. Enthusiasm seemed high for both of them. They walked slowly toward a favorite goose pass at the end of Whitewater Lake in southwestern Manitoba.

Reaching the gnarled, old, leafless tree, the two settled to watch the red sun sink below the horizon. Once situated there, the two rested. The man's hand softly and affectionately rubbed the dog's head. All was at peace in the world. Man and dog were as one, bent on the same goal—the evening flight of snow geese.

Then, as if scripted, a faint yelping of incoming snow geese signaled the nearness of geese. Far in the west, a waving line of waterfowl were buffeted by a heavy southeast wind. The line materialized slowly and increased in numbers and width. The waving line stretched from one edge of a wheat section to the other. The total bird numbers were in excess of a thousand.

Softly the man spoke to his companion, "Waldo, see the birds? Better get ready. Wally, we're about to be covered up in geese."

As if understanding, the old dog's tail began to wag, slapping the man's boots and the ground with an ever-constant rapping. Eyesight had begun to fail the old dog, but his hearing was as keen as it had been when he was a pup.

Waldo understood, having already picked out the faint yelping in the west. Neither man nor dog changed position as the birds approached. Even if they had, the gnarled tree's branches would have covered their movements.

Behind the weaving wave of geese came another, then another, and yet another. As far as the eye could see, waving lines of geese began to appear. The evening flight back to Whitewater was on. It would continue for an hour, returning tens of thousands of geese to their night rest.

Man and dog watched as the first wave passed over. At a point where the flock straddled the gnarled tree, the leader birds began to pitch and drop, some turning completely over on their backs to aid their need to descend rapidly. With newly gathered wheat seeds growing hot in their craws, the water below was badly needed.

Not until the fourth wave of geese passed over did the man raise his Remington 743 pump. Three times the gun sounded and with each report, a high-flying adult blue goose folded and plummeted to meet the soft marsh grass and mud at Whitewater's western edge.

Unlike so many other golden Labradors, this dog didn't run to retrieve the geese. Instead, Waldo moved at a trot to pick up the first goose downed, then walked slowly back to the man, dropping the prize at his feet.

"Good boy, Waldo. Now get the others," encouraged the man.

Slowly the old dog made the effort and finally all three geese lay beneath the gnarled old tree. During the retrieves, the man held off a temptation to shoot as line after line of geese passed overhead, each one lower than the last.

Then, as if asking the dog's permission, the man bent over and whispered, "You okay, buddy? Ready for another one?"

The tail wagged, and approval was given.

With that, the man took aim on the next wave and once again, two geese folded as three more reports sounded.

That's the way it had been since my faithful, old yellow Labrador, Waldo, met Ross George, a dear friend and waterfowl hunting companion from Boissevain, Manitoba. Immediately Ross took to Waldo . . . and Waldo to him.

The night shoot just described was typical of many I've spent with my friend. Many occurred at that same gnarled old tree or within close proximity to its shadow.

Ross George is a goose man, supreme among waterfowlers. He has no time in his schedule for duck hunting, and when it came to upland birds, they weren't worth the cost of the powder. No one knows openland goose gunning . . . or is better at it than Ross George.

Ross is the one who first showed me the trick of allowing the first flocks to pass over you when working a line of field-bound birds. It's a technique for engaging lower-flying birds. When the first waves of geese establish a pattern into a field of their choice, those that come after observe them descending into a field. This, in turn, causes the following geese to lower their travel path to the target field. Thus, by allowing the first flocks, three or four, to pass overhead, lower birds to shoot at are generally provided as the following flocks of birds pass over. In most cases, the first flock to pass over a gunner's position are always out of range anyway.

I was with Ross when I worked my first road ditch shoot. We were between two fields of feeding geese. A strong northwest wind was blowing, and singles, doubles, and small family groups were trading back and forth between the fields.

As generally is the case, the majority of the birds held near the center of their respective fields, thus preventing any chance of sneaking up on them. Ross suggested we take cover in the east side of road ditch, closest to the eastern section flock. He further suggested we split up, one of us picking a spot a third of the way down the ditch from where an east/west road crossed above the section in the north.

The other of us would select a spot one third of the way up from the east/west road in the south. Ross explained that the geese from the eastern pod would lift into the wind, then fall off and cross the road south of its central region. The western pod birds would lift into the wind, circle north of the flock, then fall off slightly to pass over the road north of the central region. (See diagram on the next page to better understand.)

But, first we must sit and watch what was happening. It took nearly twenty minutes for Ross to analyze the flight pattern. Satisfied, he suggested I take the top position (north), while he worked the lower (south) spot. Ross's reason for suggesting we find cover in the eastern edge of the north/south road ditch was that geese coming with the wind tend to drop down as they pass over a road, while birds flying into the wind tend to lift at a roadway. By placing ourselves on the east side of the road, we'd take advantage of these lower flight positionings.

At this point, I must mention three things are necessary if a successful road ditch shoot is to be obtained. First, there must be a fairly stiff wind blowing. Second, nearly equal amounts of geese must be stationed in nearby fields. Third, possibly the most important, the gunners must watch the scene for a good length of time to ensure that a flight pattern between the fields has been established.

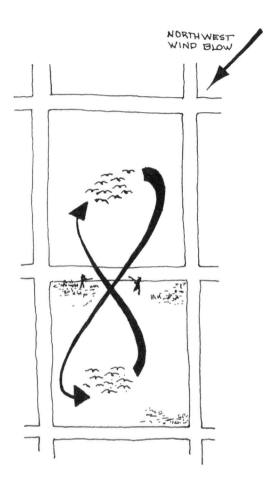

On that first shoot, Ross and I killed our limits. However, it didn't occur immediately. It took three hours of patient waiting. Ross never moved from the spot he selected, electing to allow the traveling birds to work back over him after each series of shots. Sometimes several dozen birds traveled to one side of him before the followers allowed their path to cross back over him.

Not having that kind of patience, I would sneak down the ditch after each firing, adjusting to the new path taken by the following birds.

Note: Birds tend to avoid passing over the very spot their predecessors had just traveled when shot.

One would think that, by adjusting, I might have completed my limit of birds ahead of my companion. Not so! As a matter of fact, I still had a couple of birds to go when Ross was done. I realize now that each time I adjusted, the birds that came over me were like new birds, and their distance off the ground had increased. Thus I was shooting at birds, much of the time, just out of range. If I'd waited in one spot, by the time the flocks had reset their flight path over me, they'd have been at a decent shooting range once again.

Patience is the key to ditch shooting! Not many gunners have enough patience to successfully gather limits while working the roads.

Then, there was the time the southwestern prairies saw no wind for ten days. All attempts at gathering a goose, let alone limits of geese, failed.

One night Ross suggested we wait out a flock of snow geese and catch them on their return to Whitewater Lake, a resting area miles to the south. The three of us—Ross, Dan Stewart (another hunting buddy), and I—would crawl into position along a fence line south of where the geese were feeding. The closest goose to our position was better than 250 yards away.

Once settled into our respective positions, we would wait for them to lift off and follow a natural return to water. It took over an hour, but once the birds did take flight, their path was directly over the three of us. Ross had positioned us directly between the main flock on the ground and the distant lake where they would head. Not disturbing the flock prior to firing was the key to success.

Several small groups of birds lifted off early and passed over one of us, but we'd agreed previously that we would not shoot until the main flock ascended over all three of us. Restraining from shooting was hard, but an agreement had been made.

Then, as shooting time was nearly at an end (one-half hour after sundown in Manitoba), the main group took to the air. It was a magnificent sight to behold. Five thousand geese lifted skyward, their yelping a deafening roar. They pushed over us, obscuring the evening light.

Guns resounded; geese began to fall, and as quickly as it began, the hunt ended. In all, the three of us downed thirteen birds. It was the largest batch of birds taken that week among the groups of waterfowl hunters in the small town of Boissevain.

Yes, Ross George was a master goose hunter. The key to his success was always patience and observation of the shooting situation beforehand. But, as with all masters of their trade, time takes its toll. It began with the uexpected death of my old, yellow Labrador, Waldo.

One morning in late August 1997, I was awakened by the incessant barking of my young black Labrador, Smudgy. Upon peering out the back door, I noted Smudgy was running over to Waldo, who appeared to be sleeping on the lawn.

Several times she nudged Waldo, then ran back to me and barked. Somehow I knew he was gone, even before I got to him. Waldo had passed on in his sleep, gone to the happy hunting grounds.

It took me three weeks to get up the courage to tell Ross. I knew the love my old hunting companion had for that yellow dog. It would shorten his life, of that I was sure. Without Waldo at his side, the goose hunting season would fail to glimmer for my friend Ross.

But finally I managed to tell my friend of our loss. His reply startled me. "Dan, I knew somehow that Wally and I wouldn't see another season together. It wasn't meant to be, and I don't think I'll see another day in a road ditch either. I'm pretty sick; got lung cancer," explained my friend.

The conversation shocked me. Even with lung cancer, my goose hunting mentor would surely be able to get out a few more times.

It was not to be. Ross George left the land of southwestern Manitoba at 4:55 P.M. on October 22, 1997, with his family and friends surrounding him. As much as we tried to get Ross out on one last hunt during the first three weeks of October 1997, his sickness had taken its toll. His strength and weight loss had left my dear, old goose hunting buddy unable to shoot just one more big, blue goose.

Yes, my friend has gone from this world of waterfowling, but his love and knowledge of goose hunting lives on. Each and every time I lift a shotgun skyward toward a flock of incoming snow geese, Ross George comes alive. It will be that way until I pass on to the world where Waldo and Ross now hunt the evasive white goose of the north.

A strange thing happened the day Ross George died. Dan Stewart, Ron Fancher, Pat Ludgate, and I were hunting a concentration of blues and snows that had left Whitewater, flying to the east. They then began a migration to the west. It was a migration that would see geese travel close to the ground along a given path across section after section of prairie farmland. They flew from noon 'til nearly 6:00 P.M., then mysteriously stopped and disappeared. Watching the migration, with a western sun gleaming off their white wings, made one think a flight of angels was weaving its way across the southwestern prairie land. I like to think it was a tribute to the greatest goose man I've ever known.

Today Ross George still lives among the birds he loved so dearly. His ashes rest beneath the gnarled, old tree at the western end of Whitewater Lake. I like to think my friend is there to greet the arriving snow geese each year as they pass through on their northern and southern migrations.

Chapter 24

The Land of Mosquito

The virgin white sand ran for miles across the multi-colored tundra, evidence that an ice-age riverbed had been deposited across this land 10,000 years ago. It began far to the south, snaking its way and zigzagging north to the point where it entered Mosquito Lake. Even then it refused to disappear as mile-long islands appeared and disappeared, always heading north.

At the northwestern corner of the gem-green lake, the ancient esker emerged once again to form a mile-long slit of sand and gravel that sliced its way north along the lake, dividing and isolating a second body of pale green water.

Along the sliver of ancient sand, a mass of horns slowly walked south, heading for the shelter of a treed land. Caribou by the hundreds were doing as they had always done, migrating along the ancient ice-age highway.

In the west, an orange-red sun rested just above the horizon, its colors painting wind clouds red, orange, and purple. To the east, open water glimmered silver-gray as the eastern sky darkened to the coming of night.

This scene greeted Steve Childres, "Bobber" Anne, and me as the Beaver aircraft, flown by Bob Huitikka, returned to base camp on Mosquito. The camp, pure white in color, appeared on the south shore of Outlet Bay where the lake's main river departed. Anyone flying over this land could hardly miss Tukto Lodge. It appeared as a beacon in the late day light.

The date was August 7, 1997. This wasn't my first trip into Mosquito Lake country. With my friend, Bob Vos, and a pilot named Vern Gutman, I'd stopped at Mosquito's north end to collect fuel from a deserted gas dump left by some long-departed mineral explorers. That was in July 1978. One other time I dropped in on Mosquito at Tuktu Lodge after it had been deserted and ravaged by tundra bears. I traveled with a rather odd Arctic outfitter named Tom Fauses. The second stop came ten years after my first stop. On both occasions caribou had been much in evidence along the shoreline of the main lake. This time was no different.

Slowly the Beaver settled toward bay water. Below, the camp island loomed larger, its fauna becoming isolated in detail. Then, as if erupted from earth, three giant caribou bulls raced directly before the descending aircraft. Had I not known the skill of our pilot and held complete confidence in his ability to maneuver the plane, I might have feared an imminent collision.

Rather than dart to one side or the other, the three magnificent animals raced directly ahead of us, racks resting back along their shoulders. A moment later, we past directly over the bulls, clearing their racks by fifty feet. At that moment they crossed a tan-colored beach and crashed into Outlet Bay waters. I'll not soon forget the wild-eyed look those three bulls had as we passed over them. In their primitive minds I'm sure our aircraft had become a giant eagle or primitive bird of prey after one of them for dinner.

Latitude 62.6°

Longitude 106.4°

Once you reach this area of the Arctic barrens you are cut off from the normal manner of travel and all the perks that come with a close proximity to the civilized world. You have entered a wilderness world where nature rules. You travel at the mercy of weather and often are forced to survive on your knowledge of the land and its resources.

Our party of four had just spent two days exploring the world north of base camp. The objective of our journey was a large caribou herd that summers near Outlet Bay on Dubawnt Lake's north end. Dubawnt is also known for its massive schools of trophy lake trout.

Day one of our flyout began with a touch down twenty-five miles northeast of camp on a small unnamed lake for a "look see" at a herd of thirteen muskox. They were spotted by Steve and Bob as the small herd crossed an esker ridge just south east of the lake on which we'd elected to land. Since our intent was to film a documentary on the Arctic barrens and its wildlife, these muskox would make excellent subject matter.

Once down, the four of us began a stalk across a bug-infested plateau, moving from one large rock to another. By the time our party reached the suspected spot where the muskox were last seen, they'd moved farther west and were grazing down along a small white-water river. Much to our surprise, there were not one, but three large bulls in the herd, one of them immense. The balance of the herd was made up of six cows and four calves.

Normally there would be only one large bull, several cows, a couple of yearling and calves to match the number of cows. It was obvious the herd's makeup was a result of heavy wolf predication. Probably the killing off of this herds' yearlings had occurred during the winter. The two missing calves probably were picked off by wolves the previous spring, soon after birth. Getting close to this group would be difficult, as wary as they must be after as many wolf attacks as they must have endured.

Selecting a path to carry us down to the river's edge, we managed to crawl within 200 yards of the closest animal. Bob led the way with Steve and his camera next. The closest animal was a cow without a calf. It was obvious she was wary. She may not have been able to see us (muskox have poor eyesight), but her senses were in tune. Her head slowly turned our way. Her hooves stomped twice, and she sounded a soft snort. That was all it took to alert the balance of the herd. All heads turned our way.

We froze! Time stood still.

It took twenty minutes for the animals to relax and begin feeding again. Then, slowly, we began our stalk, this time on all fours. If you have never crawled across the bug-infested tundra, there is an experience in pure misery awaiting you. It's not the mosquitoes that create the agony. It's those black flies and sand flies that wreak havoc. They find any and all openings in your clothing and crawl, biting their way along all parts of your body. They get in your eyes, nose, and ears, causing the immediate urge to slap, hit, and spit . . . none of which were allowed while attempting to sneak up on some very wary muskox!

Note: Even though most people believe that the Arctic tundra abounds in hordes of blood-thirsty insects, it isn't so. Surprisingly, the number of bugs will vary greatly with each season, and from year to year. A good rule of thumb is to expect a heavy bug population ever three or four years. Often there are summers when most bugs fail to hatch in some areas. Much depends upon the moisture available to the breeding population. If the winter and spring are dry, the chances of a large hatch are virtually eliminated. Even so, it is also good rule to go prepared. Always carry a good supply of mosquito repellent that contains 100% Deet. A headnet is also advisable for every member of the party.

It took better than an hour to get within decent photographing range of the muskox herd. I'm not sure what spooked them at the end—maybe the clicking of my 35mm camera or Steve's changing video tapes was all it took. At eighty feet, it could have been anything.

Alerted, the big bull charged us, stopping a mere twenty-five feet away. Had I been a wolf, I would have cut and run, but knowing that a dominant herd bull's charge is mainly bluff, I managed to coax our group into holding. Bob and I both had previous experience with these long-haired throwbacks to the ice age. That helped as the enormous bull pawed the ground and snorted a number of times before turning and taking off at a full gallop. In turning, he startled the rest of the herd, which beat a fast track up over the far hill.

You would think that would have been enough for the four of us. Not so! Wanting one last shot, Steve suggested that Bob and Anne try to get around on the other side of the hill and push the muskox back past us. It wasn't going to be easily done. In other words, "easier said than done."

Anne thought we were crazy, but she reluctantly agreed to being a member of the roundup party. It took Bob and her fifteen minutes to work their way around the nervous herd. Once there, the two of them took off their coats and, in cowboy fashion, began to run directly at the herd, driving them toward Steve and me. We'd figured, once spooked, the herd would trot along the highest section of the ancient esker. Thus, Steve and I had tripoded our cameras directly in the path we'd surmised the muskox would travel.

Boy, were we right! So right that the charging animals, now racing at full speed, ran directly at us. You can only imagine what its like to attempt to stand your ground when caught between thirteen badly frightened muskox and the spot to which they were determined to escape!

The charge came directly at us. The noise of the animals—beating hooves and bodies thudding against one another as they raced through the short tundra brush—descended down on the two of us. Add to this the grunting of these animals, and it was unnerving, to say the least. One hundred feet away, the herd stopped in a cloud of dust and bugs. They milled around a bit, not knowing which way to go. Obviously the two humans in front of them weren't going to move.

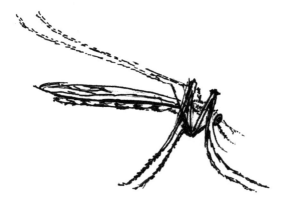

"What do you think, Dan? Do we get the hell outta here?" questioned my partner.

Before I could answer, we saw Bob and Anne begin to top the hill behind the hesitant beasts. That's all it took. On they came, directly at us. I'm not sure about Steve, but for me, it was one of the scariest moments of my life.

Twenty feet from our position behind a short stand of Arctic willow, the herd broke in two and raced by on either side of us. For the life of me, I couldn't say how many went left and how many went right. I really didn't care. The important thing was that they all passed around us without trampling over us. Imagine a herd of frightened prehistoric beasts, armed with razor-sharp horns, racing by you at a distance of less than twenty feet. I'm betting it would make your stomach turn a bit, too.

We watched the herd pass over the next hill on the esker. Only then did either of us suck in a breath of fresh air.

"Gawd, fellows. Bob and I thought they'd run right over you," came Anne's voice from behind us.

Neither Steve nor I had noticed the arrival of our companions. We were all smiles. The danger was passed, and we both had taken some terrific photos. All is well that ends well.

Then Bob suddenly yelled, "They're coming back, guys!"

There, where the herd had vanished, came that single massive bull, trotting directly at us. A hundred yards away, he stopped, shook his massive head from side to side a number of times, grunted a couple of loud snorts, and stared at us. It was a tense moment, but in the end, the angry bull turned and slowly walked back toward the path the herd had taken. All of us breathed a sigh of relief. This time, I'm sure, we would have run!

*Note: Muskox could be called the animal of the "big bluff."
The Inuits, who know them best, say that when a bull
muskox charges, the one being charged needs only to position himself higher than the charging beast to bluff it into
submission. Keith Sharpe, a good friend from Rankin
Inlet, tells the tale of a time when a rather large muskox
bull charged him only to stop three feet away.*

*As the animal began its charge, Keith raced uphill and
positioned himself on the largest rock available. The rock
was but three feet high, but, as it turned out, it was big
enough. As the bull raced uphill toward him, Keith began
to bellow as loudly as he could. As he explained it, if the
muskox could snort, so could he. He could outdo it by bel-
lowing at the top of his lungs. It worked! The bull came
to a skidding stop an arm length away, snorted twice,
then turned and trotted on downhill. Keith claims the
animal was so close that he could smell its foul breath
and hear the air rattle through its lungs as it snorted. If*

you knew Keith, you, too, would believe his tale, for he looks a lot like a muskox bull himself. When comparing beards, I'm not sure which of the two has the better one.

Back in the aircraft, we headed north. Our destination this time was a spot on the Dubawnt River . . . a spot I had visited thirty-two years before. That time, Bill Scifres of *Outdoor Life* magazine, and I had caught and released some huge river lake trout. I wondered if they still swam beneath the wild rapids of Dubawnt.

We arrived at Dubawnt by noon. There would be time to fish a little before once again heading north to our final objective, the north end of Dubawnt Lake.

It took twenty minutes of weaving down and over the river's channel before I spied the divide in the river that matched my memories of the past. The water was lower, but two heavy main channel rapids were still there. We'd land between them, as before. Such action required that our floats touch the breakaway waters of the downstream rapids and come to rest 200 yards upstream, below the upstream rapids. Only a skilled pilot could or would attempt such a landing. Bob was our man.

Once we were down, the rubber, inflatable raft was blown up, rigged with a six-horse motor, and we took off to explore the incoming rapids. Before departing the plane's tie-off spot, I had checked out the old campsite. Sure enough, the lower half of the old tent frame remained as well as a set of rusting bed springs on which Bill, Doc Herb, and I'd slept. Thirty-two years before, this spot had been the farthest outpost camp available in the Arctic north. So deep into the hinterland was it that an extra flight of gas had to be positioned ahead before we came in. At that time, our departure point was the small Indian community of Stony Rapids on Saskatchewan's northernmost border, 390 miles to the south. Today, from Mosquito, we'd traveled a mere 100 miles.

Out on the river, we immediately headed upstream to the descending rapids. With any luck, lake trout would be waiting . . . and waiting they were. The four of us cast toward the deep pool beneath the rapids, and instantly all four of us engaged fish. Three were landed, one lost. For the next fifteen minutes we engaged a lake trout on nearly every cast. None of them was of the size I'd expected. The largest tipped scale just over fourteen pounds. Where were the trophy lakers?

Finally, by analyzing the time of year I had come here before (late June) and that we'd now come in mid August, I suggested we try trolling down to the lip structure just above the lower rapids. Lake trout in rivers stage where they can get to food the easiest. At this time of year, grayling and whitefish would be migrating upstream. Whitefish would be traveling up to the lake above in preparation to spawn. Grayling would be heading upstream to enter the same lake water to winter. Both species are extremely vulnerable to attack as they break out on the top side of rapids.

Not till we entered the pull of the rapids' upper lip did a large fish strike. She struck a huge Dardevle spoon, one of my favorites—a shad finish, scaled in black/gray and white. Bob, who was running the outboard, barely had time to beach the raft before being swept down over the rapids.

It was from shore I landed the twenty-six pounder. The battle lasted ten minutes during which the stubborn fish was nearly swept over the lip three times. The only thing that prevented such a tragedy was to give the fish slack line so it could swim back upstream on its own. Instinct governs such a reaction from large fish when feeding above rapids drops.

After pictures, the fish was released, and we began another run along the shoreline above the rapid lip. In all, we landed six fish over the twenty-pound mark, the largest a few ounces under thirty pounds. It was all the proof I needed that monster river lake trout still roamed the waters of the Dubawnt River system.

With time slipping away, our party reluctantly called a halt to the river fishing and headed back to the waiting float plane. It was nearly 3:00 in the afternoon. The big lake still waited.

Once in the air, Bob noted that it looked like the lower end of Dubawnt Lake was covered in a mass of low clouds. We might have trouble getting up to the lake's north end.

Approaching the south end of Dubawnt is like heading out over the Gulf of Mexico. Because of the flat land and enormous width of the lake's south end, the viewers get the feeling the world before them has suddenly turned to water. Ahead, about fifteen miles off shore, was a group of islands beyond which the huge cloud bank descended to the water surface. We'd not be able to fly beyond that point.

"Gang, this looks like those islands are as far as we're going to be able to fly for the time being," commented Bob, after looking over the skyline ahead of us.

That was fine with his guests. None of us were in the mood to attempt to travel into the thick blanket of fog and clouds.

It is said that Dubawnt makes its own weather. As large an area as it covers, I can believe it. With its size being a major contributor to weather creation and the fact that it sits on the edge of the Arctic's weather break ridge, Dubawnt is subjected to a constant flux of fronts. Whenever I've visited this body of water, I've been greeted with unstable weather fronts, most of them bad. This may be the reason no tourist operation started on Dubawnt has ever succeeded. With a mere four-week season and unpredictable weather, no tourist operator can make money. Transportation costs are enormous. Those who tried, most in the 1980s, failed and went bankrupt.

Selecting a small southern bay in the largest of the islands ahead, Bob throttled the aircraft back and landed. We'd sit the front out. Surely it would retreat up the lake soon. With a northwest wind blowing, the plane was taxied as far up into the bay as possible. Below, the water appeared crystal clear, just as I remembered it to be. If ever there was lake trout water, this was it.

Slowly we began to drift back out into the bay. Below, huge rocks, the size of cars, appeared as we passed. Beside one of them I spied a trout. Suddenly a thought came to mind. As long as we were here, why not fish? Climbing down onto the plane's right side float, I retrieved my fishing rod from the storage compartment.

"Any of you want to try catching your first Lake Dubawnt laker?" I queried my traveling companions. The three of them looked at me in disbelief and shook their heads. It was obvious they thought I was crazy.

Retrieving a two-ounce white Ugly Bug jig from my tackle pack, I tied it directly to the twenty-pound mono on my seven-foot casting rod and reel. I was ready. To hell with those poor sports. They could stay in the plane's cab and talk about how a great big, thick steak tasted or wonder what was happening back home. I was going to fish.

By the time I dropped my jig, the plane had floated into twenty feet of water. It appeared to be only five- or six-feet deep, but as the line departed, I soon learned that wasn't the case. No sooner did the white jig reach the bottom than a shadow darted down after it. The fish didn't look big. Quickly I raised the lure, gave it a couple of twitches, and was pleasantly surprised to see the fish seize it. Once the hook was set, that small fish seemed to gain weight and sustain a rather decent fight.

"Got one, gang. Seems fair, but I'm not sure. The water's deeper than it appears . . . and . . . there's another one trying to take the jig out of my fish's mouth!" I yelled as a second trout came into view.

"Sure, Dan; show me. I'm from Missouri," came Steve's sarcastic response to my report.

Finally I managed to get the fish to the surface. Now the trick was to land the thrashing trout while balancing on the plane's float.

"Anne, I need help . . . please? Bring the landing net. I think it's behind the back seat," I pleaded.

By this time my fishing partner had become interested in what was going on outside the plane. It didn't take her long to grab the net, hop down onto the float, and net the twelve pounder. Yes, the fish was much larger than I thought at first. Clear water can confuse the viewer, making large fish small or small fish large, depending on how deep it is.

"Dan, is there another rod and reel handy? Think I'll give it a try, if you don't mind," commented Anne as she released the fish. The fact that two more trout followed mine up to the net may have been a contributing factor to my partner's sudden urge to fish. One of those appeared to be in the twenty-pound range.

Now there were two of us working off the right side float. It wouldn't take too much prancing around to see one of us slip and descend into the icy cold water of the lake. Later I would slip a couple of times, only to be grabbed by my partner's hand helping me maintain my balance.

In the next ten minutes, Anne and I caught a fish on nearly every drop with jigs. She used yellow, and I continued with white. Both worked equally well. Anne succeeded in catching that twenty pounder which turned out to weigh nineteen and one-half pounds. It was on the netting of that fish that our lazy partners decided they'd give the Dubawnt trout a try. The left hand float would be their boat.

Steve begged an orange, two-ounce Ugly Bug off me and went to work. Bob held off and used his favorite spoon, a yellow Five of Diamonds. It would prove to be a mistake. There was no need to cast. All one needed to do was drop directly below the plane, jig your Ugly Bug jig a couple of times, and a half dozen trout would descend on it from all sides. Continuously those fish not hooked would attempt to snatch the jig out of the mouth of the one hooked, as it was reeled in.

Because of wind drift, Bob had to start the engine up and taxi us in toward shore several times. Soon he gave up his spoon and switched to a jig.

We were having so much fun that none of us noticed the cloud bank as it descended down over us. Before we knew it, the plane was surrounded in white mist. At 100 feet the island became barely visible. Dubawnt had done its thing. There we sat, trapped in a world of white. Because we couldn't see the small outer islands or the reefs around us, we'd become stranded without the ability to depart.

Dubawnt is a relentless foe. She doesn't give in to those who make mistakes. She had seduced us with her trout and now enveloped us with her unforgiving weather. We were here until she allowed us to depart.

Taxiing up to shore, Bob instructed us to jump off and rope the plane by the floats' rear tieoffs to the largest rock we could find. Fishing would have to wait. Right now Mother Nature and Dubawnt had taken control.

Softly the fog and clouds became dark, and within an hour, we could hardly see from one end of the plane to the other. What was worse, it was a wet whiteness that surrounded us, so wet, that those of us who had chosen to stand outside the plane donned our rainsuits for protection against the wetness and the bitter cold that came with it. Daylight temperature had descended thirty degrees in a matter of an hour and a half. It had dropped from seventy-five degrees in the sun to nearly forty degrees under the white shroud. It appeared we were in for an overnight stay.

Luckily, Bob kept a cook kit and a small tent in the plane's back end . . . just for such occurrences. Along with these necessities were a couple of heavy Hudson Bay blankets. In the end, we would end up sharing them . . . with Anne, Steve, and me sleeping in the tent and Bob in the plane.

Supper was easily had. It took only a couple of casts off the rocky point to produce a pair of small, five-pound lake trout. The cook kit contained salt, pepper, lard, and flour, as well as a couple of cans of beans. Fried fish and beans made up our late evening meal. To say it was delicious would be an under statement. The golden fillets of trout were the best I'd ever eaten. They were so good that, right in the middle of the meal, Bob went down to the water and caught another trout to be added to dinner. No one objected.

Morning dawned with the same white shroud surrounding us. If we had to stay one more day, the boys back at base camp might send out the message that we were lost and missing. That wouldn't be good. They only give you two day's leeway in the Arctic before calling search and rescue. The plane's radio didn't pick up base camp until we were in the air, thus there hadn't been any way to tell base camp our problem.

Shortly before noon, the fog began to lift, and within an hour, patches of blue sky could be seen to our southwest. It was time to leave, but not before giving the float fishing technique one more try.

Wind direction had changed to the southwest, allowing us to drift along the island's eastern shore at about the twenty- to twentyf-five-foot depth. At times, all four of us had fish on at the same time. It was a similar situation to the day before. No one took a lake trout under ten pounds, and Steve managed to land the lunker of the float fishing experience, a twenty-nine and one-half pounder. At first we thought Steve's fish to be thirty-five to forty pounds, but once landed, we found it be rather thin and without the broadness that normally makes up this size trophy. It had length, but was lacking the weight for its size.

A decision was made to skip the north bay herd of caribou. About halfway up the lake that ominous fog bank still held. None of us were of a mind to challenge Dubawnt again. If she was kind enough to give us the opportunity to depart, we'd take it.

Back at camp that night we were greeted with smiles and voices of concern. Some camp guests had us piled into the desolate tundra in some god-forsaken place. Others thought we had had engine problems and were stranded on some unnamed lake.

Only Bob Vos, my old fishing partner who was spending his summer at the Mosquito Lake camp, had theorized that we'd run into bad weather on Dubawnt and had to sit it out. Bob and I had been on Dubawnt before. He knew the threat that mean old lake could produce. It was an adventure all of us in that float-rigged Beaver aircraft will long remember.

Note: To learn more about Mosquito Lake and the land around Dubawnt Lake, turn to the last chapter in this book.

Tips and Bits
OF THE NORTHERN NATURAL WORLD

It is always the largest male animals in the muskox and caribou species that die first during a severe winter. Reason: Fat and strength lost during the previous fall's mating season make these largest and most dominant animals susceptible to death through starvation and freezing.

Chapter 25

Demons of Dubawnt

Latitude: 63.20°
Longitude: 102.15°

As long as the Inuit people of the island barrens could remember, immense Dubawnt Lake contained enormous fishlike demons known to devour anyone brave enough to venture out into the lake's central region. There were many who claimed to have seen such beasts. They claimed the beasts would breach lake surface only during the short time between summer sundown and the sun's reappearance two hours later. At that time of day the northern sky blazed bright orange, and yellow spears of light shafted skyward from within Mother Earth.

Never were the demons sighted after sunup or during the bright, daylight hours. Appearances were always brief and only came to shoreline-hugging kayakers who were alone and without witnesses. The demons had existed for as many winters as the oldest of the elders had lived. Some claimed the demons had lived beneath Dubawnt since before the coming of the people to this land.

To confirm their fear of these lake monsters, the oldest of the people told the tale of Sitiyok August (hard male), the bravest of all Inuit. No one knew exactly when the events in the tale of Sitiyok August occurred, but that they happened they were certain.

The Tale

Long before grandfather's time, Sitiyok August, mighty killer of muskox, lived among the people. He was the mightiest hunter ever to be. His father, Tolotaeksak Tuktu (Killer of Caribou), had also been a great hunter and provider of caribou and muskox for the people. But, it was Sitiyok August, who had killed the enraged muskox bull with only a stone knife, who the people considered the mightiest of all hunters. He killed the enraged bull by leaping on its hairy back and, with two swipes of a stone knife, blinding the beast. Then by entwining his legs in the beast's three-foot mane, Sitiyok August repeatedly stabbed the thrashing animal until it tumbled to the ground and died. Sitiyok August, from that moment on, became a legend and the mightiest of all Inuit hunters.

Bestowed with such a reputation, it was only natural that Sitiyok August be the one chosen to rid Dubawnt Lake of its demons. With that decision made, it took a year of careful preparation to ready for the great hunt.

A giant kayak must be constructed. Special bone spears, their heads chipped from ivory-white quartz, had to be manufactured. There would be eighteen in all, three each for each hunter in the party. Sitiyok August would choose five others besides himself. Only the bravest of the hunters would go.

Construction of the thirty-foot kayak took most of the winter. Only the skins of adult male muskox would be used. It would take ten animals. They had to be killed and processed during the late fall season when the hair was new and the skin thickest. Male muskox skins were used because they are the thickest and toughest of all animal skins.

Special bone and stone knives were made for each hunter. Their length exceeded the arm length of each hunter. These special long weapons might be needed for close-in fighting in case the quartz spears failed to do their job. Along with the weapons, special clothing was made—waterproof clothing that would withstand the icy waters the hunters would encounter in the central region of Dubawnt.

By the end of June all was ready. Reports said that the demons had been seen miles off shore near the island where the giant river entered. Other reports claimed that the biggest demon of them all had been spotted mid-lake east of the great esker that graced Dubawnt's western shore.

Sitiyok August's hunting party would depart from the people's camp where the great river entered Dubawnt, then proceed to the lake's central region, traveling north by northeast.

On the last day in June, at high sun, the six hunters left. All the people went down to see them off. Everyone smiled and nodded their good will. Ridding Dubawnt of its demons would open a vast hunting and fishing ground for the people.

As the kayak passed beyond the last island, heading for open water, the people called one last farewell. They would now wait, confidant that Sitiyok August and his chosen crew would return within a moon change.

Two weeks passed. Word came that a scout, headed south along the great western esker, had seen the mighty hunters in full pursuit of what he thought was a demon. Standing atop the high esker (450 feet above Dubawnt), the scout, Pissuinnarpok Okalerk (Walking Hare), had seen the giant kayak racing east into the midsection of the giant lake in hot pursuit of a demon-like fish that surfaced every so often to blow air. It had appeared to the scout that the demon was fleeing for its life. The people were overjoyed by the report. Soon the mighty Sitiyok August would return with good news.

Time passed! The full moon came and went. Winds turned north and carried the chill of things to come. Still no word. Soon a second moon came close to earth, its fullest rays now bright with the scent of winter. Where were the mighty hunters? Surely, by now, they had ridden Dubawnt of its demons. Why hadn't they returned?

Caribou had begun to gather in huge herds when some of the elders began to fear for the hunters. The people must not be told of their thoughts. Instead, caribou must be gathered for the long winter to come. To hint that hope for the hunters was waning, might see the people become discouraged, and discouraged people didn't hunt well. Spirits must be kept high. The elders planted rumors that Sitiyok August and his men had been sighted coming south along the western shore where the great esker rises to the west.

Planting rumors was against the elders' mind set, but food must be gathered, or the people would starve during the long winter to come.

The hunt went well. Ten caribou for each adult and four caribou for each child were gathered. No one would starve this coming winter. To make things even better, the Inuit hunters of the people had harvested fifteen caribou for each of the demon killers. Upon their return, the hunters would be hungry and need even more nourishment than usual.

Time passed. Cranberries ripened, their leaves turning vivid red. Arctic willows faded from green to yellow. Then, without warning, the first snow of winter descended. With it came the harsh, cold, northern wind. Where could the demon killers be? Why had they not returned? Hadn't they been seen coming south near the great esker? Had they seen another demon and pursued it north? If so, why hadn't any of the people's scouts seen them?

It was in mid-November, three full moons after the demon hunters' departure, that the elders called the people to council. A decision must be made. It was long past the time to depart for their wintering grounds far to the south. To wait longer could find the people trapped on the shores of the great lake. Ice had long covered the lake's southeastern bays. Soon snow and deadly north winds would prevent a migration south to the treeline. The caribou had already entered the treeline and would stay there until spring breakup.

It took four days of council to convince all that migration must begin. On the morning of the fifth day (November 10), the entire band of men, women, and children departed. Spirits were low. The demon hunters had not returned. Were they dead? Eaten by a demon? Could they survive the winter? Even hunters of their greatness would be hard pressed to survive under the horrid, harsh conditions of an Arctic winter on the open barrenlands.

Winter passed. The people returned to the shores of Dubawnt Lake. Still no sign of the hunting party. Sitiyok Augut and his mighty hunters had disappeared somewhere out on the great lake where the curve of Mother Earth connects the water of Dubawnt with the sky above.

Summer's hot days came and went. Those who carried hope that the demon hunters would return, resigned themselves to the fact that they would not. What had happened to the mighty hunters could only be speculated. Some felt they had done their job, but, in so doing, had exhausted themselves and were caught by the winter storms and ice. Others believed that a demon, so big that a giant kayak could be swallowed whole, had sealed their fate. Others, mostly older in their years, believed a great battle had ensued when the first demon was met. But, as history had always proven, even the mightiest hunter of the Inuit was no match for the demons of Dubawnt. The mightiest of all Inuit hunters, Sitiyok Augut, had failed. Never again would any Inuit hunter venture out into the open water of Dubawnt Lake.

Thus the tale of Dubawnt's Demons has persisted through generations of Inuit people. In 1932, caribou by the hundreds attempted to migrate across the open water of Dubawnt. Early ice complicated their swim. Many were trampled and drowned. Hundreds of carcasses washed up o the lake's northeastern shoreline as spring thaws came. By midsummer, only the bleached, white bones remained. In some areas, the piles of white bones reached ten feet in height.

Kadzait (Wandering Wolf) and his family of seven were on their southward migration when they first spied the bleached bones. From a mile away, the bones seemed to stretch for miles along the lake's shore. Some could even be seen far out on the lake where rock reefs touched water surface.

It was obvious a great killing had occurred. The people had not done this! If not the people's hunters, then who? What deadly being could wreak such havoc?

The answer was obvious. It had to be the Demons of Dubawnt. No others could kill so many *tuktu*, the animal of the people. It must be that the demons were still angry at the people for having sent Sitiyok August. It was the only explanation. Why else would the demons kill so many of the animals from which the people attained life? Was this the beginning of the end for the caribou of the people? Would the demons continue to kill the caribou as each season passed?

Then, as if to confirm his belief, Kadzait spied a number of baby demons, rising to surface, blowing water high into the air, then sinking below the surface. The demons were many now. He must tell the people.

Hurriedly, Kadzait and his family headed south to tell their tale of horror. They would return this way no more. The demons had become many, and any attempt to fish the waters of the great lake would be an open invitation to death.

Today the legend and myth of the Demons of Dubawnt continue to persist among the native tribes of the Far North. Even though the original Inuit people have disappeared from the land, those who live along the coastal regions of the tundra never venture inland to test the tale.

Note: It is a known fact that some seal and sea otter species have been spotted far up the river system that connects Dubawnt to Hudson Bay. In 1968, a group of four fishermen spied a number of giant otter playing in the northeastern reefs of Dubawnt, near the caribou killing area of 1932. All four anglers, skilled in the ways of Arctic adventure, were startled at the animals' size. In the fog-shrouded waters of the lake's northern region, it was easy to see how such animals might be mistaken for children of some sort of demon.

Tips and Bits
OF THE NORTHERN NATURAL WORLD

Polar bear cubs must stay with their mothers until they are at least two and one-half years old. Reason: They do so to learn the art of seal stalking and the gathering of other food, plus the need for protection from male bears.

Older large males are often susceptible to death in the winter by starvation due to fat and strength loss sustained during the previous fall's mating season.

An 800-pound female polar bear, with cub at her side, will generally drive off the amorous attentions of a 2,000-pound male partly due to her aggressiveness and the males' weakened condition during the mating season. Males do not take on nourishment from the beginning of the fall season until numerous encounters and matings with female bears has occurred.

Chapter 26

Kasba's Secret

"You've been holding out on me, Tim," I chided as a two-pound grayling broke surface a second time.

"In all the years I've been coming here for trophy trout, no one, not even Doug, has mentioned that grayling were available in the main lake!"

Early that morning Tim O'Shaughnessey, our guide, requested that Laurie and I take along fly rods and ultra-light spinning gear. There was no explanation as to why. The request seemed odd since it was trophy lake trout we were after. But, you never attempt to second guess your guide while in the north. (You don't, that is, until he hasn't produced at the end of day two.) This was our second day. It would be another hot one. Not the best conditions if it's trophy trout you're after.

We fished "Jimmys" and the "shark" with no luck. The largest finny one to come to the boat was a ten pounder. The graph didn't show any large arcs. The big fish had disappeared. As on the day before, big fish were avoiding us once again.

Suddenly Tim called a halt to the search for big fish. "Let's put the heavy gear aside, gang, and go for grayling," the announcement was made.

Grayling? Where would we find grayling out here in the middle of this huge lake? When asked that question, our Irish guide just grinned.

"Oh, I have several places we can pick up lake grayling. It'll take about ten minutes," grinned Tim as the motor was gunned into action.

There was no river close by that I knew. Northern grayling are always associated with rivers. But, they are found in most northern lakes that host rivers where grayling are caught. Few, if any, resorters promote this fish in lakes. The reason, in most cases, is that they are sporadic feeders in lakes and tend to travel in schools that move about.

The northern grayling, or Arctic grayling, as it's called, migrates into the lake-connecting rivers each spring and returns to the sanctuary of the lake each fall. They do so because of the insect life available in rivers. Grayling are primarily insect feeders, though they are known to feast on small minnows when bugs aren't available.

Fishing this species is a fly fisherman's dream, but grayling will strike small French spinners (0 and 00 size) as well as crappie jigs.

According to Tim, Kasba has numerous places where grayling are found along the main shoreline. Most of these places seemed to be on rocky points in the shallower bays.

Arriving at one of these points where crystal-clear water revealed a melange of varying size bottom rocks, Tim suggested I try a #14 muddler fly on a #6 fly rod. Laurie would use four-pound test on her five-foot ultra light on which Tim suggested she attach a #00 no-tangle French spinner.

On my second cast a two-pound grayling struck. Minutes later, after a few additional leaps, the fish came to the boat and was then released.

216

Was it just luck, or were we in for a treat? The nearest river was the Kazan, outlet to Kasba Lake, and it was an hour away by boat.

During the next two hours, the three of us boated and released two dozen fat, colorful, surface-breaking Arctic grayling. It was the treat of the day, a day on which a hot sun drove temperatures to exceed the ninety-degree mark, and the lack of wind made a day on Kasba's open waters very warm.

Had we continued watching the 120-foot lake trout holes for fish that refused to feed under such hot conditions, the day might not have gone so well.

I don't know how everyone feels about fighting the odds, but this angler loves action. Thus, it is my recommendation that when lakers refuse to bite on hot, still days, prod your guide into taking you grayling fishing. Hot, still days are ideal lake grayling feeding days. The more bugs that hatch during such times, the better the grayling bite.

What were the average weights of our grayling? About one and one-half pounds. But the biggest came close to two and three-quarter pounds. Of course, I lost one on a #14 Irresistible dry fly that may have hit the three-pound mark. The biggest ones always get away, don't they?

What my fishing companions and I experienced on Kasba Lake that hot summer day isn't unusual. In the far north, any cold water lake that hosts rivers entering or leaving, generally hosts Arctic grayling. Knowing where to look for them and at what time they feed can make the difference between success and failure. Catching this colorful trophy of the north, or going home skunked depends on these tips.

Let's examine what, where, and how you can be successful on your next trip into the Far North.

Grayling are insect feeders. Being such, they are found in close proximity to the area in which insect larvae hatch. Look for points, rocky ones, close to both deep water and a black-loam bay. Black loam is a bedding area for most insect larva such as shad fly, black gnats, mosquitoes, and other insects that lay eggs in open water. Such insects require bottom loam in which to hatch and grow into the larva stage.

Deep water is required to hold grayling during their staging time prior to feeding. Since grayling are a cold-water species, deep water is needed to maintain the northern lakes' cold temperatures. Because grayling are a river fish most of their lifetime, while feeding, they prefer holding to rock structures. Look for bottom rock that varies in size from a gravel texture to two-foot-diameter boulders. The greater the variety in the bottom rock on such structure, the more likely it is that grayling will hold on the point.

An ideal shoreline point, such as we found in Kasba Lake, Northwest Territories, runs out into forty-foot-deep water, hosts a variety of different size rocks and gravels, contains pockets of loam between rocky ridges, and penetrates out into the lake proper 100 to 150 feet. The slope can be gradual or can drop in a variety of plateaus, each one staging a foot or so beneath the other.

Knowing if the lake fished hosts Arctic grayling can normally be determined by these factors: Does the lake host lake trout? Do the rivers and streams attached to the lake contain grayling? Is there an abundance of other species such as northern pike and walleye in the lake? Is the lake a cold-water lake, one that maintains a water depth, in some areas, of 100 feet or more?

If the lake has no other gamefish but lake trout, whitefish, and eel pout, is a cold-water lake with several pockets of 100 feet, and rivers entering that contain grayling, the likelihood of this fish being in the lake is good. If there is a heavy concentration of northern pike and walleye, or either one, even if the incoming and outgoing streams have grayling, it's a good bet that the lake won't.

On a still evening when the bugs are hatching, in many cases the angler will see the soft dimpling of grayling feeding on the rocky points formerly described. The other fish the angler could be seeing are northern cisco or whitefish.

Lake grayling, unlike their stream cousins, do not jump nearly as much. Their fight is similar with that one exception. In a sense, they are the same fish. One year, as spring breakup comes on, a lake grayling may take it upon itself to migrate up the incoming lake streams. The next year, it may choose to stay in the lake. No one has discovered why this happens, only that it does. One thing is true . . . the larger a grayling becomes, the more likely it is to migrate. Stream grayling tend to be larger than their lake cousins.

Another fact: As winter comes on, all grayling depart the rivers and streams and migrate back into lake where they spend the winter.

For information on Kasba Lake, mentioned in this article, turn to the information index in the last chapter.

Tips and Bits
OF THE NORTHERN NATURAL WORLD

Tree Growth in the Tundra

Three types of spruce grow in the Arctic tundra. The first is a low, thick, creeping bush which, at times, reaches ten feet across and a mere one foot high. This bush continues in this state, at times as many as fifty to eighty years, until rooted enough to send up a single servicing shoot, which eventually becomes a tree. As the tree grows, the surrounding creeper bush dies away. Often these creeper spruce bushes will produce more than that single tree. Observation has revealed as many as a dozen adult trees grow from low creeper spruce bushes.

What may seem strange is that creeper spruce bushes have stems that reach a diameter of up to four inches, and they can be as old as one hundred years.

White and black spruce can both be found in the Arctic barrens in protected draws. The farthest, northernmost trees reach a height of eight feet and a diameter of two inches. This is a huge tree for the region north of the Thelon River. Its age may be between 250 and 400 years. Protection from the harsh environment and its natural surroundings govern how long these northern trees exist. So close are the growth rings in such trees that determining one's age by counting its rings is nearly impossible. To the naked eye, it is impossible to count the rings. Even under magnification, the growth rings of such a tree seem to be a gray blur.

Chapter 27

God's Lake

The year was 1962!

Below, the waters of Johnson Bay whisked by beneath the floats of our ancient DeHaviland Beaver. My partner and I were about to be deposited at Tom Ruminski's God's River Lodge. All my life I'd heard stories about the huge fish that swam beneath the waters of God's Lake and River, a multi-species body of water in north central Manitoba.

Finally, with a new bride, I was going to fish the sportsman's paradise. We'd be the fishing guests of Tom Ruminski for seven days. We'd not only fish God's, but spend three days at a newly opened outpost camp on Nagilini Lake, far to the north. At Nagilini, we'd be the second party to work its waters. Nagilini was at the very top of the province. The new lake straddled the border of Manitoba and the Northwest Territories.

Tom and Joe Ruminski, brothers of Ukrainian descent, a pair of farm boys from Sclater, Manitoba, left the farm early in life. They had dreams of making their fortunes in Canada's far northern frontier. Lacking the normal talents of piloting or timber crewing, which draw most young men into the north, Tom and Joe elected to become traders in natural products. There was a heavy harvest of commercially netted fish available and awaiting those tough enough to transport this catch back to the civilized world. Any entrepreneur smart enough to bridge the miles between the northern harvesting areas and Manitoba's northernmost railhead would make a better-than-average living.

Winter roads, a way to transport material and food goods to the mining operations of the north, had been in existence a long time. Why not use them to transport the commercial fish harvest? Thus began a new business for the Ruminski brothers. The year was 1948.

During those first years, stories flourished about lost fish shipments, disappearing cat (Caterpillar) trains, and loss of human life when cat trains crossed lake ice not capable of carrying their weight.

Note: Winter roads and the vehicles that use them are the mainstay of the North, providing vital material for the northern native communities. Winter roads aren't really roads but are hard, snow-packed right-of-ways constructed each year in early winter by D8 tractors pulling heavy-laden sleighs. Winter roads traverse stump-filled cuts through the forest areas, holding to nearly perfect constructed straight lines. They cross lakes, rivers, and rocky hills. When fill is needed to cross a ravine or river, the cats push in tons of ice and snow. Then freight-laden snow trains can cross the north country during the coldest of Canada's harsh winter months.

Many of these winter roads cross lakes where ice thickness varies from five to nine feet. At times, trains are forced to cross waterways where warm lake or river currents thin the ice. In early spring, these thin areas can spell disaster for freighters. Many a train has vanished beneath lake ice.

*Most of northern Canada's winter roads service com-
munities beyond the northernmost railheads. Any visitor
privileged to fly over this vast, vast wilderness of northern
Canada during the summer months can easily pick out
the cuts made by winter roads. They travel from one large
body of water to another—lines cut from the green forests
as straight as an arrow flies.*

Tom Ruminski often had spare parts for the freighting operation flown in via float aircraft during summer. In 1949, needing a
spare toggle wheel for one of his cats, he ordered a flight in. Since
the wheel was the only part needed, there was more than enough
room for a couple of passengers.

As luck would have it, in the States there were a pair of eager
fishermen who had always wanted to try God's Lake. Prior to
ordering the flight, Tom contacted the two and asked if they'd care
to share the cost of the flight. Happily they agreed.

Tom arranged for the two anglers to be housed and guided by
the local natives during their week-long stay. At that time Tom
and his brother had only a small building at the spot where God's
River exited God's Lake. It acted as a trading post and living quarters for the Ruminski brothers. The fishermen would leave a week
later when another planeload of freight arrived.

Unknowingly, Tom had begun a fly-in fishing service that would
turn into a full-time living. So thrilled were the two anglers at the
results of their fly-in to God's Lake that they insisted on returning the
next year and bringing some of their fishing buddies. From that meager beginning sprung a full-plan, fifty-guest, American-plan operation
for the Ruminskis. It would provide work for the locals and a good living for the brothers. By 1958, the Ruminski brothers had backed off
from the hard and heavy work of winter freighting. Instead, tourism,
which catered to United States anglers, became their life.

Today the original Ruminski resort operation is owned by the
native band which helped create it with the brothers. It was the

first lodge operation on God's Lake. Today there are three others catering to the gathering of summer tourists.

Joe Ruminski died in 1984. Tom passed on in 1988. Before his death, Tom saw to it that the native band that had helped him build the tourist operation received it after his death. Neither brother ever married, but their love for the native people continues to this day in the stories told and retold over the campfires on the shores of God's Lake.

My new bride and I caught and released dozens of brook trout, northern pike, walleye, and a goodly number of lunker lake trout during our stay at God's Lake in 1962. As far as I can remember, God's Lake was the first in the north practicing "catch and release."

The three days we spent at Nagilini were somewhat of an angler's dream. Legendary Al McClaine, of *Outdoor Life* magazine fame, was in ahead of us, but bad weather had suppressed his ability to get around the area, and good fishing results had been limited. However, Al had managed to land two lakers over thirty pounds and a bushel of trophy-size grayling.

Patty, my wife, and I did even better. We did better without having to go much beyond the first bay in Nagilini where the river exits down past the camp. In the lake and the larger pools at the river outlet, we caught and released two dozen lakers in excess of twenty pounds, the largest, slightly over thirty-eight pounds.

The grayling fishing in the main river provided immense numbers of fish, many of them over two pounds. A two-pound grayling may not sound large, but in Manitoba, it's considered a trophy fish. Nagilini didn't provide any grayling over three pounds, and even to this day, grayling size continues to average the same as it did in those days. If one really wants large grayling, he must go farther north to rivers such as the Thelon, Dubawnt, or Kazan.

The history of God's Lake is varied, with humans of many cultures contributing. The lake stands thirty-five miles wide and sixty miles in length. Spruce-covered rocky islands abound on the northern and southern shores. The native population seems to rest at 1,800, year in and year out.

The Hudson Bay Company was a major factor in drawing the natives to this area. Back in the late 1700s and early 1800s, the Bay Company built a trading post at God's Narrows. Back in the 1940s, Ruminskis' operation at the river's exit drew many of the natives to settle close to them. Today both groups of natives remain, separate, yet related by blood lines.

During the summer of 1997 I went back to God's. This time, to a resort owned by the Healey family at God's Narrows. There I learned another story about the people who migrated to this small spot on the Manitoba map.

In 1968, Jack and Goldie Healey, school teachers from Newfoundland, migrated west, looking for work. Their home area was in the depths of a depression, as it related to work availability. In the town of Winnipeg, the family's car broke down. Not able to go any further, the couple, and sons, John and Sam, elected to take the only jobs available. There were teaching jobs in the northern part of the province, among the natives. Jack took a job as principal of the newly built native school at God's Narrows. Goldie was hired as a teacher of the first through fourth grades and would act as school nurse. The family would live in a small shanty attached to the back of the school.

With no material things of their own, Jack and Goldie accepted anything handed their way by the native community. Examples were a handmade feather bed and a rabbit skin blanket that kept the family warm that first winter.

There was plenty of game in the surrounding forests to provide the nourishment needed to get through the first winter. Since Goldie's parents had been commercial fishermen back in Newfoundland, the Healeys were able to gather a supply of fish to balance off their meat diet.

Young Sam and John grew up living off the land. And, as is so often the case, the native elders took the two white youngsters under their wing, teaching them the art of trapping, canoeing, and living off the land.

> *Sam divulged to this writer that, to this day, he loves to eat fish eyes, moose nose, and fish heads. At times he lived off beaver, muskrat, and porcupine when trapping with the natives. Once young Sam was asked to try otter, but he found it tasted fishy and worse than a dead fishduck smelled. On the trapline, nothing was wasted.*

In the mid-1970s, young Sam Healey began guiding for the Stringer family who had opened the second resort operation on God's Lake. This would lead to his mother and dad, Goldie and Jack, buying the Stringer operation in the 1980s.

Jack Healey died in 1989 after operating the lodge through its first four years under the Healey family's name. Today, Sam and his mother continue to operate it, maintaining a close relationship with the native community at God's Narrows. As with the Ruminskis, it was the togetherness with the native community that made the fishing operations a success.

From Sam Healey I learned more about the Ruminski era. It seems much of Tom and Joe Ruminski's money was made in the trapping and trading fur business. At one time Tom nearly starved to death while trapping and had it not been for the community natives who took care of him, he would have died. Tom repaid the community by promoting the first gravel airstrip next to his resort at the God's River's exit from the lake. The pay scale wasn't much —ten cents a day for women who cleared the brush and fifteen cents a day for men who cut timber and tore stumps and discarded rocks. The runway was finished in 1966. It would become the first gravel airstrip in this area of northern Canada.

Our party arrived at the paved airstrip behind the community of God's Narrows. With me was my dear friend, Dennis Maksymetz, of Manitoba Travel, and Anne Orth, my TV partner, better known as "Bobber" Anne. We'd come in September. Our goal was to challenge the lake trout of God's, as they came in shallow in a flurry of fall feeding on the lake's cisco population.

Sam suggested we first try the fall walleye migration, which was taking place just around the corner from the resort. That seemed a bit strange, since the community of God's Narrows rests along either bank, right where we'd be angling.

As a matter of fact, during our mornings of fishing the rapids area two blocks from the resort, we were delighted to see the community's school children being transported by barge and boat over the river. They have a unique way of transporting the children. First the bus rounds them up on the east side and drops them off where they are ferried across the river by boat. Then the bus is put on a specially built barge and ferried across. Once over, the bus picks the children back up and deposits them at the school. This process is repeated twice a day.

The walleye angling was excellent. Unlike many regions of Canada, the walleyes of the God's Narrows migration averaged over three pounds. In most areas, a one-and-one-half-pound average would be more like it. Dennis caught the largest—an eight and one-half pounder, on a three-eighths-ounce yellow Ugly Bug jig. Several in the five-pound mark were taken by Anne and me.

After an early morning of walleye fishing, we were whisked down the lake in fast, thirty-horsepower boats to the open lake where lake trout became our target. In all, we caught and released twenty-seven lake trout, ranging in weight from four to nineteen pounds. Most were taken by jigging in water just off the spawning reefs. One-ounce white Ugly Bug jigs did the trick in the thirty to thirty-five-foot-deep water.

By day three we'd tired of catching both walleye and lake trout. It was time to challenge the late fall northern pike. As is normally the case in fall, we located the larger pike in deeper water along rock structures next to the summer cabbage beds. Most were caught on white or yellow one-and-one-half-ounce Weedcutter spinner baits. The largest I caught tipped the scales at twenty-one pounds. Anne and Dennis tied with nineteen and one-half pounders for second place. I realize twenty-pound northern pike might not seem big, but, considering it was fall and God's had been fished hard all summer, I felt our results were fantastic. One afternoon the three of us took forty-three pike. All were released unharmed. We ate walleye for shore lunch each day.

On our fifth day, a hardy storm blew in from the north, bringing heavy winds, freezing temperatures, and snow flurries. It was time to leave. Even though we'd not caught the lake trout in shallow waters, as we had hoped, it had been a good trip.

The one thing I noted about God's Lake was that its fish size and population hadn't changed much since I was last there in 1962. I didn't have a chance to fish the river for brook trout, but I'm sure it is nearly as good as it once was. Sam said there had been a period in the late 1980s when brookie fishing on the God's River had declined, but that had been corrected with the one-fish limit and barbless-hooks-only fishing. I'm sure that's true. It has worked in other areas where brookies have been fished too heavily.

God's Lake hosts four resorts and two native communities, and in spite of this, it is considered one of the best all around species lakes in the north.

Native Myths from God's Lake

It is rumored and thought to be true that a creature known as Windigo stalks the forests around God's Lake. It is a creature similar in makeup to the western Sasquatch. Belief in Windigo is so strong that while waiting for the aircraft to take us out in 1997, a young native girl, about eighteen, came up to us and mentioned the sighting of Windigo on the west shore of God's Lake a week prior to our arrival. At first I thought she was kidding me, but soon I realized this was no laughing matter. So frightened of Windigo was this young native that she was taking our plane out to visit her sister in Winnipeg until there was no longer any threat from the beast.

One of the more comical stories attributed to Windigo happened in a trapping cabin near the Oxford house. Phillip Weenusk, a distant relative of Sam Healey by marriage, was returning to his trapping cabin one evening in late December when he noted the door had been left open by someone or something.

There had been a local scare regarding the presence of Windigo, and this caused Phillip a slight hesitation before entering the cabin. Seeing no intruder, the trapper proceeded to take the contents of his sleigh in and store them. With supper cooked and consumed and darkness settling in, Phillip went to bed.

Shortly after retiring, having shut off the gas lantern, there came out of the darkness a deep breathing. Phillip sat up. It was not his own breathing he had heard. Someone or something was in the cabin with him. Next he heard the breathing interrupted with soft snoring . . . and there was a very bad smell.

Surely Windigo had entered his cabin. Not until Phillip felt his bed move did he jump to the floor and exit the cabin. As he did so, he grabbed his rifle resting near the door. The temperature outside was below zero, and the trapper wore only his long underwear. To stay outdoors would mean freezing to death. He must re-enter. Carefully, he slipped inside, reaching for his lantern and matches.

With the lantern lit, he carefully edged his way toward the bed. Beneath it he spied blackish brown hair protruding from beneath the lower bunk.

Hands trembling, he fired at the underside of the bed. Before he finished, eight shots from his lever action rifle had been shot into the hairy creature under his bed. Even Windigo was not strong enough to withstand such a shooting.

Twenty minutes passed before the trapper re-entered his cabin. It was the bitter cold that forced him back in, not his courage.

There, beneath his bed, partly exposed lay the body of, not Windigo, but a very large black bear. All but two shots had hit their mark. When later asked, Phillip admitted he'd been so frightened that he'd shook for another hour after the dead bear was discovered.

Natives hearing the story agree that such an experience takes years off anybody's life. After all, Windigo can take on the body of the most evil of all ghosts known to man.

In 1984 the natives of God's Narrows had a sighting of Windigo on the north shore of God's Lake. Within two weeks, the monster had been seen several more times in a number of other places around the lake. Goldie Healey was teaching the first graders at God's Narrows, as a part-time teacher, at the time.

Some of her students were so frightened that half the class stayed home for more than a week.

One last bit of information: Originally God's Lake was called Devil's Lake by the natives who lived close by. Many people had drowned while attempting to cross its massive body. Unable to believe that winds had swamped the canoes of the best canoemen the tribes had, they settled on the theory that "Kiche Nasnon," later named Windigo, had swamped the canoes.

Suspicions about the lake grew, and the islands at the north end of the lake received their names—Ghost Island and Spirit Island— just because of such incidents. The ancestors of those drowned would never look at the islands for fear of angering the spirits of the lake who would, in turn, send Windigo down upon them to punish them for such disrespect.

Not until missionaries renamed the lake God's Lake in 1870 did some of the superstitions disappear. Today many of the old myths remain. Not respecting such tales could see Windigo come looking for *you*.

For more information on the God's Lake area, turn to the information chapter at the book's end.

Run with the Tide

Gathering half the willow branches in his arms and a pack of decoys on his back, Alex worked his way to a spot about a quarter of a mile away from the anchored canoe boat. Here, he selected a gravel patch and began forcing willow butts into the soft ground. Within minutes, an eight-foot circle of yellow-green willow appeared. The remainder of the unused willow was forced in at an angle around the bottom of the blind. These would prevent the incoming birds from seeing the hunters' lower bodies' movement when they shifted to face the birds. These same slanted willow branches would hide Smudgie, the Labrador.

Next, Alex walked upwind beyond the blind and set out twelve white windsock decoys and ten hard-shell honker decoys. The honkers were set to the right, snow geese decoys to the left and a bit closer to the blind. Such a set would force incoming birds to pass over or to either side of the hidden hunters.

In the north, two families of Canadian honkers beat their way south above the salt flats. They numbered fourteen birds in all.

Their migration from their nesting grounds at Polar Bear Point had been easy and uneventful. The young birds, ten in all, were on their first journey south. Everything was new and exciting. Several times three of the youngsters had veered away from the family group to fly over other family groups resting below on the exposed flats. Each time, honking from their parents had forced them to return to formation. But, as all children do, these had a curiosity and a lack of fear for the unknown and new things in life.

"Geese coming from the north," warned Alex, as a flight of fourteen honkers flapped lazily toward the blind.

Crouching behind the blind, Alex began his "*Haw-hunk*," then deeper in tone, "*Hor-awnk . . . hor-awnk.*" He pleaded and repeated his call, until finally, three birds veered right. They came from the flock's rear, where the young always flew.

"Get ready, guys; they'll come right over us with the slight wind push," the Swamp Cree instructed his gunners.

Slowly the three juveniles beat their way toward the flock of honkers behind the green patch of willow. Ignoring the pleading behind them, they eagerly beat wing toward the calls of the ten resting birds to their west.

As the three passed over the circle patch of willow, a series of four thundering explosions occurred. The three curious youngsters would fly south no further. The lead bird, a young male, collapsed mid-wingbeat and plummeted to hit the salt flat in a shower of water and mud. His sister slammed into the midst of the ten geese as explosion three sounded. The third goose, a young male from the second family, came to earth as shot number four sounded. His wing had been broken at the shoulder.

"Great shooting, Anne," commented the male gunner.

The lady gunner had hit with her first shot, missed her second, and struck again with her third.

Smudgie, the Labrador, raced out to retrieve the first honker, noted the floating cripple, and returned to the blind with bird one.

"Good girl, Smudgie. Fetch up the others," encouraged the male gunner.

Again, the black dog raced through the decoys, ignoring the dead female goose but noting her position, in pursuit of the flapping cripple who was now racing as fast as possible out across the flats. It was no match. Smudgie was a race horse. Within a second or two of passing the last decoy, dog and goose met in a shower of water, mud, and feathers. Proudly Smudgie returned the crippled male honker to the blind where Alex would force the air from its lungs with his foot. Next the black dog returned the young female goose to the male gunner.

Thus began one of the several days when "Bobber" Anne and I worked the tide flats at the mouth of the Albany River in Ontario where the small community of Kashechewan lies on James Bay.

Dozens of islands have been constructed by silt and debris gathered as river wash and ocean tide waters come together. On this sediment structure millions of waterfowl gather each fall prior to migrating south. Though river flow into the bay is confined mainly to a single channel, dozens of others, much smaller in size, do exist.

Between these channels segments of exposed eel grass and other weedy foods are made available to the hordes of waterfowl. The farther out into the ocean proper, the less grasses. The closer to the mainland, the greater amount of grasses and even an abundance of willow and tall, heavy, hard grasses are found.

To locate Kashechewan, look to a map of James Bay, Ontario. One third of the way up the west coast, the Albany River enters. It is here that the small Indian community of Kashechewan rests along the north bank of the river. It is a key gathering spot for North American waterfowl as they begin their migration south.

Sixty miles south of here is a dividing spot where the central flyway birds head straight south as birds of the eastern flyway veer south and east over the native community of Moosonee. Because of this, the camp at the Albany River mouth has the greatest variety in waterfowl anywhere in North America. All five species and sub species of Canadian honkers, snow and blue geese, speckle bellies, and Brant are available. Every duck species, including all the Arctic sea ducks, pass by the Albany River delta. The western pintail ducks were there by the thousands in 1995 due to the droughts in the west.

"Goose! Goose! A dozen blue geese! Right there! Get down; they're coming in!" came the instructions from Alex, the Cree guide.

There, a quarter mile downwind, twelve blue geese had veered and set wing, heading directly toward the hunting party. Alex now changed his calling tunes to a higher pitch and began to talk the geese in. Eagerly the twelve beat wing against the wind, dropping toward the false geese on the flats. Alex's enticing invitation was working.

At the first shot from the male gunner, a large, leading blue folded. Next Anne missed, then collected another large blue with her second shot.

When the party arrived to construct the brush blind, the tide had been at its lowest. Now, an hour later, water had begun to creep up around the blind. It was time to move.

Over the years I've shot both Hudson Bay and James Bay a number of times. As a young man I guided on James Bay at Moosonee when our resort sent parties of American hunters via float plane to James Bay to hunt the fall migration of geese. During those days I spent a great deal of time on the bay hunting. However, I'd never had a chance to hunt the mud flats at low tide way out on tide flats. This day with Alex was a new adventure for me and my partner, Anne.

"Dan, you and Anne head out and wait for me back there at that spot where the little piece of bush is sticking up," Alex instructed while pointing inland along the flats.

It was a half-mile walk. While we walked, Alex trotted over to the canoe, dropped the blind material in it, and motored up to a spot slightly up the channel from where Annie and I waited. He had been lucky in his decision to move when we did. Had Alex waited any longer, he would not have been able to reach the float-

ing canoe. The tide coming in had floated it from its original resting spot and allowed it to float free. Even though Alex had it tethered to an anchor, the distance between river shoreline and floating boat had increased to better than fifty yards. Water depth at
the boat was up past Alex's knees when he arrived.

Once again, the blind was constructed, and decoys deployed. Again
we collected four geese and a couple of ducks before the process needed to be repeated. The incoming tide again forced us to move.

Our next setup, another half mile inward along the mud flat,
was done on the eel grass. Eel grass is a favorite food of bay geese,
and once it floods with a bit of water, geese flock to it by the thousands. This setup would prove to be our best spot. Between us,
Anne and I killed seven more honkers.

Before the day ended, we had move our blind five times. Our final
destination was next to a brackish-water pond at the treeline. High
tide had arrived. By the time our fourth move was completed, our first
blind site was covered with seven feet of salty tidewater.

At our last setup, I collected the largest honker of the day. It
weighed in at fourteen and one-half pounds. The goose came to ground,
its left wing broken, 100 yards from our pond blind. It had been at the
coaxing of Alex that the shot was taken. Normally I would have
allowed the birds to pass, hoping for a swing around to Alex's calling.
Maybe he knew something I didn't, because he insisted I shoot. Luckily
I hit the bird behind and down from the one at which I had aimed.

"Great shot, Dan. I knew you could do it with those steel BBs,
even though none of us Cree guides would ever think of using it,"
Alex commented as Smudgie, the Lab, struck out to run the goose
down. It was obvious our guide didn't think too highly of steel shot.
As a matter of fact, I've not been too much of an advocate of steel
since it came out. I've seen too many wounded birds, both geese
and ducks, fly off to die later. Admittedly, many of those wounded
birds are the result of gunners who haven't learned to hunt waterfowl and who just shoot at them, no matter what their range.

Anne and I spent four days running with the tide. Our limits of geese and ducks were filled. They included honkers, snows, blues, and Brant. The three Brant geese were a special bonus, not expected. They were shot on the third day at the first setup far out on the mud flats. We'd been seeing Brants trail back and forth during our first two days. Most flew well out over the ocean swells, too far to get unless the use of a layout boat was employed. The three Brant we did gather came just after setup when a flock of twenty-one birds edged their way up the river channel, then decided to veer back out to open sea by passing across the outer edge of the mud flats. I hadn't killed a Brant since I guided a group of Illinois gunners at Moosonee in 1951. Anne had never shot one and was delighted to inspect her first black-and-white sea goose.

If you love waterfowling, a James Bay or Hudson Bay shoot should be part of your schedule before you pass on to the happy hunting grounds. Even as I write this chapter, I can hear the pleading cries from Alex's throat as he called the geese to turn into the wind and on into our decoys.

For more information on a James Bay hunt, turn to the last chapter in this book.

Chapter 29

The Leuenbergers

"I can't get the damn plane to go airborne. You've got a DC3 load in this Otter, Father," yelled young Ernie to his father, who sat in the co-pilot's seat.

Looking out a side window, I had been wondering if we were going to make it. We had passed the dock at Webequie and were well beyond it, and still the plane refused to lift off. So far, three miles of lake surface had passed. There were only four miles left.

"Damn it; I'm giving it everything it's got! We're not going to make it!" yelled the twenty-one-year-old pilot.

"For gawd sakes, kid! A bit more gas would help. Let's go!" yelled Ernie Leuenberger, Sr,. as his red-faced son fought with the overloaded Otter float plane.

Inside the plane, anxiously awaiting lift-off, sat our party of ten fishermen, our gear, and a pair of native guides who had begged their way on board at the last minute. It was obvious we were heavily overloaded. When the last native hopped on board at Webequie, a native community on the Winisk River system, the plane's floats had begun to settle beneath the waterline.

To complicate matters, the weather remained hot and humid, without a wind. Attempting to fly an overloaded plane in high pressure and wind would be hard enough, but with these conditions, it was impossible.

Finally, after encouraging the passengers to rock back and forth as the plane's throttle was thrust back and forth, the Otter lifted up on step. There were but two and one-half miles of water left. Slowly, ever so slowly, the tach indicated we were gaining speed. Still . . . no lift-off!

Then, as speed finally reached take-off position, the right float lifted off. A moment later it slammed back onto the water. Next the left float came free, only to return to the water surface a moment later.

"We're not going to make it, Father," yelled young Ernie.

"The hell we're not!" came the response from his father, who was now leaning as far forward as he could.

Ahead, the treeline at the lake's end loomed ever larger. There was no way we'd clear the trees if we lifted off now. We had reached the point of no return. Were the aircraft to shut down right now, it would end up in the shoreline trees. Suddenly there came that feeling of departure from the water surface. Slowly altitude was gained.

Trees raced at us. A crash was certain!

Ernie Jr. fought the wheel, coaxing the overloaded plane skyward.

"Come on, baby . . . up! Up! Come on; you can do it!" Ernie talked to the aircraft he'd flown since the age of fourteen.

At the rate of ascent we were making, the plane would plow into the aspen trees at lake's end, about midway between the ground and their tips. My father, Don Gapen, who had been my fishing companion on the Winisk and Ashweig Rivers, grabbed my arm. It seemed a final response of affection between father and son.

Then, as if the Great Spirit was looking over the foolish occupants in the aircraft, there came a sudden lift in position. It came none too soon, for below us, the top branches of the aspen trees entangled with the plane's floats, only to be ripped away as we passed.

"See, kid; I knew you could do it!" croaked the red-faced, older Leuenberger.

"You can stick this plane where the sun doesn't shine, Father! I'm quitting the moment we get back!"

The conversation didn't last long for suddenly we began to descend as we passed beyond the tree line and came upon another lake. Once again, Ernie, Jr., fought the plane to gain altitude and before the far end of this next body of water passed by, we were 100 feet above the ground. At that altitude, the passengers could easily make out the pine cones on the jackpines beneath us.

"Father, the only reason we're staying up is that we're burning off gas and lightening our weight," yelled the pilot to his father. I'm sure Ernie, Jr., was right. The longer we stayed airborne, the more altitude we gained. It wasn't much, but by the time we were twenty-five miles south of Webequie, we'd reached a point 250 feet above ground. I can only imagine what would have happened to us had the area contained any hills.

Later, we were able to analyze the lift that had helped us avoid disaster at lake's end. It seems there was an air current created by the heat and foliage rising from the shoreline edge. It was enough to cause our ascent up and over the tree line. The same lifting air, as we reached the edge of the lake beyond our takeoff lake, was the reason we descended once the second tree line was passed over.

It was a flight I'll never forget . . . one that only a pilot with skills like those of Ernie Leuenberger, Jr., could have accomplished.

The Leuenbergers run a six-plane fly-in operation in Nakina, Ontario. They have nineteen outpost camps of their own and service a number of other resort operations in northern Ontario. Malcolm and Ernie, Jr. (Ernie, Sr.'s two sons) have flown since they were fourteen years old. The old man, a Swiss immigrant who came to Canada after the second world war, began teaching the two boys to fly as soon as they could get behind the wheel. Actually, by placing them in his lap when they were six years old, Ernie taught his sons the art of flying float planes. Both soloed at fourteen, two years before they were eligible for a flying license.

Today both boys have accumulated so many hours of flying time that they no longer log hours. As Ernie, Jr., once told me, "I've filled up so many books it doesn't matter any more. Logging, at this point in my life, only takes up valuable time; I could be doing other things to help my passengers."

Situations, such as described at the chapter's beginning, can no longer occur in the far north. Canada's transportation department has cracked down on float plane overloading. However, for years it occurred, mainly in the freighting business.

I can remember watching an overloaded DeHaviland Beaver on floats. It carried supplies into the Hudson Bay store at Fort Hope, Ontario. I saw it sink at the dock in Armstrong, Ontario. Hopping off, the pilot suggested he start the plane first, allow it to warm up at the dock, then hop on, gun the motor, and gather enough speed to take off. As he departed the plane, it gradually began to rise off the bottom. Even so, the rear end of the floats remained under water with water covering them just up past the back support struts.

Inside the Beaver, freight was crammed to the ceiling behind the pilot's seat. Even the co-pilot's seat was filled to the roof. There was just enough room for the pilot to squeeze in. This he did, once the aircraft's engine was warm enough to fly. By standing, one foot on the dock, the other lightly on the plane's ladder, the pilot raced the motor into "go," and, as the plane began to move, he leaped in, raced the motor forward and proceeded to coax it up one step. Luckily there was a good northwest wind coming down the lake. Without it, I'm convinced the aircraft would have sunk halfway through its takeoff.

Such situations were common back in the 1940s, 1950s, and early 1960s. Stories such as the two just told were an every day occurrence. The more you could carry, the more profitable your freight operation became.

Ernie Leuenberger came to Nakina, Ontario, in the late 1940s after serving a three-year stint on the Canadian railway system. Piloting had been part of his life back in Switzerland, and it soon became part of his life in the new world. With the money he had saved while working for the CNR railway, Ernie bought a small Piper aircraft on floats. He would begin freighting for the local co-op in Nakina, then eventually carry fishermen, one at a time, into the surrounding lakes.

From that start, the senior Leuenberger began to establish, one by one, outpost tent camps. These eventually became permanent camps, and thus, a fly-in operation took root. Today, on any given day, there will be forty to fifty cars at the air base just outside of Nakina . . . cars whose owners have been flown in to one of the Leuenbergers' camp operations.

Fishing at the Leuenberger outposts is mainly confined to walleye and northern pike, but there are some Leuenberger outposts that sit on some of Ontario's better brook trout and lake trout fishing locations as well. Except for the American-plan resort on Kagagami Lake, all of their camps are "you cook; you guide" camps. Each outpost is the only camp on the lake, allowing complete privacy to those who fish its waters.

As with many of the northern outfitter operations, the Leuenberger operation is a family one. Both of the sons' wives work at the air base as do a grandson and two sisters. As of this printing, Ernie, Sr., has retired but still can be found hanging around the base, handing out advice, whether wanted or not, to his children and grandchildren.

Much to the surprise of visiting fishermen, Ernie, Sr., has never lost his Swiss accent. This accent is even more pronounced when influenced by the consumption of several Canadian beers. And no one loves beer more than my friend Ernie. I pass this off to his

European heritage. Beer in hand, or without, old Ernie may know more about bush flying, the planes used, and the lakes and rivers of northern Ontario than anyone who now runs fly-in operations in the wilderness area serviced by the Leuenberger planes.

One last story: Ten years prior to the printing of this book, I had the opportunity to fish a small lake called Esser on the Ogoki River system. This lake is short, making it difficult to land a float plane there. Any plane landing or taking off Esser must begin at the very point where a rapids departs the lake.

Getting in wasn't a problem, but when Ernie, Jr., returned to pick me up, he ran into a bit of a problem. It seems a large rock, resting 100 yards off the dock, had reared its ugly head close to surface to engage any float plane that passed directly over it. With water low and dingy after a long summer of hot weather, Ernie missed spotting the obstruction on our flight in. But as luck would have it, he managed to run atop it on our takeoff.

After picking my partner and me up at the dock, Ernie guided the plane over to the top side of the exiting river rapids. At the point of no return, the engine was gunned to full throttle. Fifty yards into takeoff the plane jerked to a shuddering halt. We'd run up on that rock, which rested six inches underwater.

"Dammit, Gapen, why didn't you tell me about that rock?" complained Ernie as he frantically made the decision whether a take-off was in order or a shutdown was necessary.

"We've put a pretty good hole in the right float. I could feel it as we ran aground. No staying here. Can't repair the damn thing here. We need to get back to base," he said as he adjusted his instruments and throttle for a hazardous short takeoff.

As quickly as it happened, the plane was turned in a short circle, engine roared, and we quickly sped down lake to where the river entered. Running up on the rock had jerked the plane sideways, but fortunately, the rock didn't hold us, and we floated free . . . floated free, that is, as long as it took to fill up the float!

By the time we lifted off, Ernie was forcing the wheel sideways in an attempt at forcing the damaged float up off the surface before it filled the damaged compartments with water. Without knowing exactly what damage had been done, any hesitation might have meant disaster.

Back at the base in Nakina, Ernie radioed Malcolm to inspect the damage as he did a fly over. Malcolm reported that the right float had a rip in it from the second compartment back through compartment number four.

Landing would be tricky. The plane would have to be landed on its left float, taxied as far as possible on it, then immediately beached on the sand next to the dock before the right float could fill with water.

It would take some fancy doing, but, as with so many bush pilots, Ernie, Jr., had the confidence and cockiness to try it. Two more fly overs confirmed the extent of the damage.

On the final pass, Ernie explained to me what could happen if the damaged float came to rest on the water too soon. It wasn't a pleasant picture. We could cartwheel down the lake as the right float dug in, ripping the entire float from the plane's fuselage, or we might spin sideways as the damaged float ripped farther open upon impact. We both donned life preservers and readied for the landing.

As only Ernie could fly, the Beaver aircraft settled slowly toward the base lake, in a soft settling pattern. Two feet off the surface, he slipped the plane to the left and allowed the left float to settle in. Next the engine was gunned, and we magically ran toward the beach on the left float at a cocked angle. It was similar to one of those stunt car drivers who run their specially prepared cars on only two wheels after careening off a ramp.

Ahead, the beach raced closer. It appeared we were about to crash. At the moment I thought we were finished, Ernie cut the engines, and we settled to the surface not more than 100 feet from the waiting soft sands. As softly as a mallard skids on glare ice, the float plane slid up onto the sand and came to rest ten feet from the lake's shoreline. There was no jerk or jump, just a soft, slow settling, as the aircraft came to rest.

It was one of the finest examples of flying I'd ever experienced. In my opinion, there was not another float pilot who could repeat Ernie's performance that day.

Ernie just shook it off with a, "Well, Gapen, how's that? Slick as wiping a baby's ass, wouldn't you say?"

It was a typical expression from a bush pilot who brims with self-confidence and an uncanny ability to fly those very important planes of the far north.

For more information on the Leuenbergers, see information chapter at book's end.

Chapter 30

The Trick

Our guide came with rusty red hair, a smiling face, and an ever constant chatter about fishing. Unlike so many guides I've met in the north, Tim O'Shannessey was a delight, whether fishing or relaxing back at Kasba Lodge.

Today, with my fishing partner, Laurie Dickhart, we'd fish for some of Kasba's lunker lake trout. What we didn't know was that our smiling Irish guide was about to show me a trick I'd never seen before or could ever have conceived.

Tim made the long run up Kasba Lake to a long, finger-shaped bay on the western shore. When the lake was first opened in June, Tim and his parties had taken a pair of forty-pound lakers that were immediately released unharmed . . . as is the lake policy.

During the spring fishing, these large trout had come from fifteen feet of water, atop a shallow reef in the bay's south end. Today, Tim's theory was to work the outer edge of the bay's mouth where water dropped from forty-five to seventy feet. That made good sense since this was the first week in August. In August, Kasba's fish usually go deep, seeking cooler water and bait fish.

"Dan, how about handing me one of those ten-ounce Bait-Walkers you make? I want to rig up my special lure for Laurie to troll," commented the Irishman as the boat glided to a stop at the bay's mouth.

I had no idea what Tim was talking about. Maybe he had a special big spoon or a giant plug of some kind. Little did I imagine the concoction he had planned. Reaching under the seat, he gathered up a head from a lake trout he had saved the previous night when preparing our shoreline supper. The fish had been ideal size for eating, a five pounder. When Tim saved the head, I had wondered why but failed to ask his plans for it. I was about to find out.

"Dan, I need a really large hook, maybe a 12/0, if you have one. And I'll need a pair of trebles, about 4/0 or 5/0," instructed Tim.

It just so happens I carry along large hooks in both singles and trebles. You never know when such items may be needed while you fish the north.

Accepting the hooks, Tim inserted the large single up through the fish head's lower jaw, forcing it out through the upper jaw's nose. Next he asked for a six-inch steel leader, saying he had one of his own. Obviously two short steel leaders were needed. Placing the trebles on the leaders' snaps, Tim attached the swivel ends of the leaders to a large snap swivel he'd selected. The snap swivel was a #1/0. From the snap, the respective leaders dangled freely, hooks down. Next the large single hook eye was placed on the 1/0 snap, along with both leaders' swivels and their trailing trebles. The snap was closed and checked so that it closed solidly. Tim then pinched the snap shut with a pair of pliers, making sure it didn't open.

"Dan, this is the trick when using a head for bait. It's how you place the trebles at the back of the gills that makes it work," Tim instructed his bewildered guests. Who ever heard of using a fish head for bait? Surely not me!

"Are heads legal?" I asked.

"I talked to some biologists here in the Territories," Tim answered, "And they told me I could use certain parts of a fish but really couldn't say whether a head came under the legal line or not."

Next, he inserted one of the trebles down near the front fin, behind the left gill plate. The second treble hook was inserted near the top of the head on the opposite side. In both cases, only a single barbed hook on the treble was used to keep it in place.

"By hooking the trebles, one up and one down, at the head's rear," he further explained, "you get a slow roll as the head is trolled through the water. That roll is what makes it so effective."

Once the head harness was in place, a long, three-foot leader was attached to the rear swivel of the ten-ounce Bait-Walker. Then the head and its harness were attached to the snap at the leader's end.

What I've failed to tell is that on our way into the bay, just where the bottom structure begins to rise upwards into the shallows, we had spotted a very large blip on the fish locator. The blip had showed at forty-five feet where the bottom depth registered seventy feet.

"Guys, I'm going to try to get back over that big fish if I can. Once I do, I'll tell you what to do next, Laurie. Dan, you just keep trolling until I give Laurie her instructions. At that time you reel in, okay?" instructed our guide.

I nodded, and Tim gunned the motor forward and circled back toward the spot where we'd spotted the large fish. It took a couple of circles before the blip showed. This time the fish had descended to fifty feet but remained in the same depth on the bottom rise, seventy feet.

The blip had passed off the screen before Tim's instructions were blurted out. "Laurie! Put your reel in free spool; let the bait drop. Dan, reel up!"

As instructed, Laurie allowed her line to drop. Her rod was held high. Moments later, Tim instructed her to engage the clutch.

Nothing happened.

"She didn't take it. Reel up, Laurie; we'll try again," came the boat operator's instructions.

Again he began a troll toward the spot where we last saw the large blip on the screen. At the very spot the fish had held before, the blip appeared again, this time at fifty-five feet.

"She followed it down before. Wait, Laurie . . . wait . . . wait a bit more. Now! Drop the bait, Laurie," came the excited instructions.

"This time we'll let the head go all the way to the bottom," said Tim, explaining the need for a long drop, which took several minutes.

Laurie held off engaging the reel until finally Tim said it was time. It seemed like forever. What self-respecting lake trout would pick up a day-old head off the bottom?

The answer was obvious within the next minute. With the reel engaged, Laurie began to slowly pick up line—until the point where it appeared she had hung up on bottom. Her rod tip bent slowly toward the water surface as she continued to reel.

"You've got him, Laurie! Set the hook hard! Reef back on the rod. Hard!"

The lady, a good student, did as she was directed. Then, as if the lake bottom began to swim into deep water, her line took off, slowly at first, then faster. It was obvious Laurie had hooked into something very big. With a reel drag set heavy, there seemed to be no stopping the line, which peeled off.

Tim fired up the motor and began to follow in the direction the unseen fish was taking. That meant out into open water where the high winds made boat maneuvering difficult. Laurie hung on desperately.

Finally the fish, tired of the pressure on its jaw, came up, and the three of us got our first look at the head-swallowing monster.

It was big, really big. "Fifty pounds, if it's an ounce!" proclaimed Tim who now excitedly reached for the net. I didn't believe this size fish was going to fit in that net.

If we were able to see the fish, that meant the fish could see us. The difference was—we liked the fish, but she didn't like us. Off toward bottom the monster raced. There she sulked, holding fast and not wanting to come up again. Finally, with Tim beating on the rod butt while Laurie held on, the fish began to come up. Dozens of bubbles began to rise to the surface from the spot we suspected the big fish held. It was a sure sign Laurie's fish was tiring.

Then, as before, we got a glimpse of the huge fish just under the water, fifteen feet off the boat's right side. A close look revealed that Laurie's monster was hooked only by a single treble hook attached to the left side of its mouth. It appeared the hook was about to tear loose at any moment.

"Tim, you better get her on the first pass, or we'll loose her," I proclaimed. Tim nodded agreement.

Slowly Laurie worked the big fish toward the boat and the waiting net. Six feet from the long-handled net, the fish made one final surge toward the bottom. It wasn't much of an attempt, but . . . just enough to pull loose!

I thought Tim was going to go overboard. There we stood, watching the biggest lake trout of our lifetime slowly sink back toward the black depths.

What happened? The hook hadn't pulled loose! Failure had come when the leader wire wrap failed and allowed the hook to pull away. To make matters worse, it hadn't been the leader I supplied, but the one Tim had picked up from the bottom of the boat. Had Tim taken a second leader from me, Laurie may have landed the largest lake trout to be taken from Kasba that year . . . or maybe, ever.

"Tim, that's why I make my own leaders. Those store-bought ones aren't made to handle really big fish," I commented as Tim gazed down at the frayed wire.

Surprisingly, Laurie wasn't nearly as upset as Tim and I were. Exhausted from the fight, she breathed a sigh of relief and settled for a long swig of soda.

We did not take a fish nearly as big as the one Laurie lost that day during the rest of our trip. But, we did manage to land thirty-four, thirty-one, twenty-eight, and twenty-seven pounders via the "head" method. The thirty-one pounder was taken near a spot called Whale Rock by dropping a head directly down over the suspended lake trout in twenty-eight feet of water. The fish held at seventeen feet below the boat when first spotted.

We were fishing artificials at the time, and we were doing rather well on smaller-sized fish. Even though we tried enticing the suspended lake trout with jigs and large spoons, it refused to bite. Not until the head was dropped directly down on the fish from above did it take. If I were to guess, the descent of that head, rigged with its ten-ounce Bait-Walker sinker, had to only miss the fish by inches. On the graph, we watched as the thirty-one pounder followed the bait to the bottom, picked it up, and swam off. It was the that final testimony that made a believer out of me. Large lake trout love to feed on their own species' body parts, especially the head.

I've always known that lake trout are cannibalistic and often feed on their own. Had I not known this before, Tim's trick surely had convinced me.

The trick's success comes in the way you rig the head with its trailing treble hook harnesses and the size of the head chosen. The heads of three-to-five-pound lake trout seem to work best. It also helps if you leave some flesh behind the head. Tim prefers to cut about an inch back from the gill plate, leaving the front fins on. By doing this, maybe there is more scent produced when the bait is trolled.

No matter what you may think of this idea, I found it enticed lake trout when all other methods failed. As to its legality, I'm not sure. You're on your own as to where and when Kasba guide Tim

O'Shannessey's secret might be used. Frankly, I believe it's illegal in most states and provinces, but, having a bit of native blood in me, I found the idea very enticing.

Tips and Bits

OF THE NORTHERN NATURAL WORLD

The Arctic tundra covers a land mass of one million square miles of open land.

* * *

Snow is by far the best insulation material available to a stranded winter traveler in the north. If caught in a blizzard or lost temporarily, the traveler should bury himself as deeply as he can in a snow drift. If the comfort of a sleeping bag is not available, then a wrap—or blanket or heavy coat—should be wrapped around the body before covering oneself under the deep snow cover.

One need not worry about not being able to breath. Snow is coarse enough that oxygen easily seeps through its mass. For best breathing, the stranded traveler should position himself on his stomach, with a small breathing space dug out beneath the head and mouth, before the covering of at least eighteen inches of soft fluffy snow is applied.

You'll be amazed how comfortable you'll sleep during a below zero winter night. In the morning, it's just a matter of forcing the body upwards to exit the cozy sleeping quarters.

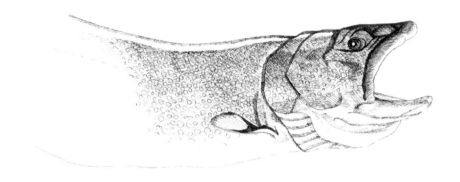

Chapter 31

The Ancient One

Eighty years of acid-cold winter waters had left the ancient lake trout weary. Obtaining food had become nearly impossible during the coldest months. Weight gain had stopped, and now weight receded with each passing day. What once had been a heavy-bodied midsection had shrunk inward between the forward and back belly fins. A thin layer of greenish-brown slimy moss encased the trout's dirty-brown back between its humped shoulder and dorsal fin.

Eyes, once cold, black and menacing, now appeared dull and lifeless. Slowly the pulpy, white mouth opened periodically to suck in water-laced oxygen across her gills. No longer did the body carry its rich cargo of life in the form of orange eggs. Instead, a single casing of bluish-white eggs held close to her backbone. They would soon disappear absorbed by her body in an effort to prolong life. Reproduction had become a thing of the past.

Spring breakup on the Kazan River north of Yakathat Lake had begun. The central region of the main lake still held its seven-foot-thick covering of ice, but where the lake's winter blanket met the river's outlet, it had begun to break away in massive ice blocks. They tumbled and tore their way through the first shallow rapids, tearing at and dislodging many of the river's bottom stones and boulders. Together ice and stone ground their way downstream, a formidable force to anything in their way. Any fish caught in the grip of this onslaught would be crushed and torn apart.

The ancient fish had survived seventy-nine spring breakups by retreating downstream into a twenty-foot-deep hole below the third rapids. Here, by holding close to the bottom in the very center of the channel, the mass of spring ice passed ten feet above her.

She wasn't the only one to seek shelter in the deep-water area below the shallow 5,000-year-old caribou crossing. Dozens of her kind joined her, an action that often led to a hearty meal as the old one ate her own kind. But that was years ago. She no longer had the stamina or speed to attack and kill a meal that was keener of eye and faster of fin than she. She would have to wait until spring breakup was over.

As with so many lake trout that inhabit the cruel waters in this area of the Arctic barrens, she had become ugly in appearance. A massive shoulder hump protruded upward just behind the gill plate—a characteristic formed by evolution.

Without the existence of bait fish or smaller lake trout upon which to prey during the winter months, she and her kind had been forced to kill and eat one another. To do this, evolution produced large canine teeth in the upper and lower jaws. So large had these teeth become that they now receded into openings in the opposite jaw when the fish's mouth was closed. When her mouth was open and she was attacking, these teeth had the appearance of those found in the mouth of a snarling mountain lion.

The use of both canine teeth and muscular shoulder hump becomes easy to understand when an attack of one lake trout on another comes into play. Instead of going for the head or forward position of its prey, this dinosauric fish attacks the belly of its prey from beneath. It's an action similar to the attacking pattern of a saltwater shark.

Once a mouthful of belly meat is securely locked between the toothy jaws, the attacker begins a whipsaw motion back and forth until the prey's belly meat comes loose. This action often leads to the victim's entrails being exposed or torn lose. Once this happens, the prey is doomed to death.

Death of the preyed-upon trout is just the beginning. The attacking fish now goes into its second phase of food gathering. Chunk after chunk of the victim's flesh is torn from its belly and consumed. The attacking trout accomplishes this by grasping a portion of the belly, near the open wound, and thrashing its own body back and forth. Thus, leverage is obtained to rip sections of meat away.

Once hunger is satisfied, the attacker leaves the remainder of the carcass to others of its breed to finish off.

It is the need to produce food in such a manner that has seen this species of lake trout evolve into the ugly, hump-backed, toothy species it has become.

Not all lake trout species in the Kazan River take on the appearance of this big-headed, hump-backed brown trout. There are two others. One is an orange-bellied, emerald-backed, insect-eating trout that seldom exceeds ten pounds.

The other is the normal, gray-sided, white-bellied, and white-spotted lake species. Both of these migrate into the rapid river waters after spring breakup and return to the deep water lakes as fall icing begins. Only the brown trout remains in the fast-water areas throughout the year. Possibly it is a species lost to the passing of time, a throwback to its prehistoric past.

Summer months on the Kazan provide an over abundance of food for the prehistoric brown trout. Not only is there the influx of two new trout species, but Arctic grayling by the thousands migrate up into the fast water rapids after iceout. They come to feed on the vast numbers of hatching insects. It is the grayling that draw the gray-sided lake trout. The lake species of trout prefer grayling, when available, more than any other food species.

With the passage of spring breakup, the eighty-year-old trout would fare better in efforts to obtain food. Body fat had been reduced by eighteen percent during the past eight months, enabling her to swim faster. Thus, it wasn't surprising that during the first week of June, she was able to overtake a small, three-pound lake fish that entered her territory behind the large, flat rock.

The eight-foot-deep hole, created by the room-sized boulder, had been her home ever since its previous owner had died of old age four years before. It provided an excellent ambush point from which to collect upstream-migrating grayling and downstream-running gray trout coming from Yakathat Lake.

The three-pound trout struggled, but a moment after the huge jaws clamped down across its midsection, life was crushed away. Surprised by her success, the old trout continued to hold her victim for several minutes after its final death struggle. It would be her first meat meal in six weeks.

Not since she'd manage to steal the tail section of a fifteen-pound victim left behind by several twenty-pound attackers in the deep-water winter pool, had she consumed any meat. Slugs and insect larva, stirred from the pool's silt bottom, had been her only food till now.

Finally the realization of her successful attack came, and she released her prey. It was consumed head first. Slowly the old trout settled to bottom. Here she would rest and gather strength . . . strength that would allow a successful attack on a one-pound grayling later that day.

By the end of June, the old fish had gained back eight percent of her weight loss, but complete recovery would never be. She was old, and death stalked her as it had her predecessor. Eighty years of life for a prehistoric river trout was a long time. All her spawn mates had long ago disappeared, victims of the cruel world in which they lived. Only six of her children, out of tens of thousands of eggs, had managed to survive, One, a large, thirty-four-pound male from her fourth spawn, lived but yards downstream behind another large river stone. It was he who would take her place after her death.

July 18 dawned early at the third rapids below Yakathat Lake. Millions of pesky insects filled the sun-warmed air. Several caribou calves and their mothers milled about, waiting for a signal from the lead cow to cross the river shallows. Upstream, at the river's outlet, a single bull muskox drank his fill at the river's edge. Once the master of the herd of twenty-four, the old bull had lost his throne, displaced by a younger, stronger, male. The rest of his life would be solitary and lonely, and never again would he rule.

Heat from the July sun had all but stopped animal activity at the third rapids when the droning sound of a 180 aircraft was heard coming from the west. Slowly the sound increased. Then, in a roaring rush of air, a large white-and-red-trimmed Cessna float plane buzzed the large boulder below rapids three. Quickly it banked north, circling the open area below the fast water. Once a complete survey of the area was made, the plane settled to the water. It would come to rest 100 yards downstream from the very place that held the old fish.

A pair of grinning humans, one with a fly rod, the other with a spinning rod, descended onto the plane's floats. As soon as the rear end of the floats touched shoreline, the pair leaped ashore, staked the aircraft off, then raced along the bank to the upstream rapids. Moments later a third human leaped ashore and checked the tie-off lines. With no trees along this section of the Kazan, a pair of large, protruding stones had been used for tieoff points.

Reaching a flat stone area above the big boulder, the human with the spinning rod made a cast. The second human, the one with the fly rod, would have to be content with the second bouldered area just downstream from where his companion now casted.

By now the old trout had not eaten in several days. Each time she had attempted to catch a colorful, high-finned grayling, the chase had failed. Add to this a failure to catch any of her own kind, her hunger had increased to the point of desperation.

So it was, when the brightly colored, flashy, fishlike spoon wobbled directly before her face. She acted on the opportunity to catch something instantly. With a lunge upward and forward, she struck the slow-moving object. Jaws came down hard, but instead of soft flesh giving beneath her teeth, there was only a hardness like bottom rock. It was a new experience. Frantically she wrenched her head sideways in an effort to tear the hard-skinned prey apart. It didn't work. Instead, she felt her head being jerked sideways as the hard food attempted to flee toward shoreline.

Above water, the human with the spinning rod was heard to yell, "Fish on!" Frantically the human wound on the small stick in his hand. He leaned back, and pressure was placed on the stick. It bowed double, and it appeared that the pressure would break the stick at any moment.

Below, the old fish torqued and twisted, but to no avail. Whatever she had attacked was now attempting to drag her toward shoreline. Twice she attempted to run out into the river bed, but because the winter loss of fat and strength had never been regained, she failed.

Opening her mouth to rid herself of the hard-skinned prey was fruitless. It had attached itself to her upper jaw in a manner that its claw had penetrated the upper portion of her nose. Wildly she wrenched her mouth several times, but to no avail. She was slowly being dragged into shallow water.

"Bob, I've nearly got her! She's a big one! Must weight forty pounds or more," the human said.

"Dan, you'll have to work on her yourself. I just hooked a real fighter. He's running me downstream, and I'll have to follow," proclaimed the human Bob.

"That's okay; I can manage. For a big fish, this one isn't fighting too much," said human Dan.

With one desperate attempt at freedom, the old fish flailed and thrashed the water surface near shore. It failed, and slowly she felt herself pulled out of the water, onto the slippery, flat rock on which human Dan stood. All her senses seemed to dull, and she resigned herself to her fate.

"Bob, she must easily weigh forty pounds, but, boy, is this fish ugly. It has a head twice the size of what it should be according to its body size. And she's long, but, man, this has to be the weirdest-looking trout I've ever caught," yelled the human Dan, as he freed the giant treble hook from the fish's jaw and she was released.

Downstream, human Bob had his hands full as the strong, fighting, male trout made run after run. Eventually the thirty-four-pound fish would be landed, then released.

As the old female felt water engage her body once again, she attempted to fin upright. This failed. Finally, with help from the land creature with the bending stick, she managed to hold erect, and once the grip on her tail was released, she ever so slowly finned off and sank deep into the hole behind her boulder home.

A number of times during the next thirty minutes, she watched as the hard-skinned prey swam toward shore above her. The old trout was completely exhausted. Thoughts of food failed to compel her into action. She was surely dying. Cooling water rippled across her body. Time passed. The old girl tilted to the side. She was unable to rebalance herself. Then, with one last shudder, the old trout allowed herself to settle on her side at the bottom of the pool. Resigned to her fate, she continued to breath, gills flaring ever so slightly with each intake of water.

This isn't the end of this tale by any means. Nature and evolution were to have a final word.

Six hours after the departure of the humans and their hard-skinned fishing lures, the old female's thirty-four-pound son discovered her dying body. His fight against human Bob had left him exhausted and with a need for food. Slowly he worked his nose along her soft underbelly until the soft flesh between her lower fins was found. Then, as he had done during so many winters before, jaws opened wide, clamped down hard, and a big chunk of belly meat was removed as the male wrenched from side to side. It mattered not that this was his mother. The mother-son relationship had never existed except at birth.

The natural world of survival was once again taking place in the waters below the third rapids, downstream from Yakathat Lake on the river known as Kazan.

Chapter 32

The Scotsman

At peace with the purpled spruce and pristine waters of northern Saskatchewan's Fond du Lac River region, lives a Scottish man of vision and soft-spoken word. His name is George Flemming —a Scottish man in the most true sense. His title: "The Man from Hatchet." This is a title endowed by those who walk this world of rushing water, northern wind, and forested granite rock. It is a stately title, won after years of perseverance against hardships cast his way by an unforgiving wilderness.

From Uranium City on the western shores of giant Lake Athabasca to Sandy Bay on the mighty Churchill River, George Flemming is known. He is a man who has survived to tell his tale.

George was born in the small town of Keith-in-Banshile, Scotland, just prior to the second world war. Keith rests within miles of Loch Ness, the world-famous lake where the Loch Ness monster is known to live. It was a fitting place for a man such as George to begin his early years—a world of unknown wonders, hidden secrets, and waiting adventure—a world which may well have molded young Flemming for what lay ahead.

Stripped of most of his Scottish ties when his father and only two uncles were killed on the battlefields of France, George left home on his sixteenth birthday. Behind he left a grieving mother and one brother.

A decision was made that would change his life forever. Lured by a story about the world-famous Hudson Bay Company, young Flemming signed on to work in a far-off land. True adventure surely awaited him in the coming days. The young Scotsman's destination: Canada!

Companioned with a pair of Irishmen, one Englishman, and twenty-eight other Scotsmen, departure from the British Isles occurred at the seaport of Glasgow, Scotland. Eight days later, after a miserable ocean crossing, the group arrived at Montreal, Quebec, Canada.

Here, the group was split up, some heading for Hudson Bay posts throughout Ontario, Quebec, and Alberta. George and four other Scots were shipped off to Saskatoon, Saskatchewan. The trip, on a slow-moving Canadian National Railway train, took four long days to reach their final destination.

Within a week, young George would head north to where his home would be for the next two years—Stanley Mission on Mountain Lake, thirty-five miles north of La Ronge on Lac La Ronge Lake.

When young Flemming signed on with the Hudson Bay company, the contract was for three years of "Far North" duty. There would be only two weeks of vacation allowed during those three years. When you placed yourself on the payroll of the Bay, you would earn every penny of the short salary they paid.

Hudson Bay wasn't known for its liberal pay policy. Much of their success then, as it is today, was due to its shrewd practice of hiring thrifty Scots. As with his shipmates, George would be placed under a miserly post manager. George would be a store clerk.

When the young Scotsman arrived at Stanley Mission, there were still a few aging birch bark canoes used by the natives. All winter travel was via dog team and toboggan-style sleighs. Stanley Mission was, and still is today, the oldest Anglican church mission in the north.

It was built by Father Moreau, who would continue to build more churches up and down the Churchill River system. The natives of the northern region knew Father Moreau for his verbal outbursts and a three-foot-long white beard. Many feared the aged Catholic priest, believing him to be a god placed among them by Great Spirit to test their faith.

The main church building at Stanley would eventually be graced with a huge stained glass window shipped from England by sea to Churchill, Manitoba, at the mouth of the Churchill River, then on upriver via York boat to Stanley Mission. Today the window remains intact, a persistent reminder of the old priest's determination to bring modern religion to the north.

During the next five years, young Flemming moved once a year to further educate himself in the way of trading with the natives. After Stanley Mission, he was moved to Pelican Narrows, then La Loche, on to Dillion, Buffalo Narrows, and finally to Ile A La Crosse.

In August 1961, George was promoted to post manager at Patwanak, and after a year there, he went back to Stanley Mission as a post manager. His contract with the Hudson Bay Company had been fulfilled. He was free to pursue other interests.

After buying tons of furs—beaver, otter, mink, fox, and marten—in trade for material goods available at the posts, George was ready for a new life.

During his travels throughout the north, George had fallen in love with a lake named Hatchet. Its crystal-clear waters were filled with enormous lake trout and northern pike. The rivers were filled with grayling and, in some areas, trophy walleye.

Knowing Hatchet Lake had a single trapper cabin on its western shore, George engaged the help of a Norwegian named Andy Flatland. As with George, Andy was an adventurous soul. Armed with a pair of axes and enough flour, salt, and lard to last the summer, the twosome set out from Wollaston Lake, road's end, on a week-long walk across land to Hatchet.

The trip was not without mishap. Crossing the Fond du Lac River was made difficult by an early spring thaw. As the men reached the southern shore of the big river, spring breakup had begun. Not wanting to wait for the completion of ice out, George and Andy gambled. It was a gamble that nearly cost them their lives.

They had arrived at the bottom of a rather large rapids which now heaved huge ice cakes into the air, only to suck them under moments later. So powerful was the Fond du Lac at this point that it was crushing fifty-foot-wide icebergs into pail-sized cubes at the down side of the rapids.

Observing the upstream side of the rapids, the duo saw a crossing was impossible. Anyone leaping on an iceberg with the intention of getting a free ride to the other side stood the chance of being plummeted over the downstream rapids and killed.

The only hope appeared to be the high ice ridge downstream from the rapids. It has been built to a height of fifteen feet. The pail-sized ice cubes had piled up in a shallow area of the river a half mile below the rapids. Beyond here, the river was open—not as wide as it was below the falls—but open just the same.

Their only chance was the temporary ice cube bridge. Without hesitation, George proceeded and urged Andy to follow him downstream to the "bridge." It was here they'd cross the mighty Fond du Lac.

Reaching the southern shore point where the bridge began, George tested the mass with his weight. It held. Encouraged, he worked his way further out. Finally satisfied it would hold him, he urged Andy to follow.

As they reached the midway section of the shattered ice structure, Andy slipped. Being slightly heavier than George, Andy's weight caused a landslide of ice, which moved toward the downstream side of the bridge. Luckily George was able to reach out and grasp his partner's hand just as the central region of the bridge gave way. Struggling, the two managed to reach the high point of the ice bridge's north side just as the central section gave way and roared its way downstream.

As fast as their tired legs would allow, the two men raced, stumbling, toward the river's north shore. Behind them, five-to-twenty-foot chunks of ice gave way to the onslaught of the river's powerful currents.

It became a race for life. No sooner would they step onto a section of piled ice cubes, then it would give way under their weight. Several times it was like running uphill against an avalanche of cascading giant ice cubes. Any hesitation would see the hesitator swept away into the wild, frigid river where they would be mangled and crushed to death in the melee.

Finally, exhausted from their ordeal, the two adventurers lay face down on the north shore. The only casualty was losing a twenty-pound pack of lard that had been strapped to Andy's pack. Later, a black bear would be gathered to provide the cooking fat lost at the ice bridge.

Reaching Hatchet, the two immediately set up housekeeping in the deserted trapper cabin. During that summer (1964), they built two more cabins. It would be the beginning of what is known as Hatchet Lake Lodge. The two had planned to live off the land, and this they did. The land around Hatchet Lake abounded in game, berries, and bulbs of all kinds. Added to this the fish they caught, and life was good.

George's original dream had been to start a resort to attract fishermen from south of the border. His dream was realized during the summer of 1965 when a Beaver float plane arrived and brought the camp's first four guests.

And . . . now comes to mind a story within a story. It began in the 1960s when the man from Scotland began to feel a need for company of the opposite sex. In George's area of northern Saskatchewan, the only women were the local native girls or the government nurses who were all taken by the area's hot-shot bush pilots.

What George would not do for the company of that sweet Scottish lass who had taken his fancy prior to his departure from Scotland! Being a man who wasn't afraid to work for his dream, George began to build a castle, which would become his home for a future wife. He didn't wait for a response to his letters, and the three-story, castle-like structure quickly took shape.

It contained everything a Scottish castle had, including a lookout high atop the central region of the building. To enhance its elegance, he constructed his dream home on the highest hill Hatchet had to offer. As the magnificent log building took form, the letters to Scotland gathered strength and daring, as well as increasing in number. George's heart was set on having the red-haired Scottish lass as his bride.

But, alas, as things go in real life, it was not to be. His childhood sweetheart married another, and George's dreams came tumbling down. The castle construction would end just prior to completion and sit empty throughout the following seasons. Today, the log castle remains empty, a monument to a love never to be. George won't talk much about it, but when he does its obvious it is the one thing he didn't accomplish in his life.

In 1977, the airstrip at Hatchet Lake began. It may have begun because of an incident that happened when George was left at Hanna Lake by a forgetful bush pilot.

Being a man with a laid-back attitude and a good sense of direction, he decided to walk the seventy-one miles back to Hatchet. His trek would take him through heavily forested land, numerous swamps, and across rivers and lakes. Without compass and food, he made the trip in three days, walking from 8:00 A.M. until 11:00 P.M. each day.

Reaching the north end of Hatchet Lake, George was hailed by the forgetful pilot who had landed his aircraft at the Scotsman's home base, in an attempt to locate him after not connecting at Hanna Lake.

When asked how he'd gotten there, the tough Scotsman replied, "I walked, you damn fool. How else would I have gotten here. I don't have wings, so I can't fly. You can see that, can't you?"

Needless to say, the pilot never flew for the Hatchet Lake Lodge again. It may have been that walk, which left George suffering from a lack of salt, that gave him the incentive to consruct the 5,800-foot-long gravel and sand runway at Hatchet Lake.

Building a runway for wheeled aircraft in the far north isn't an easy task. For most, it would be nearly impossible, but not for George Flemming. First a bulldozer had to be obtained. Road's end at Wollaston Lake was the closest point for trucking in a bulldozer. That would be over 100 miles away. The Cat would have to be brought in during the coldest winter months when the ice was thick enough to support its weight.

In February 1977 George, with a helper, walked the first D7-17A John Deere bulldozer into the Hatchet area. The trip took six days. At the Fond du Lac River, ice proved to be twenty inches thick, just enough to support the heavy machine.

The trek across the river did have its hairy moments. At about the halfway point, the ice began to crack around the Cat, causing water to shoot up in shorts bursts as the machine passed by. To protect himself from possibly going down with his machine, George steered the Cat via ropes tied to the controls as he walked fifty feet behind it. The plan worked, and the Scotsman had the key to construction of the first 3,000 feet of airstrip needed to bring DC3 aircraft into Hatchet.

That first 3,000 feet would be finished two years later, and the fishermen to follow would be treated to a much faster and easier flight to get to this world of big fish.

Today the Hatchet airstrip accommodates DC9 jets, is 5,800 feet long, and hosts maintenance machinery such as a road grader, a forty-two-ton Wabca front-end loader, and two other bulldozers, along with the original D7.

The first trip of the D7 bulldozer laid down a road for all machinery that came after. George and the D7 literally pushed over the trees in their way and created a new road through the wilderness.

Today the Hatchet Lake Lodge stands as a tribute to a Scottish lad who came to the new world of North America to make his fortune . . . and he did. Hatchet has become one of the north's finest fishing operations available to anglers who seek out trophy grayling, northern pike, and lake trout.

Remembering his past, George's guests are wakened each morning to the sweet sounds of Scottish bagpipes being played as a wakeup call to another day of super fishing.

To learn more about where to gather information on the Hatchet Lake area, turn to the chapter at the book's end.

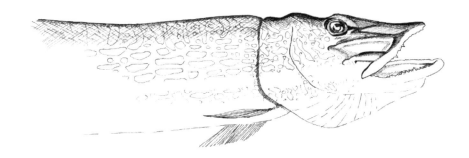

Chapter 33

Return to Wholdaia

Below, 120 feet of crystal-clear water. At seventy-five feet, a series of red arches indicated the giant lake trout of Wholdaia still remained exactly as they had been sixteen years previously.

"Anne, this is the hole where Bob Vos and I caught and released so many trophy trout on our research trip years ago. It isn't large, but it contains some giant trout," I commented as more fish flashed across the locator screen.

"Bobber" Anne, my fishing buddy, and I had returned to the North Wholdaia Camp after a four-year hiatus. This year we'd come the first week of August. Our previous trip occurred during the last week of August. At that time the outpost camp had been shut down for two weeks. Fishing on the previous trip, due to the time of year, had been so good close to camp that there had been no need to travel as far as we had this day.

Currently our location was sixteen miles southwest of the North Wholdaia outpost at a spot where the main lake inches together, then re-opens into the spacious western end. Sixteen years before, while researching Wholdaia and its sister lakes—Anaunethad and Flett, Bob Vos and I had come upon this bathtub-shaped, deep-water hole entirely by accident when motoring across the narrows with our locator on. It proved to be an awesome find. Five lake trout over twenty pounds, the largest thirty-one pounds, were quickly caught and released. We'd used two-ounce Ugly Bug jigs, tipped with whitefish belly meat, to catch those five fish. Today Anne and I would confine our lures to two-ounce Ugly Bug jigs in white and yellow.

Anne was first to drop. As she began a slow, erratic retrieve toward the surface, the rod tip jerked downward when her lure passed the forty-foot-above-the-bottom mark. Five minutes later, a healthy, fifteen-pound laker came to net, was photographed, and released. I took a ten pounder next, and moments later, Anne doubled the size of mine by wrestling a trophy trout to the surface.

Nothing had changed in sixteen years. The big trout were still here. North of Sixty's catch-and-release program, practiced since the camps were built, had paid off. If this was the case with lake trout, what about all those trophy northern pike Bob and I had caught and released. Would they still exist in the same weed beds?

"Anne, see that island on our east side? Behind it is a small, deep-water cabbage weed bed that produced two northern over twenty pounds," I recalled, while releasing another decent laker. "Let's give it a look/see; what do you say?"

My partner agreed, and within a few minutes, I rounded the island point where Bob and I had tented. As the weed bed had rested sixteen years before, it still held off the back side of the island in a sheltered bay.

Using a yellow Weedcutter spinner bait, Anne was in her third cast before she hit a fish.

"Dan, it doesn't feel big . . . maybe five or six pounds," commented the fisherwoman as the line zipped towards the boat.

Nothing could have been further from the truth. As Anne's line rolled beneath the boat's bow, the long shadow of a twenty-pound-plus pike appeared. From that moment on, the battle became a test of strength, but finally, after several strong runs, the trophy came to cradle. Weight was twenty-seven and one-half pounds. Had it not been for the seven-foot, custom one-piece rod and the 5500 Garcia reel with its thirty-pound line, Anne's first trophy pike of the trip may not have been landed. Several short runs through the weed bed's cabbage had piled the line with greenery. Before landing the pike, I was forced to tear the greenery away. Any other equipment may have failed under the stress of such conditions.

I connected next in the exact spot that had produced a twenty-five pounder for Bob Vos sixteen years before. My fish weighed in slightly over that mark.

During the balance of the day, Anne and I attempted to land a trophy pike of nearly the same size and in the exact spot success had come years before.

To understand the reasoning for this, let me explain the pecking order in the world of the northern pike. Availability of food is a key. Once a large pike reaches a certain size, she is able to force herself into a better staging area for food. Thus a twenty-five pounder reaches a weight that allows her to force all other smaller fish out of a food-staging area. The larger the fish, the better spot she is able to claim to easily ambush food. Therefore, if a weed bed hosts a twenty-five pounder this year, it will host another of equal size twenty years from now, providing the weed structure is maintained.

By day's end, Anne and I had stopped at fourteen spots that had produced trophy pike years before. In all we boated nine fish over twenty pounds and lost four others. That leaves only one trophy spot that didn't produce a big fish. At this spot, a place that Bob and I called the channel bay hole, Anne and I took a dozen fish from seven to thirteen pounds. Obviously the weed structure had changed, creating a better staging area for small fish and destroying the big fish structure. Thus, a worthy lesson was learned the first day of our trip in 1997. It was a lesson that would feed success throughout our four-day trip: If you catch a large fish on a certain structure, it is likely a similar-sized fish will be there the next time you fish the area. This could be an excellent reason for revisiting a certain body of water for a number of years. Therefore, if you are successful this year in catching big fish on a given lake, it is advised you return there next year or at least within a couple of years of your first visit.

Every camp manager has the knowledge to point the new fisherman to the hangouts inhabited by trophy fish. Be sure to ask as soon as you arrive in camp. Don't spend your first two or three days searching out large fish because your ego tells you that you're a good angler. If you are a newcomer, this is especially important.

What about Equipment?

If you've been north before, selection of fishing gear may be easy for you. However, if this is your first trip to a camp in the far north, it is advised that you follow the recommendation of your hosts. Too many anglers attempt to capture the large trophy fish of the north with bass and walleye gear. The likelihood of landing a twenty-five-pound lake trout or northern pike on the bass-casting outfit you use in Ohio or Indiana is remote. Get yourself a seven-foot, one-piece, heavy-duty rod and reel with heavy line. This style rod can be used for trolling lake trout with heavy rigs and spoons and is equally adaptable to casting the large, heavy spoons and baits used on northern pike.

If you are new in coming to the north, don't carry a lot of crank baits or walleye and bass style lures with you. They generally fail to do the trick on the northern fish you'll be after. Look to the lures recommended by anglers who have fished the waters before you or select a couple of Gapen kits for the species you'll be after.

Remember, a few extra dollars spent before your trip could determine the difference between success and failure.

Tip: Location of fish species when you arrive in one of the northern resorts can be broken down this way: The gear used on them is easily defined by the depth of water in which each fish stages.

June through July 10

Lake trout stage in water depth near the surface down to forty-five feet. The bigger trout are taken below twenty-five feet at this time. Trolling is the key. Use some weight on spoons and plugs. No more than six ounces, depending on buoyancy of the lure used.

In this same period, northern pike are found shallow (water depths less than eight feet). Use spinner baits in bright colors and spoons such as Dardevles in bright colors.

Grayling will best be caught on sinking flies and small spinners or jigs during this time. Remember to carry a #6 fly outfit or an ultra-lite spinning rod/reel combo to use on grayling which are prevalent in most northern waters.

July 10 through 30

During this period, lake trout drop into a bit deeper water. With the exception of smaller fish, the trophy lakers will be found below forty-five feet down to sixty-five feet. At this stage, they are still holding on rocky areas off reefs and land points. At this point, your best results on large trout will come on heavy jigs or plugs such as Quickfish trolled behind heavy rigs such as six- or ten-ounce Bait-Walker sinkers.

Northern pike at this time will begin to stage on weed structure just beginning to appear (mid July). Water depth that holds the larger pike will range from eight to twelve feet. The use of large, heavy spinner baits, such as a Weedcutter, as well as large spoons in yellow and dark colors, works well. It is also a time to use large surface lures such as Pop-n-Plunks. Work the surface lures during quiet days or late in the day over the young weed patches. This is also the time to use large, deep-diving plugs, such as a Crank Master for trophy pike. Try using a whitefish or shad as well as a fire-tiger pattern for best results.

Grayling fishing at this time is at its best. Use dry flies in sizes 10, 12, or 14 in dark colors for best results. Dark 1/64- or 1/32-ounce jigs and small 00 French spinner work as well.

July 30 through August 25

Now the lake trout population in the far north moves into deep water—sixty to eighty-five feet. You'll catch some small trout up shallower than that, but unless you're on an extra cold lake, these will be a small portion of your catch. Now, the angler must troll with heavy gear, ten ounces at least, and spoons or Quickfish-style plugs to locate the fish. Once they are located, a marker must be dropped, and the balance of your lake trout fishing is best done by jigging. Jig size: one and one-half to three ounces.

Northern pike—trophy size ones—have dropped a little deeper but remain on the cabbage weed beds or deep-water coontail. For best results on trophy pike during this time, work the lake side of weed beds. Once again, large spinner baits such as a Weedcutter and large spoons work best. As is the case in the earlier time slot, surface lures and giant crank baits work during this time. Late day is best for surface lures. Colors in plugs selected should be fire mackerel, whitefish, chartreuse, or red-and-white.

Grayling, though they'll soon be returning into deep lake water, are still feeding on hatching insects. Use dry and weighted nymph flies in dark colors for best results. Those using spinning gear can now use a float/bubble and fly combo or small French spinners and jigs to catch this colorful fish of the north. Work the areas of fast water that may be available or the lake side of stony lake reefs in a water depth of ten feet or more.

Our 1997 trip was completed on the fourth day when Anne and I got into grayling and giant whitefish in the big rapids above the Wholdaia outpost. We caught fish on fly and spinning gear. The whitefish were found below the rapids in the large eddies, while the grayling came from the fast rapid areas. Once we had taken a couple dozen fish, I allowed my fly to trail behind the boat. This turned out to be a special lazy technique. For another hour, as the sun settled toward the West, Anne and I trolled flies through the rapids areas of the Big Rapids, while slowly motoring upstream. It worked to the tune of thirteen more fish. The fly we used was a number 12 Muddler Fly.

A full moon greeted the two of us the last night of our stay and return to Wholdaia. It rose orange gold at first, then gradually brightened into a fire-white ball of illuminating light (with an eerie shadow-manufacturing brightness) that lit up the island and its outpost camp.

Though years had passed since last we had visited this northern place, nothing had changed. The quiet remained. The aloneness was present, and the feeling that we two were the only people left on earth was prevalent. To punctuate the feeling, lonely calls from a pair of wolves drifted across the bay from mainland. Everything was as it had been.

For more information on the Wholdaia Camp or the Gapen lure kits, see the information provided in this book's last chapter.

Tips and Bits

of the Northern Natural World

Old Inuit food proverbs—
"Fried meat is dried meat. Boiled meat is spoiled meat. Roasted meat is superb meat."

This brings to mind the ancient inhabitants of the tundra and their favorite method of roasting meat . . . a method of roasting a whole caribou leg. A leg of caribou meat, skinned with raw meat exposed, is attached by the fetlock to a woven cord of dehaired caribou skin. The cord is soaked in water until thoroughly saturated prior to using. (See diagram for better understanding.) Next, a caribou antler horn palm is woven into the cord two feet up from where it's tied to the fetlock. The weaving continues up from the caribou horn until it's long enough to support the meat over a cooking fire.

Then, a long cooking pole is selected, and the top of the cord is attached to its end. The pole's butt is thrust into the ground and weighed down with rocks. At the same time a forked strut is thrust under the pole at a point where it will support the weight of the meaty leg. The meat is raised to a point above the fire and allowed to hang within inches of the flames. In this position, it will cook equally throughout because the largest portion of the meat is closest to the flame. The least meaty part of the leg, the fetlock area, is furthest from the flame.

The horn was inserted in the cord to act as a rotisserie engine. Because the tundra regions possess an ever-constant flow of breezes, the horn acts as a device to rotate the leg of meat. Once the cord is twisted to a point where it can no longer rotate one way, it reverses and unwinds in the opposite direction. This process is constant until the leg is removed. One might call the Inuits' method of cooking large portions of meat . . . the *original rotisserie*!

Tips and Bits

In the north where spruce trees are found in abundance, the pitch they exude can be used for a repairing material. It is an ideal natural rod ferrell cement, however, it must first be melted by fire before applying.

This same pitch can be used as a cement, or glue, for patching a boat or canoe should it be damaged. To use the pitch, a handful of pitch balls must be gathered from the spruce tree trunk, heated until they begin to melt and applied to the edge of the broken area or leak in the watercraft. Next, a piece of birch bark must be obtained from a nearby birch tree. Cut this piece so that it covers the hole with an overlap of at least an inch. Press this bark into the the pitch. With another piece of birch bark and more softened pitch, apply a patch to the outside of the watercraft, making sure the pitch also adheres to the bark on the inside of the craft.

Once these two patches dry together, apply a liberal amount of melted pitch to the bottom patch, covering it completely with spruce resin so that it extends beyond the patch by at least an inch. Allow this to dry for about thirty minutes before putting the watercraft back in the water.

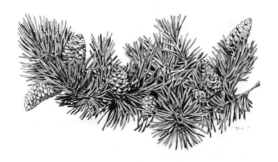

278

Chapter 34

The Gapens

A brilliant shaft of January moonlight settled across freshly fallen snow on the old logging road. Thousands of sparkling diamonds glittered upward, their lightforce enhanced by the freshly fallen snow. To either side of the snow-clogged trail, huge Norway pines reached upward to a star-filled sky. Shadows, created by the moonlight, came and went as ghostly clouds drifted across the full moon. It was cold, frosty cold.

From downtrail came a faint hissing and crunching of the snow crust intermingled with a hushed panting. The sounds persisted, becoming louder with each cloud passage. Next came the muffled sound of a human voice encouraging someone or something.

"Thata boy, Klondike! Mush up! We'll be there before you know it, fella." The words of encouragement came faint and soft.

Suddenly, from around the bend where the portage to Northern Light Lake departed the trail, came a team of sleigh dogs, a huge husky in the lead. Lead dog, Klondike, was followed by four others: Ginger, Kazan, Fanny, and Ben, all slant-eyed Alaskan Malamutes.

Behind the team of five ran a shallow-boxed sleigh, its runners waxed slick with beaver fat. Within the sleigh, covered with a huge bearskin blanket, a woman and a nine-month-old child. Resting one foot on the trailing left runner, the other foot forcefully pushing off the hard snow track, stood a man of medium stature.

"Betsey, we'll be home in thirty minutes. Mom and Dad should have a roaring fire going in the lodge fireplace," encouraged the young man, who now began to trot behind the sleigh as the dogs labored to breech the upward slope of a hill.

Reaching hilltop, the man hopped aboard the runners. This time he'd rest a bit as the sleigh raced downhill. Twice the man's hand pushed forward on the snow brake, a crude, wooden stick (attached to the sleigh's box edge), which dug deep into snow surface when forced forward.

Two more hills, then around a bend, and there before them was Hungry Jack Lake and the welcome kerosene lights of Gateway Lodge. Home was but a half mile away, nestled between tall, blackened pines on a point one third of the way down the ice-covered lake.

That is the way it was in 1933 on the Gunflint Trail. Winter travel was restricted to dog team and sleigh. Don and Betsey Gapen, my dad and mom, had made a run to the small coastal town of Grand Marais for supplies and to visit friends. The trip measured thirty-three miles one way and took a total time of ten hours in good sleighing conditions, twelve to thirteen when conditions were rough.

Reaching the log-constructed resort cabin, Don unshackled the dogs, tipped the sleigh on its side to prevent freeze in, and hurried into the warmth of his parents' cabin. As predicted, there was a roaring fire in the all-stone fireplace. The cabin glowed in yellow light from a number of candles and two kerosene lamps. The smell of burning pine permeated the room. The couple and their small child were instantly wrapped in a couple of huge handmade quilts.

Sue and Jesse Gapen, Don's parents, guided the pair to a deer-skin-covered, diamond-willow-framed couch that sat before the handmade stone and rock fireplace. Here they'd sit and sip hot coffee and warm their chilly bodies.

Jesse and Sue Gapen, my grandparents, had come to northeastern Minnesota from Monroe, Wisconsin, in 1918 to build the first log resort on the Gunflint Trail. Being an ardent trout fisherman, Jesse had traveled to this remote area two years previously to challenge the native brook trout population, which seemed to swim in every stream. So good was the native brookie fishing that Jesse decided a resort would provide a good living for his family.

Besides the brook trout, the lakes teemed with lake trout and a land-locked salmon species. Today that fish would be called a splake, a cross between a lake trout and a brook trout. In the 1920s, there were no walleye or smallmouth bass in the waters along the Gunflint Trail. They came later via planting.

The Gapens arrived with their possessions during the summer of 1918. With them came a team of farm horses to be used to pull and skid the huge Norway pine logs, which would make up the framework of the main lodge and the original six cabins.

That first summer was spent in three large, white canvas-wall tents. The first cabin built was the home cabin, which remains today, as it was then, directly across from the main lodge. It was finished in late fall just as the first snow fell.

Once moved into the cabin, things would go easier. The cabin held Jesse and Sue, their two sons—Don and Bob, and four work men they'd hired to help erect the resort. It was cramped, but considering the alternative—sleeping in tents throughout a bitter cold northern Minnesota winter—it was heaven. Sue did the cooking for all.

It took most of the cold winter months to gather the ninety- to 115-foot-long logs needed for the framework of the main lodge. They had to be cut, peeled, and then dragged over the winter ice of the lake and several other nearby lakes. At that time, none of the lakes had

English-language names. Once at the lodge site, the huge logs were rolled and wrestled into position for easy raising in the spring.

The crew lived mainly off moose meat, potatoes, onions, carrots, and rutabagas. During the previous summer, a root cellar had been constructed. Here all the food for winter had been stored. The root cellar had been built at the west end of the area that would hold the main lodge. It would be used up until the time electricity came to Gateway/Hungry Jack Lodge.

In those early years, northeastern Minnesota housed very few whitetail deer, while moose were the main meat staple for trappers and loggers. Trapping was a way of life, and packs of wolves were everywhere.

Jesse, during the fall of 1921, hired a shipwright by the name of Jack Logan. Jack was a man small in stature, so small that he'd worked in the Duluth shipworks as the man delegated to crawl up into the wooden boat's bow and stern to clinch the copper nails and rivets that held these commercial fishing boats together.

It would be Jack's job to construct the resort's furniture. In the end, every chair, table, couch, and bed in the Gapens' resort was handmade from animal skins, mainly deer and moose, and diamond willow, a native tree of great beauty.

During the winter of 1921, an overheated wood stove exploded and threw wood sparks out, which set the main lodge ablaze. Within four hours the main lodge building, with all its Norway pine logs, burned to the ground. The blaze began near midnight in late December. The crew had been using the woodstove to dry out the inner beams of the main lodge.

They would have to start all over again. But, this time it wouldn't be as hard, The crew knew what to do and where to look for the right timber. Besides, there were three cabins built by now, making it easier to house the crew, which had grown to seven.

By early April enough timber had been gathered, and as spring rolled in, a new main structure was erected. All logs were rolled into place by a block and tackle with horse and man power. Skidding a ninety-five-foot log up into a position ten feet above ground isn't an easy trick. It takes skill and power. The logs weighed in excess of a ton each. Surprisingly, by the fall of 1922, the main lodge was completed, and six cabins had been framed in.

Tourists had come the previous summer, staying in the first two cabins finished, and the three original tents. The added money they brought was badly needed by the Gapens to pay help and buy supplies.

There was one other source of money for the Gapens. Trapping and the furs it provided were paying well during those days. A fisher pelt was fifty dollars in 1922, sixty-five dollars by 1929. The hills around the lodge abounded in fisher, marten, and mink. Also, beaver and otter were abundant in the area's waterways, and payment for these pelts averaged five to ten dollars.

Young Bob, with help from his older brother, Don, did most of the family trapping. During the winter of 1923, the boys collected enough pelts to bring in $2,850.00 to help the family. Trading was done at the trading post in Grand Marais. In those days, that much money was more than a year's salary.

Most of the boys' trapping was done around the lakes now known as Moss, Bearskin, Dunkin, and Hungry Jack. The mode of travel was always snowshoes or dog sleigh. Bob Gapen, the youngest son, shot his first deer at age fourteen. It was the first deer the family gathered in those early years. The date was February 1, 1923. Bob had been on his way back from Dunkin Lake after checking his traps when he encountered the deer. In those years, there was little need to observe conservation laws. Not when survival was at stake. The skin was saved, processed, and used for chair covering.

Later Bob would earn his way to college—West Point—with money earned by trapping.

His deer may have been the first shot in that area, but it wouldn't be the last. From that point on, deer became more plentiful, while the moose population declined. With logging and forest fires' intervention, the mature forests had begun to disappear. The switch in deer and moose populations was a natural occurrence. Whitetail deer always flourish when mature timber disappears, and new growth begins. The big fire near Dunkin and Polar Lakes probably did the most to bring deer into the area.

Hungry Jack Lake and the lodge received their name the winter of 1923 when an especially bad storm held the Gapens up at Grand Marais. They had gone to town on two dog teams. Jack had been left behind to finish up a furniture project. The camp had run low on food, which necessitated the trip into town.

As the two sleighs came into sight of the lodge, there was Jack, running out on the lake, waving his arms in greeting.

"Are you hungry, Jack?" yelled Jesse as they neared the happy man running toward them.

"You bet Jack is hungry! This is a hungry Jack, for sure," replied the talented wood carver.

Thus, the lake on which sat the largest log structure in Minnesota got its name. Later the Pillsbury family from Minneapolis, Minnesota, became regulars at the resort. The result of this was to see the famous Pillsbury "Hungry Jack" pancake mix named after the lake and resort. I might add that Grandma Sue was famous for her breakfast pancakes.

Gateway Lodge, or Hungry Jack Lodge, as some wish to call it, opened officially to the fishing public in 1923. All three Gapen men guided. Jesse, my grandfather, was a trout specialist, while my dad, Don Gapen, and my Uncle Bob guided those who sought landlocks, lake trout, and northern pike which the lakes surrounding the lodge held.

Father met Mother in 1928. They were married in 1929, and I came along in 1932. Mother's father had moved from Minnesota's

Iron Range where he was the first bus driver for the Greyhound bus line. Granddad Jackson had the route from Duluth to Grand Marais for a starter.

It was Granddad Jackson's contact with the northern world at Grand Marais that soon took grandmother and him into the resort business, an industry that had begun to flourish on the Gunflint Trail.

The days of logging had departed, and any resort operation could make a respectable living for the people who had the nerve to start up. Harley and Eva Jackson bought a small cabin on a lake twenty miles north of Grand Marais. From that meager start, a five-cabin housekeeping operation blossomed. It would last until 1939 when mother's father got wanderlust once again.

Grandpa Jackson was that way. Maybe it came from his father-in-law who logged the Arrowhead country of Minnesota back in the early 1900s. Great Granddad Dumas made and lost fortunes in the logging business several times. It's claimed that most of his money was lost on ladies. Records show he was a millionaire six times over. But, as with many a great man, the ladies of the night were his downfall. He died penniless in 1917.

Living off the land and the fishermen who came north, the Gapen family managed to carve out a decent existence through the late 1920s and early 1930s. In 1935, spurred by rumors of huge brook trout, Jesse Gapen and his son, Don, headed north, across the Canadian border to the town of Nipigon. The trip took two days. Roads between Grand Marais and Nipigon were rough and winding, constructed of gravel only. Today this same trip would take a mere three hours.

In Nipigon they had the opportunity to contact the operators of Chalet Bungalow Lodge, a premier resort run by the Canadian National Railway. It was one of three jewel resorts they owned— Baniff, Chalet, and a resort in Quebec.

Customers, for the most part, came from Europe via the CNR's steamship line and railway on summer packages that would last as long as three months. Much of Europe's royalty passed through the doors of Chalet Bungalow, especially those who liked fishing.

Granddad Jesse and my father fell instantly in love with the area and the trophy brook trout fishing. Therefore, it was natural for the Gapens to jump on the opportunity when they learned the Chalet would be put up for sale in 1936. The Canadian National Railway wanted nothing to do with a resort that was about to have a road pass within a half mile of its doors. In 1935 the Canadian government had begun to build the huge bridge that would span the Nipigon River and allow for the road around giant Lake Superior to continue east.

In 1936 the Gapens bought the Chalet. Mother and Father and their four-year-old son moved north to reopen the Chalet under new management. Instead of the European tourists, the resort turned to the United State and its hoards of eager anglers.

The world record brook trout was taken seven miles from the Chalet in1929 by a Doc Cook. Such publicity created an instant surge of anglers. Along with the fishing public that had visited the Gapens' resort on the Gunflint Trail, there now came a whole new clientele. The Nipigon watershed contained some of the finest walleye, northern pike, and lake trout fishing known at that time. Add this to the world's best brook trout angling, and one can only imagine the rush to fish this new area.

Nipigon was a natural for the Gapens. Jesse Gapen was a fly tier, a talent passed down to his son, Don. In 1937, my father, Don Gapen, created the original Muddler Fly, today known as the world's greatest trout fly.

To learn more about the Muddler and Don Gapen, refer to the book, Wilderness North, *where Dan Gapen, Sr., shares the story of the original Muddler.*

By the beginning of World War II, the Gapens' new venture was flourishing. But, as with so many businesses related to outdoor recreation, the tourist business ended in 1942. There were a few diehards, but the gas rationing killed the ability to travel for many.

Once again the family went back to living off the land. My father, Don Gapen, joined the United States Air Force transportation corps and spent much of the war ferrying and preparing aircraft for transport. The United States had several bases in Canada, and he was assigned to these.

The war finally ended. Dad came home, and we once again went back into the tourist business. By then I'd become more of a man and had been gathering the winter meat, mostly moose, for the family, as well as taking Dad's place for the few tourists who did manage to spend a bit of time fishing.

My father, Don, had bestowed the art of fly tying on me when I was six years old. By age eight, I was tying commercially to earn my winter spending money. During the war years, this came in handy. Tourists who had visited our resort prior to the war continued to order flies such as the Muddler throughout this period.

Prior to going off to war, Dad had begun a fly-tying operation, using native girls from the local reservation. Mom and I managed to keep this going. It would supplement our income and allow us to maintain a certain quality of living.

Back in the resort business, with customers who had saved money throughout the war years, we flourished. Now, instead of business-men, doctors, and lawyers, our business base shifted to people such as the Iowa and Illinois farmers. They all seemed to have money saved and were willing to spend it on much-needed vacations. Now, even though brook trout were still a goodly portion of our business, the new clientele wanted any kind of fish—the bigger, the better. Northern pike and walleye became the fish of choice. They were carted back to Iowa, Minnesota, and Illinois by the boxload.

At age fourteen, I began guiding. The resort accommodated sixty-five people, American plan. Our staff consisted of twenty-two people. We had on line twenty-nine guides, three of them white, the rest natives from the nearby reservation. Names such as George Cheboyer, Dan Martin, Michelle Daba, John Cheboyer, and John Lica flood back to my mind as I remember those days. They were all guides who taught me the art of good guiding. They all had worked for the old owners of the Chalet and guided many of the European royalty such as the Duke of Edinburgh and the Duchess of Kent.

During the war, the once proud and majestic Nipigon River had been dammed, and in 1947, two more dams were planned. In the end, the world's greatest brook trout resource disappeared under the need for electricity. Dad fought to save the river, but as with so many who try to preserve our natural resources, he failed. The Canadian government refused to look to the future.

It was at Chalet Bungalow that northern Ontario's first fly-in tourist services began. Superior Airways, a freight contractor with planes on floats, stationed a Norseman and Gull Wing Stinson on floats at our resort for the summer of 1946. This enabled us to travel far into the north where fishing was at its best. We did have restrictions. No plane was allowed to fly above the Albany River. There was no search and rescue for a plane forced down above that latitude.

It was during the late 1940s that writers such as Joe Brooks of *Outdoor Life* magazine fame and A.J. McClaine of *Field & Stream* magazine came to test the world-famous brook trout fishing. Writers weren't the only dignitaries. John Hodak of Paul Bunyan Lure Company and Charlie Staff of Prescott Spinner Company came to work our fishery. It was from a lure my father created, the NEPAG, that John invented the famous Paul Bunyan 66, the original forward spinner lure.

It was Charlie Staff who gave me one of my proudest memories. One morning he came into our fly-tying cabin, the one where Dad had the native ladies from the reservation tying flies. Charlie asked me to tie up a heavily dressed Cockatush for him (Cockatush means Sculpin minnow in Objiwa). I did it, and later that day he came back up from having fished the river. He had a six-and-one-half-pound brookie caught on the very fly I'd tied. Charlie then commenced to parade me around the dining room, telling everyone that he'd caught that fish on the fly I tied for him. What a thrill it was for a fifteen-year-old boy!

Ted Williams, of baseball fame, came to our resort and became one of my father's lifelong friends. As a matter of fact, it was my father, Don Gapen, and Joe Brooks who taught Ted to fly fish. Later, Dad, Joe, and Ted would purchase homes in Islamorada, Florida, next to one another. All three loved to catch bonefish. In 1956, the bonefish of the Florida Keys was *the* species to fish if you were any kind of a fisherman.

I further remember the time an *Outdoor Life* magazine filming crew came to the lodge to film Nipigon's brook trout. Their luck hadn't been too great, and when asked by my dad to show them a seven and one-half pounder I'd taken in the river the night before, I happily obliged. Much to my surprise, they decided to use it in their film. It would be my first experience with how some films are made. Do you know that the crew actually attached that dead trout, after dousing it in Coca Cola, to a fly, and the hero of the film landed my *dead* fish!

I was later to see the film and be amazed at what a great job the editor did. It is a lesson I would not forget and one I would never practice. If the fish I filmed wasn't caught in real life, there's no way I would ever rehook a fish, let alone a dead one, for the camera.

One other time, when the national trap and skeet shooting champion of Canada came to our resort to hunt ducks, I was asked to help. For reasons I still can't understand, this fellow couldn't hit a duck. Dad suggested I hide behind the bushes where the two of them had set up for a blind. We shot mostly black ducks in the Nipigon region during those days. As the ducks settled in, my job was to shoot at nearly the same time as this world-famous gunner. Thus my duck became his duck. For a sixteen-year-old kid, this was quite an honor. It also made great bragging when I returned to school that winter.

Looking back at those years, I now realize we harvested too many fish, an action for which we all pay now. In defense of this, I can only tell my readers that in those days, there were no biologists to tell us we were depleting the population or that big fish wouldn't come forever. I can remember several incidents that reveal how we thought about fish in those earlier days.

It became a sign of pride for the guides at our resort to take the most and biggest fish with their fishing parties. The summer of 1949 I caught and killed, from a single lake, 179 pike over fifteen pounds. They came from Frazer Lake, a small eleven-mile long body of water. This feat was accomplished in sixty-seven days of guiding on Frazer. Today it still contains trophy pike, but the majority of fish continue to average around three to five pounds. This number, 179, doesn't include the rest of the fifteen-pound-plus pike taken from this lake by our other guides. In all, I'm sure there were over 500 in total. Within four years of opening up Frazer Lake, the trophy fish declined rapidly, and we were catching only small shakers, fish between one and three pounds. We had literally fished the lake out of nature's balance.

Another incident that reminds me of an over-fishing problem was the enormous catches of northern pike taken from the mouths of the rivers that flowed into Lake Superior along the north shore between Nipigon and a small fishing town called Schreiber.

Following the annual sucker run, huge pike would flood the mouths of these rivers. Most of the rivers had weed growths at their mouths at lake side and a block or so upriver. It was here, in the weed patch edges, that pike would ambush the migration of suckers. Once again, we, who guided then, returned every fish under fifteen pounds, keeping only the largest.

I remember one party of six businessmen from Minneapolis. They caught forty-two pike over nineteen pounds, the largest thirty-four pounds. The picture taken of this group and its guides, myself included, was published on the front page of the *Minneapolis Star and Tribune*. As guides we were thrilled, to say the least. Never before had our operation received such publicity. Fishermen came for years after, expecting the same results. That large a catch was never taken again.

Within five years, the fishery, born in Lake Superior, dropped off dramatically. Over fishing and pollutants from a paper mill nearly killed Nipigon Bay of its trophy pike population. The mill was built in 1947, about the time we discovered the fishery. In 1952, it had all but disappeared. Today you can still catch a few big pike in these river mouths, but it will never be as it was in 1948.

During my years at the resort on the Nipigon River, I had the opportunity to learn the ways of the wilderness through the best teachers in the world, the native Indians who know it best. I shot my first moose, bear, deer, caribou, and wolf. I landed trophy lake trout, walleye, northern pike, brook trout, sturgeon, and rainbow trout. It was the best of worlds for the young white boy who grew to be a man in the toughest, yet best, of the outdoor world. It was a world never to come again . . . for today, in the world of computers, no such existence remains.

By the time I was twenty-one, I'd killed thirteen moose and four deer for food. I had been forced to rid our property of forty-nine bear and countless wolves. I had caught a forty-nine-pound lake trout, an eight-pound twelve-ounce brook trout, a ten-pound walleye, an eighty-five-pound sturgeon, and six northerns over thirty pounds, the largest—38.5 pounds.

I'd run a trapline on which I had taken mink, fisher, beaver, marten, otter, and lynx. I was a very lucky young man. What other young man of today has the opportunity to learn and blend with nature in such a manner?

Many know the rest of the story. This writer, Dan Gapen, restarted the lure business in Minneapolis, Minnesota, in 1962. The Muddler Fly, which my father created, was much in demand, and many wanted only the original fly. At that time, jigs were just beginning to take hold in the fishing world. They'd been introduced by Bill Upperman, during the second world war, as a lure that would easily catch salt water fish. Each survival kit placed in aircraft that crossed open water, had to be equipped with a kit for each flyer.

Our first jig was one we called Hairy Worm and Hairy Worm Plus. The "plus" was added to the name by a friend of mine, Bill Scifres of the *Indianapolis Star*, one day while fishing Monroe Reservoir in southern Indiana. I had placed a jig spinner on the Hairy Worm jig and asked Bill what it should be called.

He responded with "Hairy Worm plus . . . uh, plus . . . plus . . . oh, Gapen, just call it Hairy Worm Plus, and leave it at that!" We did, and that was three years before the Alka Seltzer people came out with Alka Seltzer Plus.

Next came the Ugly Bug jig in 1965. The hot little jig caught all fish species that hit on crawfish or hellgrammites. Eight years later, the Shakespeare Company would come out with a line of rods called Ugly Sticks. The Ugly Bug brought with it the first wedge-shaped leadhead that walked rock bottom in a snagfree manner.

Today the Gapen Company stills exists. They specialize in lures that are not of the ordinary . . . lures that catch fish. I, the author of the book, spend much time angling and exploring the land of my youth. Yes, Canada, with her endless wilderness, draws me back each year to challenge just one more fishery and one more trophy fish. It will be that way till I pass on to the other world.

Dad, Mom, and all my grandparents have already gone, leaving behind a legacy that can never be repeated. In their time it wasn't anything different, but looking back, I feel the foundation I received was one I'd never trade.

My wish is that each and every child growing up today could experience what I lived in those early years. Were it possible, I'm sure our world would be a better place because of it.

Tips and Bits
OF THE NORTHERN NATURAL WORLD

The Northern Red Fox

Most people recognize the red fox as the one seen on farmland chasing chickens or mice and measuring twenty to thirty inches in length, with a reddish coat and gray to black leggings. In the far north, this same red fox measures twenty-five to forty inches in length and can be a number of colors. The silver fox is really a red fox, as is the cross fox. Far northern foxes are treasured for their fur more than foxes are south of the border in the States. The hair of the northern foxes taken in heavy winter conditions is longer and the texture is finer.

Trappers in the far north use an unusual technique to lure trap-wise red foxes. Once a trap is set, usually on an isolated clump of grass in an open field or on a frozen lake, the trapper relieves himself, urinating on or within two feet of the trap. This is the scent that draws the ever-curious red fox to the set. It is a case of curiosity killing the fox, so to speak.

Chapter 35

The

Trout

Hole

"Dan, this fish slammed that blue Crankmaster hard. And it feels really heavy. No normal twisting like those small lakers we've been catching closer to shore," commented my fishing companion, "Bobber" Anne, as she heaved back on the seven-foot rod.

Steadily, she worked the unseen fish closer to the boat, lifting hard on the rod one moment, then picking up line as the rod was allowed to lower. Whatever it was—a lake trout we presumed—had to be fairly large, for it wasn't giving in easily. The fight was steady and deep.

Once directly beneath the boat, the heavy fish gave way a bit and allowed itself to be lifted to within fifteen feet of the surface.

"Lordy lordy, Anne, that's the biggest fish of the trip so far," I commented as the trophy turned sideways and took off.

This run, his first, went deep and out towards the open lake. Considering that we sat on a slope that went from thirty-two feet into 250 feet of water, there was no telling how deep or how far the run might go. Finally, after a pulsing run, which started slow, then gained speed and eventually slacked off after 120 feet of line disappeared, the fish stopped. Here, the laker held steady and sulked. There seemed to be no way of prying him loose from the deep water hole, no matter how hard Anne reefed on the rod. This fish may be larger than the forty-five pounder she boated one year earlier off Russian Reef.

"Phillip, better get a move on and follow that fish," I suggested.

Phillip was our native guide, a somewhat lackadaisical person. Old in years, he had a habit of drifting off in thought, even when there was a fish on.

Startled by my instructions, Phillip turned the boat lakeward and began to follow Anne's line. The locator registered 135 feet when we pulled up directly over the fish.

"Dan, that last tug I gave him caused him to begin to move again. He seems to be moving inshore once more," Anne commented after she had hit the large fish a couple of times with a heavy jerk on the rod.

Sure enough, the trout was on the move once again, but instead of going toward shore, he was paralleling the 135-foot mark. As best we could tell, he swam close to the 100-foot depth mark.

Anne continued to raise and lower her rod in a heavy pulling action that seemed to gather some reel line back. Then, as if irritated about the whole thing, her fish took off shoreward in a surface rising run. Two hundred feet off our bow, the lake surface boiled heavily as the trophy trout breached. It had to be a good fish. Never had I seen a laker act this way unless it was thirty-five pounds or more.

The fight became easier at this point. The runs were shorter, and finally, with the fish directly below the boat, a prolonged series of air bubbles erupted to the surface. That was the sign we had awaited. The monster beneath us had tired and soon would be netted. Less than a minute after the bubbles surfaced, Anne's trophy rolled at boatside and was netted by Phillip. On the scales, the fish reached 41.5 pounds, not as big as the previous year's trophy but a huge fish nonetheless. With pictures taken, the fish was released after a considerable amount of coaxing. It had been a tough fight for both parties.

Unlike the year before, Anne and I had come to Lake Athabasca earlier in the season. The best lake trout window on this premier lake trout lake runs from June 1 to July 25. After that, northern pike become the target of choice. Today was July 1.

Today we fished one mile off the mouth of the McFarlane River, direction northwest by north. Water depth, where trout held, ranged from thirty to thirty-six feet. The large trout Anne had taken came from a small outcrop structure, pear-shaped in appearance, which jutted out into the deep-water area of the giant hole descending into the main lake off the McFarlane River Reef. Previous to hitting the trophy, Anne and I had taken two other lakers of trophy size, one twenty-two pounds, the other a twenty pounder. These two fish, plus a huge one that broke Anne's thirty-pound Fireline the instant her gaudy yellow, polka-dotted Crankmaster plug hit the surface.

As the boat had come to a standstill while I had boated the twenty-two pounder, Anne had casted back toward the drop. Impatience and silliness had caused my partner to heave the large bait back over the thirty-two-foot shelf as my trophy was being netted by Phillip. It became instantly obvious, as the line snapped the instant the bait was pulled under, that a large fish struck the bait going in the opposite direction to that of the lure retrieve. There was a huge boil, a loud crack as the line snapped, and a "Damn," as Anne voiced her amazement at being broken off. I can't say it was all Anne's fault, for these new Kevlar lines tend to break easily if their outer cloth coating becomes worn or frayed. One must always check to see that this hasn't happened prior to fishing. If the line appears white or fuzzy, cut the troubled portion of the line off.

With the twenty-two pounder released, we began the trolling pattern along the structure drop that would bring the strike of the 41.5-pound trophy Anne would eventually land.

July 1, 1998, would see more lake trout over twenty pounds boated. Our second largest, a thirty-six pounder, was taken by this angler on the same style blue-backed Crankmaster. All twelve of our large lakers were taken on either blue or green Crankmaster plugs. It became obvious that Athabasca harbored a baitfish that resembed this oversized ten-inch sunfish-shaped Crankmaster. The fact that the Crankmaster dove to a depth of near thirty-five feet may have also contributed to its success. Each time we felt the bait touch bottom or stop touching bottom and swim off into the deeper water, we seemed to be rewarded with a strike. Even more surprising were the numbers of small lake trout taken on the oversized bait. A number of five to ten pounders were caught and released before we hit the pocket on the pear-shaped outcrop where the large fish seemed to have gathered. In all, we released five fish over thirty pounds that day.

Lake Athabasca stretches 200 miles east to west from the small native settlement of Stony Rapids to the western edge where the Peace River enters and the Slave River exits. At its widest point, south of Uranium City, the lake widens to sixty miles in width. There aren't a lot of islands in Athabasca, but the central area hosts a north-to-south structure, the Russian Reef, which protrudes south from a large group of north-shore-hugging islands for a distance of nearly thirty miles. The maximum depth in Athabasca is 459 feet, a large hole in the western basin. From this hole the largest lake trout was obtained, captured in a commercial net and weighed 109 pounds. There are a number of 250-foot holes that dot the massive body of water. In between these structures the lake bottom rises and lowers around deepwater reefs that come within fifty to sixty feet of the surface. The open lake doesn't lack for rocky, lake trout-holding structures. The major baitfish on which lake trout feed are the hordes of native whitefish, ciscos, and lake shiners that roam its open-water areas.

Unlike so many other lake trout lakes in the far north, Athabasca hosts a wide variety of gamefish. Walleye, northern pike, lake trout, whitefish, sturgeon, and grayling all can be found within its system. Three varieties of suckers, as well as eelpout, are all part of this huge lake's ecosystem. On any day, an angler can expect to catch four of these—the lake trout, walleye, northern pike, and Arctic grayling. But it is the lake trout that reigns king of the lake. Even after several years of extensive commercial netting (see Chapter 13), when the take was in excess of a million pounds each year, Athabasca remains a staple lake trout producer. In my opinion, this lake is the best producer of medium-sized (between twenty and thirty-five pounds) trophy lake trout in the continent.

Several factors lend to this observation. The lake sits below the treeline, thus nutrients flowing into the main lake via the multitude of rivers which feed Athabasca form a staple base for the aquatic food chain. Because Athabasca rests below the sixtieth parallel, it has a longer growing season than many of the believed trophy lake trout waters of the far north. Due to its size, it gets little fishing pressure from anglers, tourist or native. No longer is the lake commercially netted. Even the native communities along its shore resist commercially netting its waters. If they net, it is for food only. Athabasca has the tremendous volume of deep water needed to host a hardy breeding population of lake trout. The fact that there is but one active tourist resort, Athabasca Lodges, on the lake also helps. This operation, run by Stella and Cliff Blackmur, has practiced catch and release from their beginning in 1973. This too has been a major factor. Yes, Athabasca just doesn't get enough fishing pressure to see its lake trout population decline. It just may be the best lake trout lake in all of North America.

The eastern end of Athabasca, into which the Fond Du Lac River runs, is narrow and riverlike. This thirty-five-mile-long stretch of water is no more than eight miles wide at its widest point and is dotted with countless numbers of rocky, tree-covered islands. It is here that some of the lake's best walleye fishing is found. This region of the lake is also noted for its northern pike population but does have a healthy number of lake trout. Not as many trophy-sized lakers are taken here when compared to the wider open area of Athabasca to the west. However, in late fall and very early spring, the resort records a dozen or so trophy trout a week caught and released on the more open pockets of this narrow eastern end. The main reason lake trout don't play as big a part of the eastern fishery is because these waters warm up much faster than the lake's central and western end. This is due to the number of warm-water rivers that dump into the eastern end. Even so, the eastern end has provided this angler with some excellent trout fishing. During the first two weeks of August, by trolling the deeper water with devices such as a ten-ounce Bait Walker Sinker and a flashy spoon behind, the angler can catch lake trout. In one area, five miles from Athabasca Lodge, in August 1997, my fishing partner "Bobber" Anne and I managed to catch and release fifteen lakers in one afternoon. They were spotted on the graph at sixty to eighty feet of water, working over a 140-foot deep hole. By slow trolling a seven-inch silver and copper spoon behind the Bait Walker, we managed a decent afternoon of trout angling. Shore lunch that day consisted of fried lake trout fillets, fried potatoes, and baked beans. And, yes, it was good!

Athabasca abounds in history and natural wonders. It hosts America's most northern desert (see Chapter 18). Athabasca is home to two native villages, one in the northeast—Fond Du Lac—and another at the west end—Fort Chipewyan. See Chapter 12 for a bit of this area's native history. On the north end, Athabasca is dotted with deserted gold and uranium mines. Names such as Eldorado, Gunnar, Uranium City, and Bushiet are steeped in history of mining operations long deserted by their founders. One day, while inspecting the old Gunnar mine, Anne and I were shocked to see tons of yellow sulphur left behind in a walled open trench. Old machinery, buildings, narrow-track rails, and storage facilities sat as they had been left forty years before. Nothing much had changed, not even the normal rusting and rotting processes had set in significantly. Everything lay as it had been deserted years before, millions upon millions of dollars worth of material goods, abandoned to those who might have a use for it. It was evidence that greedy white men had come, raped and pillaged the land, then left as suddenly as they had arrived, a common practice in the north.

Today, all the outsiders are gone; only the natives remain. Gone are hard-hat miners who searched for gold and dug for uranium. Gone are the Russian fishermen who might have depleted the waters of Athabasca of its true treasure, the lake trout. Gone is the massive houseboat that once roamed the lake's shoreline in search of trophy fish. Once a going operation, the giant houseboat run by two brothers from Minneapolis, Minnesota, with its dozen metal fishing boats has long since rotted away, a result of mismanagement and greed. Only the natives and Blackmur's Athabasca Lodge remain. They remain because they blend together, one leaning on the other. Instead of attempting to commercially net the monstrous lake, the natives of Fond Du Lac have become consultants and guides for the lodge operation. If the Russians found commercial fishing unprofitable, certainly to do so today would remain as fruitless as it was thirty years ago. Why fight this wilderness with modern ways or thinking? Allow nature to show the way. Respect the land and live off it by taking only what you can use and giving back when it's needed. Here, in this land of open water, rock, and millions of trees, it is the old ways that will see the human species survive.

Athabasca Lodge sits on the southern shore, near an incoming river, off the lake's southeastern arm. Walleyes abound throughout the summer just off the dock, next to the incoming river's current break. There are twelve cabins, a main lodge where guests are fed, and several outbuildings for storage and employees quarters. It is a modest operation, built by Cliff and Stella through years of hard work and dedication. The atmosphere is cheery and friendly, the way you would expect a tourist operation should be. The food is excellent, and why not—Stella and her sister do the cooking. A single-propeller Otter float plane sits tied to the dock, ready on a daily basis to ferry anglers to the hidden secret fishing spots Athabasca has to offer, spots that might not otherwise be available due to the weather the large lake can muster up. Beside the plane, a high horse-power Cruiser lays at dockside. It is a boat that ferries anglers to the main open areas of Athabasca at a top speed of forty-eight miles an hour. No longer are the choice fishing spots a three-hour boat ride away. The Cruiser does in fifty to sixty minutes what once took a guide boat three hours. Once arriving in the open lake area, the Cruiser waits while small boats, stationed at certain points early in the spring, scurry to places like the McFarlane River mouth or Poplar Point or the Russian Reef. At these special spots lodge guests fight and boat the monster trophies Athabasca has to offer.

Athabasca Lodge is a homey place, one you might like to take your father for a late-in-life fishing trip, or a friend who had never caught a trophy fish. Though laid back in atmosphere, the lodge is a well-run operation, one that rolls along smoothly each summer through three months of operation. Despite this soft, casual atmosphere, the numbers of trophy fish taken at this lodge would amaze even the best pro fisherman. Trophy pike and lake trout by the hundreds are caught and released each season.

In 1997, south on the Russian Reef, "Bobber" Anne, my fishing companion, took the largest lake trout of her lifetime, a forty-five-pound monster. Even though it was August and weather remained hot and sunny, our guide insisted that we troll the eastern side of the reef with our deep-diving Crankmaster plugs. Anne was using a whitefish patterned plug, while I trolled a huge devil spoon. We worked the deep, forty-five-foot break. Seeing that Anne's plug ran at thirty-five feet of depth when trolled with 140 feet of line out, our native guide felt such presentation would work. I took the first two fish on the spoon, small ones, an eight and a ten pounder. I was about to suggest Anne change baits when the trophy hit. It was a hard, stubborn fight, like most trout fights, but, in the end, Anne prevailed, and the monster was boated. With pictures taken, the fish was released and we continued to troll southward far out into the lake down the reef. We had covered nearly four more miles of the reef before another trout struck; this time I did battle with the thirty-four pounder. I had changed baits to that ugly oversized Crankmaster bait like Anne was using. It paid off. In the end, we took five trophies off Russian Reef during our five-hour stay, just enough to whet our appetites for a return trip in 1998. We once again discovered the old adage remains true in the north: "Big bait means big fish."

At the beginning of this chapter, I described the fishing the two of us had one day at the mouth of the McFarlane River on the first day of July 1998. What I failed to tell was the rest of the story.

Anne and I fished the McFarlane River reef three times during our stay at Athabasca in 1998. Bad weather kept us from doing much on two other days, and on the balance of our seven-day trip, we elected to chase northern pike, which provided each of us with a forty-seven incher, about twenty-six to twenty-seven pounds. In all, the two of us caught and released off the McFarlane River reef and the reef at Poplar Point, thirty-one lake trout over twenty pounds plus an equal number of fourteen to nineteen pounders. That is excellent lake trout fishing no matter where or in what body of water you fish in North America. What we used to catch these trophies and the equipment that took them might be of interest to you, my readers. Let me fill you in.

For the most part, the largest trout were caught on a large crank bait called the "Crankmaster" in a blue or green finish. Blue seemed to work the best during daylight hours, but as soon as the sun began to recede towards the western horizon, green became the color of fashion. We did try the old favorites like the Dardevle in yellow-five-of-diamonds and silver quickfish plugs and found they worked fairly well. However, it was that huge ugly plug that produced the best results. Possibly the reason these plugs worked as well as they did was the fact that they dug into the proper feeding zone where the largest trout fed and that we had failed to present the other lures at this feeding depth. We'll never really know. When something is working well, why change?

The method of approach was trolling. Normally, vertically jigging would have been in order when lake trout are bunched up such as they were off the McFarlane River reef, but we had tried that and found that jigging didn't work at all. Even when a fish would follow one already hooked, jigging failed. There was no explanation for this. Maybe that's what makes fishing, even in a paradise like Athabasca, as interesting a sport as it is. You can't always catch fish via a similar method that worked on the trip before.

Equipment used for catching larger lakers, in both our cases, was a seven-foot, one-piece rod, medium/heavy action, mounted with a 55 Garcia 3C reel. For line, we used thirty-pound Fireline with twenty-pound monofilament backing. During the trip, a couple large fish were lost to the flawed character of the Kevlar line. As a matter of fact, because of this, I've gone back to a hard-based monofilament for trolling. Kevlar line, as mentioned previously in this chapter, tends to fray when used for any length of time, and to prevent breakage under certain conditions, the angler must be alert enough to cut off the worn part.

One-piece rods were used because of their sensitivity and shock absorbing quality. Many resorters in the north don't like one-piece rods because their cases make them difficult to store in a float plane. But if the resorter with whom you book flies an Otter float plane, they can be stored easily in the back compartment.

By the time you read this final chapter, I may have returned to Athabasca, as I plan to do for as long as I'm privileged to live on Mother Earth. Each year, God willing, I'll return to this paradise in northern Saskatchewan. As stated previously in this chapter, Lake Athabasca has to be the finest lake trout fishery in North America, bar none.

And they get bigger and bigger!

Chapter References

To obtain more information on the places, resorts, and guide services mentioned in this book, look to the following chapters.

Chapter 1.　Wholdaia Outpost is run by—
　　　　　　North of Sixty
　　　　　　14375 23rd Ave. No.
　　　　　　Plymouth, Minnesota 55447
　　　　　　612-745-7888

Chapter 2.　The Kamilukak River system can be reached by contacting—
　　　　　　Kazba Lake Lodge
　　　　　　P.O. Box 96
　　　　　　Parksville, British Columbia　V9P 2G3
　　　　　　800-663-8641
　　　　　　　and
　　　　　　North of Sixty
　　　　　　14375 23rd Ave. No.
　　　　　　Plymouth, Minnesota 55447
　　　　　　612-745-7888

Chapter 3.   The Dubawnt River system outposts are run by:
North of Sixty
14375 23rd Ave. No.
Plymouth, Minnesota 55447
612-745-7888

Chapter 4.   This chapter takes place along the northern shore of Ford Lake off Wager Bay. Further information on this area can be obtained by contacting:
Nunavut Tourism
P.O. Box 1450
Iqaluit, NT
Canada X0A 0H0
1-800-661-0788
     and
NWT Arctic Tourism
Postal Service 9600, YK Centre, Suite 310
Yellowknife, NT
Canada X1A 2R4
1-800-491-7910

Chapter 5.   This chapter, though fictional, is based on historical facts. Information on this area of the Kamilukuak River is available by contacting:
NWT Arctic Tourism
Postal Service 9600, YK Centre, Suite 310
Yellowknife, NT
Canada X1A 2R4
1-800-491-7910

Chapter 6.   Kashechewan, Ontario, goose camps are available by contacting—
Charlie Wynn's Goose Camp
P.O. Box 165
Kashechewan, Ontario P0L LS0

Chapter 7.   Information on the Goose Camp on Hudson Bay where Teto was can be had from:
Nanook Goose Camp
Frontier, Saskatchewan
Canada
306-296-4403

Chapter 8.   Information on Manitoba's goose and caribou camps can be obtained by writing:

        Manitoba Travel
        c/o Dennis Maxsymetz
        7th Floor, 155 Carlton & York
        Winnipeg, Manitoba R3C 1T5
        204-945-2292

        Dymond Lake Goose Camp
        116 Rainbow Crescent
        Thompson, Manitoba R8N 1B2
        800-665-0476

    Cookbook information available from:
        Whitewater Publications
        17910 87th St.
        Becker, Minnesota 55308
        612-263-3558

Chapter 9.   Information on Sportsman Lodge can be obtained by writing—

        Sportsman Lodge
        P.O. Box 369
        Winnipeg, Manitoba R3M 3V3
        800-668-4558

Chapter 10. For more information on pike flies and their use, write or call—

        The Gapen Company
        17910 87th St.
        Becker, Minnesota 55308
        612-263-3558

    Information on the lake is available from:
        Wollaston Lake Lodge
        322 Verlicke Road
        Saskatoon, Saskatechwan
        Canada B7K 6M3
        1-800-328-0628

Chapter 11. To obtain information on the places mentioned
in this chapter, contact—
      North of Sixty
      14375 23rd Ave. No.
      Plymouth, Minnesota 55447
      612-745-7888

Chapter 12. To obtain information on the area in which this
chapter takes place, contact—
      Athabasca Lodges
      P.O. Box 7800
      Saskatoon, Saskatchewan S7K 4R5
      306-653-5490

Chapter 13. To obtain information on the area in which this
chapter takes place, contact—
      Athabasca Lodges
      P.O. Box 7800
      Saskatoon, Saskatchewan S7K 4R5
      306-653-5490

Chapter 14. Information on this chapter can be obtained from:
      Athabasca Lodges
      P.O. Box 7800
      Saskatoon, Saskatchewan S7K 4R5
      306-653-5490

Chapter 16. Information on this chapter's sites is available from:
      North of Sixty
      14375 23rd Ave. No.
      Plymouth, Minnesota 55447
      612-745-7888

Chapter 18. Information on Saskatchewan's desert is available from:
      Saskatchewan Tourism
      500 -1900 Albert St.
      Regina, Saskatchewan S4P 4L9
      800-667-7191
        and
      Athabasca Lodges
      P.O. Box 7800
      Saskatoon, Saskatchewan S7K 4R5
      306-653-5490

Chapter 20.　For more information on whitefish, contact:
　　　　　　　The Gapen Company
　　　　　　　P.O. Box 10
　　　　　　　Big Lake, Minnesota 55309
　　　　　　　612-263-3558

Chapter 21.　For more information on the Wager Bay area, contact:
　　　　　　　Sila Lodge
　　　　　　　c/o Frontier North
　　　　　　　P.O. Box 630
　　　　　　　Rankin Inlet, NWT XOC 0G0
　　　　　　　800-663-9832

Chapter 22.　More information on hunting Manitoba's west
　　　　　　　is available by contacting:
　　　　　　　Manitoba Travel
　　　　　　　c/o Dennis Maxsymetz
　　　　　　　7th Floor, 155 Carlton & York
　　　　　　　Winnipeg, Manitoba R3C 1T5
　　　　　　　204-945-2292

Chapter 24.　For more information on Mosquito Lake and the
　　　　　　　area north of Tuktu Lodge contact:
　　　　　　　Tuktu Lodge
　　　　　　　c/o Wilderness North
　　　　　　　P.O. Box 249
　　　　　　　Nester Falls, Ontario P0X 1K0
　　　　　　　807-484-2512

Chapter 26.　More information on Kasba Lake Lodge is
　　　　　　　available by contacting—
　　　　　　　Kasba Lake Lodge
　　　　　　　P.O. Box 96
　　　　　　　Parksville, British Columbia V9P 2G3
　　　　　　　800-663-8641

Chapter 27.　Get more information on God's Lake Lodge
　　　　　　　and the surrounding area—
　　　　　　　Healey's God's Narrow Lodge
　　　　　　　General Delivery
　　　　　　　God's Lake Narrows, Manitoba R0B 0M0
　　　　　　　204-335-2405
　　　　　　　　　　　　　　or

Manitoba Travel
c/o Dennis Maxsymetz
7th Floor, 155 Carlton & York
Winnipeg, Manitoba R3C 1T5
204-945-2292

Chapter 28. More information on James Bay hunting is available by contacting:

Charlie Wynn's Hunt Camp
P.O. Box 165
Kashechewan, Ontario POL-LSO
705-275-4499

Creebec Airlines: 705-267-1722

Chapter 29. Information on the Leuenberger Air Service in northern Ontario is available by contacting:

Leuenberger Air
P.O. Box 60
Nakina, Ontario P0T 2H0
807-329-5940

Chapters 30 and 31. Information on Kasba Lake and the Kazon River mentioned in these chapters can be obtained from:

Kasba Lake Lodge
P.O. Box 96
Parksville, British Columbia U9P 2G3
1-800-663-8641

Chapter 32. To obtain information on the man and his fishing lodge mentioned in this chapter, write or call:

Hatchet Lake Lodge
P.O. Box 611, Post St. G
Calgary, Alberta T3A 2G5
403-286-2717

Chapter 33. To obtain information on the area mentioned in this chapter contact:

North of Sixty
14375 23rd Ave. No.
Plymouth, Minnesota 55447
612-745-7888

Chapter 34. To obtain more information on the lures, videos, and
books the Gapens have available, write or call:
The Gapen Company
17910 87th St.
Becker, Minnesota 55308
800-484-4001, plus code 3954
612-263-3558

Chapter 35. To obtain information on Athabasca Lake, write or call:
Athabasca Lodges
P.O. Box 7800
Saskatoon, Saskatchewan S7K 4R5
306-653-5490